1982

CHILD ABUSE—AN INTERACTIONAL EVENT

CHILD ABUSE

AN INTERACTIONAL EVENT

Alfred Kadushin and Judith A. Martin
with the assistance of James McGloin

COLUMBIA UNIVERSITY PRESS
NEW YORK   1981

Alfred Kadushin is Julia C. Lanthrop Professor of Social Work in the School of Social Work at the University of Wisconsin, Madison.

Judith A. Martin is Assistant Professor of Social Work in the School of Social Work at the University of Pittsburgh.

James McGloin is Clinical Assistant Professor, Department of Family Practice, in the Medical School at the University of Wisconsin, Madison.

LIBRARY OF CONGRESS CATALOGING IN PUBLICATION DATA

Kadushin, Alfred.
Child abuse—an interactional event.

Includes bibliographies and index.
1. Child abuse.   2. Parent and child.
3. Children—Conduct of life.   4. Social inter-
action.   I. Martin, Judith A., 1945–   joint
author.   II. McGloin, James, joint author.
III. Title.
HV713.K32   362.7'044   80-39654
ISBN 0-231-04774-6

COLUMBIA UNIVERSITY PRESS
NEW YORK   GUILDFORD, SURREY

COPYRIGHT © 1981 COLUMBIA UNIVERSITY PRESS
ALL RIGHTS RESERVED
PRINTED IN THE UNITED STATES OF AMERICA
Printed on permanent and durable acid-free paper.

Dedicated to

The Abused Child
and the Oppressed Parent
Victims and Victimizers

CONTENTS

ACKNOWLEDGMENTS ix

CHAPTER 1 PHYSICAL CHILD ABUSE: AN OVERVIEW 1

CHAPTER 2 CHILD ABUSE AS AN INTERACTIONAL EVENT 47

CHAPTER 3 METHODOLOGY 91

CHAPTER 4 RECORD REVIEW OF ABUSE INCIDENTS 105

CHAPTER 5 INTERVIEW STUDY OF ABUSE-EVENT INTERACTION 141

CHAPTER 6 FACTORS ASSOCIATED WITH THE ABUSE EVENT 225

CHAPTER 7 CONCLUSIONS AND IMPLICATIONS FOR PRACTICE 251

APPENDIX A. Letters 281

APPENDIX B. Standard Report Form 283

APPENDIX C. Tables 287

INDEX 299

ACKNOWLEDGMENTS

THE PROJECT DESCRIBED HERE could not have been completed without the help and support of many cooperative people. We are principally thankful to the parents who shared with us their experiences in such detail. Professionals in the state and local agencies graciously contributed their time, energy, and know-how in providing access and information we needed to do our work. In every instance, this was done with scrupulous regard for the rights of the clients to confidentiality and anonymity. We are grateful to Robert Lizon, director, Bureau of Children, Youth and Families; Jerry Majerus, William Ghanz, Wayne Kudick, and James Honnold of the State of Wisconsin Department of Health and Social Services; to Arthur Silverman, director, Milwaukee Department of Social Services; Edith Blackhall, former section supervisor, Child Protection and Parent Services, Milwaukee County; Gary Shaw, Rock County Department of Social Services; Patricia Dixon, supervisor, Child and Family Services Unit, Dane County Department of Social Services; John Stowe, supervisor, Waukesha County Protective Services; and Michael Radke, Kenosha Department of Social Services.

We are thankfully appreciative of the help and consultation provided by Leonard Berkowitz, Psychology Department, University of Wisconsin-Madison, who throughout, shared with us his very considerable knowledge and expertise regarding aggression and helped in the formulation of the project design.

The project was supported, over a two-year period, by a research grant from the National Institute of Mental Health (ROIMH2745), additional supplementary support being provided by the Graduate School Research Committee, University of Wisconsin-Madison. Our gratitude to both organizations for this help; and to Jean Allen, who patiently and very competently transcribed the interviews and typed the manuscript from often almost indecipherable hieroglyphics.

NOTE

Word usage presents both a general problem and a particular problem. The general problem is one of gender. While some attempt was made to randomize gender in the general discussion material, the use of the pronoun "he" should be regarded as referring to both male and female. The particular problem relates to child abuse. The parent who abuses a child might be referred to as the "abusive parent" or the "abuser." While the latter term is more convenient, it tends to label the parent and suggests habitual consistency in such behavior. Despite this, we have tended to use the term "abuser" because of convenience but with some apology.

CHILD ABUSE—AN INTERACTIONAL EVENT

CHAPTER 1

PHYSICAL CHILD ABUSE: AN OVERVIEW

C HILD ABUSE AS A SOCIAL PROBLEM is a relatively modern phenomenon. Parental behaviors and actions which are currently defined as child abuse were, until recently, accepted as nonproblematic parental prerogatives of no concern to the community.

Where children have very limited rights, they cannot easily be violated. Children "belonged" to parents who had considerable latitude in how they might choose to treat the child.

The advice of religious leaders and medical authorities supported and reinforced harsh treatment of the child if this was the parents' choice. The view of the child as inherently evil and requiring harsh discipline resulted in unquestioned punitive prescriptions in defining acceptable parenting.

Biblical advice echoed folk wisdom that to spare the rod was to spoil the child:

⁍ Foolishness is found in the heart of a child, but the rod of correction shall drive it far from him (Proverbs 22:15).

⁍ Withhold not correction from the child; for if thou beatest him with the rod, he shall not die (Proverbs 23:13).

In recapitulating the history of childhood, DeMause says, "The evidence which I have collected on methods of disciplining children leads me to believe that a very large percentage of the children born prior to the eighteenth century were what would be today termed 'battered children.' Of over two hundred statements of advice on child rearing prior to the eighteenth century which I have examined, most approved of beating children severely and all allowed beating in varying circumstances except three . . ." (1974:40).

In a general way, the neglected and abused child has always been an object of concern in America (Folks 1902:167–69). But agencies specifically concerned with physical abuse trace their origin to the dramatic case of Mary Ellen in 1875. The child was cruelly beaten and neglected by a couple with whom she had lived since infancy. There seemed no appropriate legal measure available to protect her. Community leaders, concerned with the situation, appealed to the Society for the Prevention of Cruelty to Animals. This organization brought Mary Ellen to the attention of the court as an "animal" who was being mistreated. Because the law did protect animals from abuse, the complaint was accepted, protection was granted Mary Ellen, and her guardians were sent to prison. As a result of this case, a Society for the Prevention of Cruelty to Children was organized.

The organization of the New York County Society for the Prevention of Cruelty to Children in 1875 was a signal for the development, within a short period, of similar societies elsewhere: San Francisco, Boston, Rochester, Baltimore, Buffalo, and Philadelphia. By 1900, 161 such societies had been established throughout the United States (Folks 1902:173). (See also McRea 1910.)

Public interest in and concern with the problem gradually subsided and protective service agencies, as they are called in child welfare, experienced a gradual decline until the 1960s. While the early protective service agencies were voluntary, nonpublic agencies, there was a gradual shift in responsibility for this function from such voluntary agencies to county departments of public welfare. There was a gradual shift also in the orientation of such agencies from a legalistic, child rescue focus to a family oriented social work rehabilitation focus. Throughout this period social workers had primary responsibility for providing the community with child protective functions.

A nationwide study conducted in 1954 by the Children's Division of the American Humane Association (DeFrancis 1956) indicated that there were only 84 private agencies in the United States offering a clearly defined protective service function. Of all such agencies, 72 percent were located in New England and in the Middle Atlantic states; 32 states had no such agencies. In some of these states, public agencies accepted the responsibility for protecting children from abuse, but the report showed that in 8 states there was neither a voluntary nor a public social agency offering protective services. The report sparked an increase of interest in child protection on the part of the Children's Bureau, but little action.

The 1960s witnessed a rediscovery of child abuse, this time by radiologists and pediatricians. A number of reports by pediatric radiologists called attention to X-ray markings of multiple, healed injuries suffered by children, which appeared to be the result of abuse. Following nationwide inquiries from hospitals and district attorneys about experience with child abuse, Kempe at al. (1962) published a report of a condition they identified as "the battered child syndrome." The survey of children hospitalized owing to abuse uncovered some 749 cases, including 78 fatalities.

The American Academy of Pediatricians, the American Medical Association, the Children's Bureau, and the American Humane Association reacted to the report, national meetings were organized, relevant legislation was proposed, and child abuse became, once again, a problem of considerable public interest and concern. A conference called by the Children's Bureau to consider the question was followed by the adoption of legislation requiring the reporting of child abuse in state after state within a very short period of time. As Paulsen notes, "Few legislative proposals in the history of the United States have been so widely adopted in so little time" (1966:47).

A Federal Child Abuse Prevention and Treatment Act was passed in January 1974 and extended in 1978. This act provides for direct assistance to states to help them develop child abuse and neglect programs. The act further provides for support of research in the area of child abuse and neglect and establishes a National Center for Child Abuse and Neglect within the Children's Bureau, Office of Child Development, Department of Health and Human Services (HHS).

In adopting the new social services title to the Social Security Act in 1975 (Title XX), protective service, including services to physically abused children, was made mandatory. By 1978 protective services were provided universally in all states. Some 8 percent of the total 2.5 billion Federal Title XX funds were being allocated in 1977 to protective services.

The very rapid development of interest in, and increased concern about, maltreatment of children, with particular focus on physical child abuse, is exemplified by the fact that in 1978 an annotated child abuse bibliography was published listing 2009 citations, most of which had been published after 1970 (Kalisch 1978).

Some component of the rapid growth of interest in child abuse results from what has been termed "low-cost rectitude" and "slack resources" (Nelson 1979). Child abuse legislation permits politicians and the public to feel that they are doing something significant in behalf of children. The cost requirements of programs legislated have been of very modest proportions. At the time when the "battered child syndrome" first achieved some visibility, the Children's Bureau was seeking a new mission and had resources available to deploy in support of a special effort. Child abuse was a relevant, significant, politically attractive choice.

The declining birthrate in the 1960s resulted in the availability of pediatric resources in hospitals seeking a new constituency. Physically abused children were such a potential client group.

Public interest lawyers identified children's rights as a hitherto neglected area. A specialized concern with children's rights intensified interest in child abuse as a social problem.

Others attribute such growing interest to the more general concerns with violence which developed in the 1960s (Gelles and Straus 1979).

Success in arousing public interest in child abuse was ensured by having an influential group of professionals and organizations as active partisans of child abuse legislation, energized by effective leadership and having no organized opposition in support of child abuse.

The rediscovery of child abuse in the 1960s came primarily, however, as a result of the activities of pediatric radiologists, pediatricians, and psychiatrists (Pfohl 1977; Antler 1978). The resurgence of interest in child abuse has, consequently, a more distinct medical orientation, as contrasted with an almost exclusive social work orientation in protective services of an earlier period.

While the child has the right to expect protection from both abuse and neglect and while the incidence of neglect is considerably greater than the incidence of abuse, major interest and concern has been focused most sharply on abuse. Since child abuse is also the concern of the project reported on here, the rest of this chapter is exclusively concerned with this one aspect of the more general problem of child maltreatment. It is in fact even somewhat more narrowly oriented than this. According to federal legislation and state laws, child abuse covers physical abuse, emotional abuse, and sexual abuse, which—despite some overlap—are perceived as different diagnostic entities requiring different treatment interventions. Our concern is with physical abuse. But further, physical abuse can be perpetrated in a variety of different contexts—institutions for child care and the public schools, as well as the family, engage in the physical abuse of children. Institutional physical abuse involves special considerations differentiating it from abuse in the family. Our focus in this overview is exclusively on physical abuse in the family context.

Problems in Definition, Context, Numbers

At the very outset there is a problem in defining physical abuse. The line between physical abuse and harsh parental discipline is difficult to determine. As Arnold says, "Forms of punishment considered proper and even wholesome in Elizabethan or Victorian days would be considered as abuse today" (1962:3).

The problem lies in distinguishing discipline which is "legitimate violence" toward children from abuse which is excessive and inappropriate and, hence, unacceptable violence toward children. The transition from discipline to abuse may be variously defined in different social-cultural contexts, some groups being more accepting of corporal punishment (Korbin 1977). The definition of abuse not only changes with the social-cultural context, it is different for children of different ages; the same parental action might be abuse for an infant and not for an adolescent.

It was not, therefore, unexpected that in interviewing some 1,700 respondents affiliated with hospitals, schools, courts and social agencies, Nagi (1977) found that 69 percent agreed with the statement that "It is difficult to say what is and what is not child mistreatment."

A number of different studies confirm the fact that there are differences in the definitions of child abuse and neglect among different sections of the general public, but also among members of the different professions concerned with this problem (Nettler 1958; Boehm 1964; Giovannoni and Becerra 1979). Despite the differences, there is a core of consensus about what is minimally acceptable child care.

Most simply, physical abuse is defined as nonaccidental physical harm to the child inflicted by persons responsible for the child's care. Some modify this to include only instances where there is "serious" physical harm, eliminating mild physical harm from inclusion in the abuse rubric. Some definitions emphasize the intentional, willful nature of the physical injury inflicted. Other definitions give intent less consideration on the supposition that what is happening involves a danger to the child, whether it is intentional or not.

The American Bar Association Juvenile Justice Standards Project, in its report on standards relating to abuse and neglect, takes a very conservative position in defining child abuse. It is defined in the report as a nonaccidental injury which "causes or creates a substantial risk of causing disfigurement, impairment of bodily functioning or other serious physical injury." Interpreted literally, this view of abuse, covering only serious or severe abuse, would eliminate a very large percent of reports currently identified as abuse.

While the terms "battered child" and "abused child" are often used interchangeably, there is a clear distinction which might be made in terms of severity of injury. The "battered child syndrome" was originally applied to a hospitalized population of children, generally very young, who were so severely injured as to require medical attention. The greatest majority of "abused" children suffer limited physical harm and require no medical attention.

The spectrum of concern ranges from the seriously injured "battered child" through "child abuse," (the largest percentage of instances involving children who suffer mild physical injury) to "violence directed toward children," which includes corporal punishment of any degree of severity against the child. As the definition broadens to include a greater variety of actions on the part of the parent or parent surrogate toward the child, an increasingly large group of children are identified as objects of concern.

Our concern here is primarily with the "abused child," not violence directed toward children, and further with the abused child who has been identified through a formal report to an agency where such a report has been substantiated by the agency.

A second general problem which needs recognition in understanding child abuse is the general attitude toward corporal punishment as an acceptable child-disciplinary procedure.

The level of violence in society generally, and in the mass communication media, suggests an acceptance of the use of force in settling interpersonal disputes. The general acceptance of, and acquiescence in, corporal punishment as a disciplinary procedure calls attention to collective sanction of possible abuse. While there is some dispute about whether lower-income families are more predisposed to the use of corporal punishment than middle-class families (Erlanger 1974), studies show that the largest majority of parents of all classes see such disciplinary measures as acceptable (Stark and McEvoy 1970; Blumenthal et al. 1975). Reports from 10,000 middle-class respondents to a national survey conducted in 1977 indicated that 77 percent thought "children should be disciplined by physical punishment whenever necessary" (*Better Homes and Gardens* 1978:66).

Interviews with a random group of 100 mothers attending a well-baby clinic indicated that one-third of the mothers whose children were less than one year of age had physically punished the child. One-fourth of the mothers with children under six months of age had already started "spanking" the child (Korsch et al. 1965:1883).

In detailed interviews with 57 families concerned, in part, with parent-child disciplinary episodes, "only one parent stated that physical punishment has never been used on their children" (Steinmetz 1977:65).

Community sanction of corporal punishment of children in public schools is a further manifestation of the general acceptance of corporal punishment as a disciplinary procedure. In the case of Ingraham Wright, the Supreme Court ruled that "spanking by schoolteachers did not violate the Constitution's 8th Amendment ban against cruel and unusual punishment even if the spanking is 'severe,' 'excessive,' and medically damaging. The decision was a recognition of the teacher's common law privilege to inflict reasonable corporal punishment" (*New York Times*, April 20, 1977).

A task force study (1972) by the National Education Association found that 67.5 percent of elementary school teachers questioned advocated corporal punishment in the schools. In 1979, forty-six states allowed the use of corporal punishment in public schools (Hyman and Wise 1979). Collective consensual norms thus permit parents to justify use of corporal punishment which runs the risk of becoming abuse.

There is an additional difficulty in attempting to determine the comparative seriousness of child abuse as a social problem. It is difficult to evaluate the significance of child abuse from the point of view of the numbers of children affected. The actual number of children abused supposedly is far in excess of the number of children reported abused. Here estimates vary widely from 60,000 to 500,000 (Light 1973) to 1.5 million children (Fontana 1973) abused in a year. Straus, extrapolating from interviews about family violence with a "nationally representative sample of 1,146 American families who have a child age 3 to 17 at home" (1979:214), concludes that 1.7 million children are abused each year.

Variations in estimates result from differences in the definition of abuse. Some include in their estimates only serious cases of abuse, while others include abuse of any degree of severity. Some estimates include neglect as well as abuse and are more properly estimates of general maltreatment rather than abuse. Variations result from including all reports whether substantiated or not. A considerably reduced figure results if only substantiated reports are included. The sources of data for estimates vary. Results may be obtained from interviews with the public, interviews with professionals concerned with the problem or review of agency report records. Cohen and Sussman, reviewing state reporting statistics nationally for 1972, conclude that a "total of 27,569 actual cases of abuse is indicated" (1975:440). However, on the basis of intensive interviews with professionals involved with the problem, they estimated 167,000 cases of abuse for the same year (p. 16).

With such wide variations in estimates, it is difficult to quote with confidence any figure regarding the incidence and prevalence of physical child abuse. In an effort to get a more accurate picture, a National Clearinghouse on Child Abuse and Neglect was established in 1973 under the auspices of the American Humane Association, with funding from the Office of Child Development, Children's Bureau (HHS). The Clearinghouse (now called the National Study on Child Abuse and Neglect) collected statistics on a standardized form from thirty-one states and three U.S. territories, and collated statistics submitted by nineteen other states and the District of Columbia.

The National Study on Child Neglect and Abuse Reporting, which provides the most definitive information on abuse reporting currently available, based on information from each of the states, notes that "it is currently impossible for reporting systems to provide incidence data because it is known that not all incidents of maltreatment are reported; all states do not mandate the reporting of the same types of maltreatment and the requirements for determining substantiation differ among states. What can be conclusively stated is that reporting statistics underrepresent the actual maltreatment on a national basis" (AHA 1979b:8).

Collating the reports from all of the individual states, the National Study totaled 510,324 maltreatment reports in 1977 and 575,506 reports in 1978 (p. 15). There was considerable variation in reporting rates (number of children maltreated per 1,000 population) ranging from a low of .65 for Minnesota to a high of 6.83 for Idaho (p. 20). The largest percentage of reports in 1978, as was true for earlier reports as well, were of neglect rather than abuse. The actual number of *substantiated* physical abuse cases is difficult to disaggregate with any confidence. For the thirty-four states submitting individual case data enabling some designation of the nature of maltreatment in 1978, the National Study lists 25,656 cases of *substantiated* child abuse and an additional 4,654 cases of substantiated mixed abuse and neglect (total 30,310) (p. 25).

The thirty-four states submitting individual case data accounted for 191,739 of the total of 575,506 abuse and neglect reports received in 1978. If one applied the same percentage of substantiated abuse and abuse plus neglect cases to the 382,767 cases of maltreatment reported by the other states, this would suggest approximately an additional 61,242 substantiated cases of abuse and abuse and neglect, for a total of approximately 91,500 cases of substantiated abuse nationwide in 1978. The total of abuse cases includes sexual abuse and emotional abuse as well as physical abuse, so that the number of physical abuse cases is somewhat smaller.

Profile of Abusee, Abuser, Injury, and Services

Summarization of statistics from state reports in 1976 compiled by the National Center on Child Abuse and Neglect showed that 72 percent of the phyically abused children required no medical treatment, the injury being, most frequently, bruises and welts. Only 6 percent of the abused children required any hospitalization and the fatality rate was .5 percent. Sixty-five percent of the abused children were 6 years of age or older and a minority, only 17 percent, were under two years of age. Boys were more frequently abused than girls, but this was true only for children up to age 10 or 11. Girls were more frequently reported abused from ages 11 to 17. The change results from inclusion of sexual abuse in the statistics—a type of abuse which is reported much more frequently with females as victims and concentrated in older-aged children (American Humane Association 1978). If sexual abuse were deleted from the tabulation, males would be rated as the more frequent victims of physical abuse at all age levels. Subsequent, less-detailed reports in 1977 and 1978 confirm this general picture in terms of ages and sex of abused children, and limited severity of the largest percentage of injuries (AHA 1979a; 1979b).

Reports from England show a similar highly skewed pattern in the direction of limited injury as a consequence of abuse. The National Society for the Prevention of Cruelty to Children, collating reports from a group of its units covering 13 percent of the total child population of England and Wales, found that 84 percent of 618 physical child abuse reports received in 1976 consisted of moderate injuries—"soft tissue injuries of a superficial nature" (Creighton 1979:602).

Friends, neighbors, and relatives were the most frequent source of child abuse reports; law enforcement agencies, schools, social agencies, and medical agencies being other sources of reports.

Parents were most frequently the abusers, being the perpetrators in 87 percent of the cases. Fathers were somewhat more often the abuser (55 percent) than the mothers, who were the abusers in 45 percent of the reports. Most abusers were over 30, the group of male abusers being older than that of female abusers—66 percent of the males being 30 years of age or older, 48 percent of the females 30 years of age or older (National Study of Child Neglect and Abuse, October 1979:31).

The picture of the abusive family presented by the 1976 abuse reports collected by the National Clearinghouse is that of a low-income family with three or fewer children. The families were disproportionately mother-headed, single-parent families (35 percent) and disproportionately nonwhite (20 percent). There was evidence of "family discord" and stress due to "insufficient income" in many of the families. Parents had limited education and employment skills, less than 3 percent being college graduates and less than 7 percent in a profession (AHA 1978: appendix 2).

Social agencies carried the major responsibility for helping the parents and children after abuse was reported. In 78 percent of the cases the children remained in their own homes. "Casework counseling" was most frequently the service offered. This service, offered to more than half the families, contrasted with much more limited use of other services—foster care in 12 percent of the cases in 1976; day care and homemaker services in 6 percent and 4 percent of the cases, respectively, in that year.

Although abuse is found among all socioeconomic groups, it is most frequently reported among the poor. This may be an artifact of reporting, it may be a function of the heavier emphasis on physical discipline among lower-class families, or it may be a consequence of the fewer opportunities, among the poor, for temporary "escape" from children—through baby-sitters, an evening out, a vacation weekend.

Selective sources of referral tend to accentuate the skewed class affiliation of reported abuse. Public hospitals and clinics, and police and welfare agencies, are much more frequently sources of abuse reports than are either private hospitals or family physicians. Low-income people are in contact with the first institutions; middle-class and upper-class people more frequently in contact with the private, voluntary sources of help.

Reviewing the research on the socioeconomic characteristics of abuse and neglect families, Pelton (1978) concludes that, even after allowing for such justifiable explanations of discrepancies in reporting, lower socioeconomic groups are disproportionately represented among maltreaters, so that it is not, in fact, a "classless" phenomenon. Studying an unselected sample of families, Gelles and Strauss (1979) found violence was more frequent in lower-class family interaction.

If there is truth in the assertion that child abuse is distributed at random throughout all socioeconomic classes, this invalidates the supposition that social stress is a significant factor in determining abuse. If such stress is a factor, then poverty and deprivation and discrimination should result in a disproportionate percentage of abuse being located in the community among the poor and the nonwhite.

In recapitulation, the more typical physically abused child is a school-age child who has sustained minor physical injury not requiring medical attention of any kind. The child was abused by one of the biological parents, the report of abuse having been made most frequently by friends, relatives, or neighbors. The child lives in a low-income household, from which he is not removed.

Process in Protective Services

INTAKE

An effort has been made to encourage parents who have physically abused their children, or who feel that they are at risk of such action, to voluntarily request agency service. Posters and spot radio and TV announcements indicate the availability of parental-stress hotline services which the parent might call. Such services are accessible in many communities on a 7 day a week, 24 hour a day basis. The service offers supportive listening, advice, and reassurance to a parent who is about to "lose his cool with a kid," or to a parent who has just abused a child and wants to talk about his feelings with an interested, accepting person. However, abusive parents do not generally voluntarily apply for agency service. Case finding and the initiation of contact results from the action of other individuals or community agencies. Currently, initiation of services frequently results from response to the legal requirement for mandatory reporting. The laws require that professionals aware of a child who is physically abused have the obligation to report this to an agency designated responsibility for taking action.

The agencies to which reports are to be made are generally the public welfare agency or the legal agencies of the community. The laws grant civil and criminal immunity to the professionals required to make such reports and provide penalties for failure to report. The abuse-reporting laws are essentially a case-finding device that helps the community to identify the abusive family and the abused child. Regulations require that the investigation be made within a short time after receipt of the complaint as a protection to a child in possible danger. Investigation needs to be done expeditiously before bruises or welts disappear.

Contact is made with the family by letter or phone or, on less frequent occasions, by an unannounced visit in a follow-up of the abuse report. However initiated, the approach is direct and frank. It involves a clear statement by the agency that it has learned that a situation of potential danger to the child exists; and that, representing the community, it would like to enlist the aid of the parents in determining what is happening. The focus of the inquiry is not on the investigation of the truth or falsity of the allegation, which would put the parents on the defensive. The focus is on what should be done—by agency and parents together—for the optimum benefit of the child. Protective service agencies prefer to "evaluate" rather than "investigate." Semantics suggest an important attitudinal difference. An investigation may be conducted without involving the client; an evaluation implies a joint process, with the parents' active participation.

The parents are not given the right to refuse an exploration. In response to the responsibilities for child protection and in accordance with the community mandate, the agency must conduct some assessment of the situation.

It might be noted that as a result of the agency review, a substantial number of reports prove to be unsubstantiated. For instance, the National Study on Child Neglect and Abuse Reporting found that in 1976 46.6 percent of abuse reports were "not validated" (AHA 1978:4).

PROCESS: DIAGNOSTIC ASSESSMENT

One objective for which the worker has responsibility in making the study of the situation is to determine if abuse has, in fact, taken place, and if the child is in any immediate danger in remaining in the home. A second major objective of such a study is to obtain a diagnostic understanding of the physical abuse situation for the purpose of formulating and proposing treatment interventions which might be helpful to the family and effect changes in the situation.

Available reviews of the literature on child maltreatment, including physical abuse, summarize the research findings regarding the diagnostic configuration of the abuse situation, the abuser and the abused child (Polansky Holly, and Polansky 1974; Spinetta and Rigler 1972; Parke and Colmer 1975; Holmes 1977; Maden and Wrench 1977; Allen 1978; Shorkey 1979). The literature reflects the problem of identifying the differentiating diagnostic configuration which clearly distinguishes the physical abuse situation as a discrete entity. Neglect and the different kinds of abuse—physical, emotional, sexual—are often not clearly separated in the research findings.

The picture is further complicated by the fact that within both the abuse and neglect groups there are subgroups which have little diagnostically in common with each other, except for the fact that ultimate behaviors toward the child are similar. Merrill (1962) lists 4 types and Delsordo (1963) describes 5 types of child abuse. Zalba (1967) defines 6 types, Gil (1970) suggests 17 types, Walters (1975) lists 10 types.

Gelles (1973) notes that of 19 traits listed by various researchers supposedly identifying the personality of the child abuser, there was agreement on only 4 traits by two or more authors, the other 15 traits being cited by only one author.

Summarizing the results of a review of the available research, Allen notes that "there is no such thing as a 'typical example of abuse' which represents the majority of cases, nor is there one factor conclusively present and relevant to all cases. Instead, the research picture suggests that violence is the end product of a complex interaction of individual environmental and interpsychic factors in which the balance between all these influences varies with the individual" (1978:68).

Despite the exponential increases in articles and books on child abuse, a critical reading of the literature leads to uneasiness about the "state of the art." Widely different conclusions are often presented, depending on the locus of the reporters—reports by doctors and reports from hospitals are focused on the younger, more severely injured children and one ethnic or socioeconomic group to which the hospital offers service. Community protective service workers often see older children with mild injuries.

While much of the literature contributing to a diagnostic understanding of physical abuse is descriptive and clinical, there is an increase in the number of studies using nonabusive control, contrast or comparison groups of parents (Lauer et al. 1974; Smith 1975; Baker et al. 1976; Egeland and Brunnquell 1979; Disbrow et al. 1977; Jameson and Schellenbach 1978; Burgess 1979; Burgess and Conger 1978; Elmer 1977; Jakobsson, Lagerberg, and Ohlsson 1979; Oates et al. 1979; Robertson and Juritz 1979; West and West 1979; Wolock and Horowitz 1979).

Even in the control group studies, differences between groups in one study are not found in another study. Sometimes there is even a reverse contradictory finding. Where there is some consistency in findings, the degree of difference between control and experimental group often does not reach statistical significance, and when it does, the result is achieved at modest levels. This means that the factors studied are very weak discriminators. It suggests what is likely to be more true of abusers, but is also true of a sizable percentage of nonabusers. Extreme, clearly defined differences are not easily uncovered (Starr 1979:874).

Although findings from clinical and empirical research are complex and often contradictory, there is some low-level consistency, despite the caveats noted above, in a configuration of factors frequently found associated with abuse. These include a history of abuse and/or rejection in childhood; low self-esteem; a rigid, domineering, impulsive personality; social isolation; a record of inadequate coping behavior; poor interpersonal relationships; high, unrealistic expectations of children; and lack of ability to empathize with children. Abusive parents are seen as having limited ability to tolerate frustration and delays in gratification. They have a "low boiling point" and, as a consequence of low self-esteem, react impulsively and intensely to even minor provocations.

It is suggested that abusive parents are strict disciplinarians who have rigid expectations regarding child behavior without empathic regard for a child's needs or feelings or particular individuality. The parent is seen as "owning" the child, as being solely responsibile for molding the child, and as having a sense of righteousness in making autonomous decisions as to what is best for the child. It is also suggested that abusive parents tend to regard the behavior of even very young children as willful, deliberate disobedience. Strict discipline is then perceived as justified, since the child is consciously disobeying the parent.

Abusive parents supposedly show a tendency to role reversal, in which parents turn to their children for nurturing and protection (Morris and Gould 1963). The child is seen as a source of gratification for meeting the parent's needs. The parent, when disappointed and frustrated by the failure of the child to meet the parent's needs, reacts with hostility toward the child. The failure of the child to meet the parent's needs is seen as willful and deliberate behavior on the part of the child and reactivates the parent's own disappointment, as a child, in his parents.

While it is generally agreed that only a limited percentage of abusive parents are psychotic, a review of studies concerned with the general psychological functioning of abusive parents "sustain the conclusion that abusive parents exhibit considerable psychological dysfunction compared with control groups" (Maden and Wrench 1977:209).

Comparative studies of abusive and nonabusive families tend to show that the pattern of parent-child interaction is apt to be less positive, less child-centered, less tolerant of child behaviors in abusing families. Abusive parents, as compared with controls, are found to be generally more inclined to resort to corporal punishment as a disciplinary procedure.

The above factors center on a psychodynamic "explanation" of child abuse. This approach suggests that the causes of child abuse lie predominantly in the parent and that abusive parents can be clearly distinguished from nonabusive parents in terms of personality, emotional functioning, and psychosocial developmental history.

A more sociological orientation presents another group of factors as being most potent in "explaining" child abuse. According to the sociological approach, the explanation for abuse lies in the general prevailing social ideology, which sanctions violence, and in the particular deprived, stressful socioeconomic situation of the family. Stress resulting from illness, marital friction, unemployment, poor housing, discrimination, or limited income stimulates frustration, which is manifested in aggression directed toward the child. The configuration additionally includes the supposition that social isolation and the lack of a support system are related to abuse.

Clinical and research reports persistently point to a poor relationship between the marital pair in the abusive family. Not only are the participants denied support from each other in dealing with their problems, but the conflicted relationship is a source of additional stress and tension predisposing toward aggression, which is displaced onto the child.

Social isolation from relatives, friends, and neighbors—and a low rate of affiliation with, and participation in, community institutions and organizations—seem to be problems presented by a high percentage of abusers. As a consequence, they lack the availability of an effective social support network. They have a higher rate of residential mobility than nonabuser controls (Lauer et al. 1974), and more often being new neighbors intensifies their tendency toward isolation. There is a question as to whether social isolation is a function of lack of opportunity for contact with others or the result of personality factors which predispose the parent to isolation and/or behaviors which result in their rejection by others.

The fact that a high percentage of reported abusers are young may suggest stress associated with parental immaturity—involvement in youthful marriage and parenthood before being ready for such experiences. Abusing parents tend to be younger at the time of the birth of their first child than nonabusing parents; more frequently the pregnancy is out-of-wedlock or, if in wedlock, unplanned and unwanted. There is a higher probability of difficulty during pregnancy and more often some complication in the delivery.

The fact that a disproportionate percentage of the reported physical child-abuse population are low-income families and single-parent families suggests, further, the contribution to abuse of situational stress and the lack of opportunity for respite from unremitting child-care responsibilities. Gabarino (1976) notes that increased rates of unemployment are associated with increases in child abuse.

While there is general agreement that a stressful living situation—i.e. low income; inadequate, crowded housing; unemployment or intermittent employment; discrimination—is associated with maltreatment, the question is raised as to why most other parents in the same population, living with the same stresses, do not abuse their children.

In comparing abusive with nonabusive parents and controlling for social class, Smith found that there was little difference in the adequacy of housing and financial resources among the two groups. He concludes that "personality disorders . . . are more important than environmental factors in contributing to child abuse" (1975:207), and that "constitutional personality differences are more fundamental than financial factors in the causation of baby battering" (p. 209).

In comparing abusers with nonabusers from the same population—where both groups were living in a stressful, deprived environment—abusers were found more likely to have had a history of disordered childhood development and subsequent personal difficulties in social functioning than the nonabusive controls (Holmes, 1977:148). (See also Smith 1975; Baher et al. 1976).

Comparing 30 abusive mothers and an equivalent matched group of 30 nonabusive mothers, Gray (1978) found that the groups did not differ significantly in terms of the levels of life stress to which they were exposed. There were, however, significant differences between the two groups of mothers in their ability to respond empathically to their children's dependent and aggressive behavior. Standardized instruments were employed to measure levels of life stress and empathic competence.

In comparing identified abusive parents with a like number of nonabusive parents, Pierce (1979) once again found that the stress profiles of the two groups were not significantly different. However, children in the two groups of families were different in terms of the types of provoking behavior exhibited and in the parents' typical response to that behavior.

The greater weighting of personality variables, as contrasted with situational variables, in "explaining" abuse is noted in a study of a large sample of abusers. State reports submitted to the national study on Child Neglect and Abuse Reporting (AHA 1978) included data on selected factors associated with maltreatment incidents. Recapitulation of relevant information on 16,000 reports where sufficient information was available showed that "although there are commonalities, factors involved in child abuse are different than in child neglect. In neglect, the relative importance of environmental stress factors (poverty, broken homes, poor housing) is greater than the personal characteristics or inability to cope factors (lack of tolerance, loss of control during discipline) inherent in cases of abuse" (1978:7). Environmental stress was more characteristic of neglect families, faulty interpersonal dynamics more characteristic of abuse families.

A psychosocial explanation which combines both the social stresses which might act as the "triggering context" for abuse, and the psychological factors which predispose the caretaker to resort to abuse as a selective response in dealing with child management problems, appears to be a more comprehensive interpretation.

Situational stress is an incremental load imposed on psychological stress, increasing the total stress overload to which the individual is subjected and with which he has to cope. More recently the tendency has been to include psychological, sociological and ideological factors in an ecological configuration (Parke, 1976; Gabarino, 1976).

The preponderance of research efforts concerned with trying to formulate a diagnostic understanding of maltreatment has focused on the parent or parent surrogate. There is a beginning effort to look at the interaction of parent and child rather than at the parent alone in trying to understand the abuse situation. It is suggested that the abuse event is not the product of the exclusive input of the abuser but is, rather, the result of the interaction of behaviors of both the child and the parent. Since this content is most directly relevant to the focus of this study, a more detailed review of this aspect of physical child abuse is reserved for, and covered in, chapter 2.

In summary, physical abuse might be best understood as a consequence of a complex interaction of a limited number of identifiable factors in each abuse event. There is a potential abuser with some predisposition to act aggressively toward the child, there is a child behaving in some way that instigates an aversive feeling in the potential abuser, there is some history of relationship between the potential abuser and the child with some negative residual components, there is a stressful situational context (sometimes general, sometimes more immediate and specific) which impacts negatively on the abuser, incrementally fueling aggressive feelings—all coming together in a crisis situation, which triggers the abusive act. The probability of abuse is increased in a setting of social isolation, which reduces the ready availability of help and support from other people; cumulative situational tensions which have lowered tolerance for additional stress; and a community context which sanctions interpersonal violence.

One repeatedly cited diagnostic indictor, only briefly alluded to above, requires a more extended comment at this point. This is the supposition that maltreatment is associated with the fact that abusers have themselves experienced abuse as children. This has achieved the status of an axiom. The supposition suggests the perpetuation of intergenerational abuse where the abuse of one generation of children is inflicted on another generation when the victims themselves become parents.

As a consequence of his experience, the abused child learns to employ violence in parent-child interaction. He takes the abusive parent as a role model and patterns his own subsequent parental behavior accordingly. The outcomes are consistent with learning theory. The outcomes are also consistent with child development theory. Having been abused and rejected as children, having lacked a stable, consistent love relationship in childhood, these parents have experienced inadequate gratification of early affectional and dependency needs. In response to such deprivation, abusive parents are themselves still children—in their narcissism, their selfishness, their dependency, their impulsiveness—in short, in their immaturity. The idea of intergenerational transmission of maltreatment is thus consistent with theoretical suppositions regarding the effects of emotional deprivation in infancy, which suggests that the deprived child, not having been loved, is incapable in adulthood of loving others.

The idea of intergenerational abuse is not only theoretically attractive, since it is consistent with learning, modeling, psychodynamic, and socialization concepts; but it is attractive because it permits the social worker to approach the parent with a greater feeling of acceptance. The abusive parents are not to blame. They too are victims—victims of their own childhood experiences.

While these considerations explain and support the contention that abuse is intergenerationally transmitted, Jayaratne (1977), in reviewing the relevant data on this, finds little empirical support for the proposition. Following a similar review of the research, Holmes notes that "while there is general agreement that abusive parents were themselves treated with hostility and lacked nurturant care in childhood, there is virtually no empirical substantiation of the often repeated view that abused parents were themselves actually abused as children." Furthermore, "In the absence of normative data, it is impossible to determine the extent to which a childhood characterized by hostility and lack of nurturance is particularly characteristic of abusive parents" (1977:143). A longitudinal study (Lefkowitz, Huesmann, Eron 1978) of parental reports of punishment administered to their 8-year-old children and reports from these same children 10 years later concerning the hypothetical use of punishment on their own children, found that there was no simple direct relationship between childhood experience and later attitudes toward use of physical punishment in child rearing.

An atypical group of disturbed, multi-problem families do clearly show, on genealogical examination, intergenerational recurrence of abuse (Oliver 1977). Some studies of abusive parents compared with a sample of nonabusive parents generally show abusive parents as having had less favorable relationships with their own parents (Melnick and Hurley 1969; Schneider, Helfer, and Pollock 1972; Bedger 1976; Green 1976; Smith 1975). In all instances, however, sizable percentages of abusive parents had positive developmental experiences and sizable percentages of nonabusive parents had unfavorable parent-child experiences. Detailed data on some 13,000 abusive parents collected by the National Study on Child Neglect and Abuse in 1978 indicated that only 20.1 percent of these parents presented a history of having been abused as children (AHA 1979b:41).

Much of the clinical "evidence" for the "axiom" rests on the retrospective recall of childhood experiences by abusive parents, which may or may not be congruent with the reality of such experiences. In addition to a sizable number of abusive parents who have not themselves experienced abuse as children, we know little about the, perhaps, sizable numbers of parents who, having been abused as children, grow up to be nonabusive parents. This group, whose behavior would contradict the supposition, would not be protective-service-agency clients.

Sometimes clinicians, advocating the concept of intergenerational abuse, report that the "abuse" experienced by the abusive parent in his own childhood was not necessarily physical abuse. It is often significant deprivation or neglect. The injury is that of a "lack of empathic mothering," a term used to "describe a variety of less than ideal responses of the caretaker (usually the mother) to the infant" (Steele 1976:14). Since few mothers offer their children "ideal responses," a very considerable percentage of the general population can be identified as having been abused in childhood. The hypothesis then loses some differentiating utility.

The questions that have been raised above about one of the most consensually accepted axioms regarding child abuse might stand as a paradigm of similar kinds of questions that might be raised about many of the other findings stated in the summary describing the abusive parent. The picture that research has as yet provided, while providing some useful clues and leads, is far from definitive or unambiguous.

TREATMENT AIMS AND APPROACH

Following from the diagnostic study, which results in some understanding of the parent-child relationship, attempts are made by the worker to formulate a treatment program to effect change in the situation. The core of the agency's work is with the parents, the objective being to prevent further neglect and/or abuse of the child and to alleviate or correct those problems that have led to the situation. The ultimate aim is to preserve the home so that the child can have his needs adequately met within his own biological family.

Currently there are two general approaches toward effecting change in the abuse situation in efforts to promote prevention and/or amelioration. One approach is directed toward effecting change in the parents, strengthening their ability to cope with stress, modifying their patterns of coping with it. Attempts are made to effect changes in parents' behavior through parent education, behavior modification, and self-help organizations, through counseling, casework, psychotherapy, and group experiences. Broadly defined, this is a psychotherapeutic approach.

A second general approach, a sociotherapeutic-oriented approach, is directed toward reducing stress impinging on the abuser family unit through provision of social utilities, social supports, facilitative services, and broader opportunities. Day care, homemaker service, foster care, income-maintainance programs, baby-sitters, Parents Anonymous, job opportunities, and more adequate housing are employed in implementing this approach. In the most comprehensive interdisciplinary, multimethod program, psychotherapeutic and sociotherapeutic approaches are utilized in tandem.

The very fact that the agency is required to make and maintain contact with the family, as well as the fact that the worker representing the community is invested with some authority, results in more acceptable parental behavior toward the child in some percentage of cases. The judicious use of authority by the social worker can help effect change (Studt 1954; Moss 1963; Foren and Bailey 1968; Yeleja 1971). What is achieved in such instances is compliance, overt changes in behavior in response to suggestions and/or directives from the worker.

Clients have accepted the social worker's efforts because of their concern over the possible social consequences of their behavior and their desire to avoid certain specific punishments. The new behavior is not adopted because the client believes it to be good or desirable. The new standards remain external; they have learned to do or say what is necessary, but there is no inner conviction in the values followed. Continued supervision is necessary because the client has to be kept constantly aware of the possibility of negative consequences for failure to provide adequate care.

The more desirable goal is to change behavior through the internalization of new standards of child care. To support such a change in values and beliefs, the agency must be certain that the living situation—housing, income, and so on—provides a realistic possibility for the parent(s) to act in accordance with a changed attitude toward child care.

Effecting changes in behavior through internalization of changed attitudes toward the child and toward child care is very difficult, however, with abusive parents. Professionals who have worked with such parents have remarked on their emotional inaccessibility, the persistence which one has to display in going out to them physically and emotionally, and the difficulty in liking them while aware of what they did to a child (Davoren 1968).

Protective service clients are generally resistive to social work contacts. A study of intensive services offered such families found that few families initiated a request for an appointment, and that families often failed to keep appointments scheduled by the workers (Baher et al. 1976). Consequently, the social worker has to accept the expectation of limited goals and small gains.

As in all treatment situations, the worker attempts to develop a relationship of trust by being empathic, accepting, and genuine. In working with an abusive client population, more emphasis is put on providing a structure of unambiguous expectations and being more than ordinarily supportive. The worker attempts to act as the model of a "good parent."

In part this is designed to provide abusive parents with examples of non-punitive child management skills that they may lack. In addition the worker, acting as a "good parent", gratifies client dependency needs. The approach is based on the idea that maltreatment results from a deprived childhood, resulting in a lack of trust and inability to love and nurture. A significant element of the protective-service treatment program, then, is concerned with "reparenting" so as to make restitution for a deprived childhood and to help the client "unlearn mistrust."

Efforts have been made through the use of such programs as Parent Effectiveness Training to increase the parents' repertoire of disciplinary procedures. The parent is educated to the use of skills in child rearing which emphasize nonpunitive approaches. The assumption is made that abusive parents have not had an opportunity to learn desirable parenting procedures because they lacked effective models for this in their own parents. Further, such parents know little about child development and need both information and training in good parenting. They need training in expanding their repertoire of procedures for child management beyond a supposedly almost exclusive use of corporal punishment.

Behavior modification approaches have been used in some child-abuse-control programs directed toward the behaviors of both parents and children. Parents have been trained to use behavior modification procedures based on operant conditioning concepts in changing the behaviors of the children that stimulate abusive responses on the part of parents. Parents have been trained through the use of behavior modification procedures, such as modeling and role playing, to change their behaviors in response to the child (Reavley and Gilbert, 1976).

A wide variety of additional treatment resources have been utilized in attempting to meet the needs of this group of clients. One group of innovations involves "shared parenting" to provide the parent with some relief from the stresses and burdens of unremitting child care which might lead to maltreatment. Among these are crisis nurseries, drop-in centers, parental surrogates, and extended-day-care centers. Parental surrogates (parent aides) are paraprofessional "friends" who are available to take over care of the child in the home when some relief is necessary to prevent abuse.

Crisis nurseries operate on a 24-hour, 7-day-a-week basis. They accept children at all hours in order to divert or relieve a potentially damaging crisis situation by providing short-term relief. As emergency shelters, they do not solve an ongoing problematic situation and are most effectively used in conjunction with, or as supplementation of, other services. A crisis nursery may impose a maximum 48 or 72 hour residential stay for a child, and may accept a maximum of 5 to 7 children. The danger of parental misuse of the center as a convenience rather than a facility for avoidance of abuse, needs to be monitored.

"Drop-in" nurseries permit a mother to place children for a few hours "without much explanation or preparation—in moments of great stress— for no other reason than the mother wants relief" (Kempe and Helfer 1972:48). In San Francisco the extended family center provides a "home away from home" for abused children and their parents. The center cares for children between 9 A.M. and 6 P.M., acting as an extended family to relieve the mother while she receives treatment (Ten Broeck 1974).

Special live-in treatment facilities have been developed. The New York Foundling Hospital has established a temporary shelter at the Center for Parent and Child Development in an effort to help parents who have abused their children. The program permits mothers and children to live in at the hospital for periods ranging from three to six months. During this time the children are cared for in the hospital nursery or day-care centers and mothers receive intense individual and group therapy from a multidisciplinary team which includes social workers. The staff provides a modeling of good mothering by actual demonstrations of desirable child care. Discharge from residence in the hospital is followed up by a year or more of supervision in their own home by "surrogate mothers," who are paraprofessionals selected from the neighborhood in which the mothers live.

Because situations triggering maltreatment can sometimes be improved by money, agencies have experimented with emergency relief funds. Such emergency funds have been disbursed as a cash grant to meet emergency housing costs, including rent payment; to return heat and electricity to a home; or for emergency supplies of food. The funds have had the effect of increasing client confidence in the worker's desire, and ability, to be of help (Horowitz and Wintermute 1978).

In addition to individual psychotherapeutic and sociotherapeutic interventions, agencies have organized family-life education group programs, group therapy, and family therapy groups for abusive parents. A self-help group of abusive parents has been organized and provides an effective adjunctive group treatment resource. Parents Anonymous was organized in

California in 1971 with the help of a social worker. Membership requires that the mother make an open admission of child abuse and express a desire to change. By sharing "positive behavior alternatives" to abuse, P.A. educates its members to more acceptable patterns of parenting. The organization is involved in socializing the abusive parent to the role of parent in terms of role behaviors which are socially acceptable (Collins 1978).

In June 1978 Parents Anonymous was estimated to have about 8,000 members in some 800 chapters. It is defined as a self-help organization providing a "nurturing and therapeutic service" (MacFarlane and Lieber 1978). Parents Anonymous membership is primarily white, middle-class, young, and female. In 1977, of some 500 chapters in the country, only two were identifiably black and three Hispanic. Membership was about 4 percent black (Mahomoud 1978); 45 percent of the members had incomes of over $10,000, 25 percent had some college education (Lieber and Baker 1977). Affiliation with, and participation in, Parents Anonymous is involuntary for only some 7 percent of parents and is mandated by the court. However, beyond the stage of initial resistance, those who come to Parents Anonymous through this route are indistinguishable from those who are self-referred (Collins 1978:8).

All of the treatment interventions which bring abusive parents together in a group—Parents Anonymous, group therapy, family therapy, parent education programs, living-in programs—have, as one of the intended therapeutic derivatives, diminishing the social isolation of abusive parents and providing them with social supports. Agencies are also concerned with meeting the treatment needs of the abused child. The child may need help in dealing with his feeling about the abuse experience, his relationship with his parent, as well as treatment for the physical and emotional consequences of abuse.

Concern for the treatment needs of children is substantiated by the adverse physical, social, and emotional consequences of child abuse (Martin 1976; Kinard 1979). Treatment then involves offering education, role modeling, support, clarification and a variety of concrete services within a constructive limit-setting context, in an empathic, warm, noncondemnatory relationship, the workers representing a symbolic accepting parent.

If a protective agency is to do its work effectively, it needs access to a wide variety of resources. The agency needs baby-sitters or homemakers who are able to go into homes and care for children who are temporarily abandoned. It needs a corps of emergency parents (Paget 1967) for a variety of crisis situations which place the child in some danger. The agency may make regular payments to foster families who stand ready to accept a child for care on short notice. It needs, in addition, more traditional kinds of foster homes for longer-term care. A comprehensive program of such resources may be developed and organized into a program from which the worker can select the resource, or group of resources, most appropriate to a particular physical-abuse situation (Burt and Balyeat 1977).

Because physical abuse is a multidimensional phenomenon, both diagnosis and treatment may involve a variety of different professions. Consequently, multidisciplinary team programs have been developed. Such teams collaborate in establishing an assessment of the situation and cooperate in a broad program of treatment (Schmitt 1978).

COURT ACTION IN PROTECTIVE SERVICES

The process of assuring more adequate care for the child may involve changes in the child's own home or, if this is impossible, provision of a substitute home. If the parents are unwilling or unable to plan the necessary changes, or if the situation involves so clear and present a danger to the child that he can be protected only by being removed from the home, the agency may have to obtain court action. In taking such a course, the principle followed is that "use of the court should be constructive—as a resource, not as a last resort." The court process needs to be seen as "a means of protecting the child rather than prosecuting the parents" (Thomson 1971:44). The caseworker attempts to exercise authority in a positive, supportive manner.

The general estimate is that about 10–12 percent of protective service cases actually require the exercise of the court's authority against parental voluntary consent (Polier, and McDonald, 1972; AHA 1978). In deciding in favor of court action, the agency is concerned with preventing a recurrence of abuse. This general concern is warranted. Recapitulating the findings of 10 studies between 1968 and 1975 which give figures on children who had been previously abused, Maden and Wrench find that some 51 percent had been previously abused (1977:204). In a more recent study of abuse in 328 families referred for protective services, Herrenkohl and Herrenkohl (1980) found a repetition of abuse in 54.1 percent of the families.

In most jurisdictions, if either a social agency or the police have to remove a child from the home because there is no caretaker available, or because the situation is dangerous, a court hearing must be held within 24 hours to determine the appropriateness of the action. Unless the court is satisfied that protection of the child requires his continuation out of the home, the child would have to be returned to his parents.

Primary emphasis has been on the treatment of manifest abuse as against concern with intervention to prevent abuse from taking place in the first instance. However there has been a trend toward attempting preventative services.

Abuse Prevention

At the widest primary preventative level, some, such as Gil (1979), call for a total reorientation of society so as to reduce the general level of violence. The hope is that society would make unacceptable the use of violence of any kind in interpersonal relationships.

A general preventative measure lies in the elimination of all corporal punishment as applied to children. This would outlaw any violence toward children, even the mildest spanking. In July, 1979, Sweden adopted just such a policy making child spanking illegal. It is not likely, however, that a procedure which is currently so widely prevalent in the U.S. is likely to be interdicted, and if interdicted, could be enforced.

Periodic visits to the family by health personnel during the child's first two years has been proposed as a primary child-abuse-prevention program (Kempe 1976). Other industrialized countries provide for such regular visits as a service to the family. During the course of such visits, any evidence of child abuse can be discussed with the family.

Family-planning services and Medicaid support of elective abortions are primary preventive measures. They prevent the birth of unwanted children at a period in the parents' lives when care for a child would be very stressful—a situation which is high risk for abuse. Programs of parent education and child care offered in high schools to a generation of prospective parents are viewed as a large-scale effort to prevent child abuse.

Preventative child-abuse treatment programs involve identification of high-risk-for-abuse mothers. This is done through the use of a questionnaire, the answers to which supposedly distinguish between mothers who show an attitudinal acceptance of their recently born child and those who indicate a rejection of the child. The questionnaire responses may be supplemented by staff observation of mother-infant interaction shortly after birth.

Negative "nesting" behavior and "claiming" behavior of mothers are noted as indicative of high risk for abuse. If the mother has made little preparation for the child's care on leaving the hospital—or is hesitant about naming the baby, holding the baby, and feeding the baby while in the hospital—this is suggestive of rejection. If the mother is actively repelled by the child's odor, drooling, excrement, or regurgitation, this supposedly points to later difficulty. The preventive program provides education and support of the mother, active involvement of community agencies that might be of help, and explicit follow-up.

A variety of questionnaires have been developed that are designed to uncover attitudes and feelings about children and child care which indicate danger of abuse (Lynch and Roberts 1977; Gray et al. 1978; Knight, Disbrow, and Doerr 1978; Altermeier et al. 1979; Geddis et al. 1979).

In checking the precision with which such instruments clearly distinguish between potential abusers and nonabusers, subjects have been followed up for some time after the birth of the child. The instruments in general proved to have a low level of predictability. Although potential abusers are often correctly identified, many identified potential abusers are not found to have actually abused their children, and some percentage of those identified as nonabusers actually do abuse their children (Daniel et al., 1978.)

The problem in precise identification of likely abusers lies in the fact that the search for reliable and meaningful psychological, developmental, and social differences between abusing and non-maltreating parents has as yet proved both illusive and inconclusive. While some characteristics have been identified as distinguishing between the two groups, success in identification of such characteristics has varied from study to study. In identifying the same variable distinguishing abusive from non-maltreating parents (social isolation, recent stress, history of abuse in childhood, etc.) there has been considerable overlap. While somewhat more of the abuse group may display such characteristics, a sizeable percentage of the non-maltreating group have also manifested the same difficulty.

The findings are generally on the order of a very modest increment in probability that the variable will be somewhat more likely to be true of one group than the other. There is very rarely any certainty or definiteness that a particular factor would be true of any particular abusive family or individual abusive parent.

EVALUATION OF OUTCOME

Studies concerned with determining whether the protective services programs actually achieve their objectives of reducing maltreatment of children might be divided into the period which preceded the recent "rediscovery" of the problem and the period of the late 1960s and 1970s, which followed the discovery of the "battered child."

Evaluation research conducted during the earlier period in protective-service-treatment intervention, which includes studies by Kelly (1959), Scherer (1960), Merrill et al. (1962), Bourke (1963), Varon (1964), Young (1964, 1966), Rein (1963) and Johnson and Morse (1968), enable us to conclude that the agencies apparently achieved some modest measure of success. Almost all of the studies had a strong clinical orientation and none included control groups or comparison groups.

The more recent period—from 1965 to date—is characterized by similar deficiencies in outcome-evaluation research. The situation has not changed significantly from the earlier period. A consultant's report to the National Institute of Mental Health, reviewing the state of the art in child abuse and neglect programs in 1977, notes that "the impact of various treatment approaches and programs has not been measured in any systematic way to date" (Holmes 1977:167). A recent evaluation study of protective services, which attempts, for the purpose of comparison, to review the literature, notes that "evaluation of treatment services for abusive and neglectful parents constitutes a major gap in the child abuse and neglect literature" (Berkeley Planning Associates 1977:62).

A review of English, as well as American, literature on child abuse notes that "there is little reliable evidence available on how far it is possible to help parents who have hurt their children and to what extent future abuse can be materially reduced" (Jobling 1976:7; see also Smith 1975:218).

Evaluation outcome statements are frequently made indicating possibilities of "satisfactory results" with 75 to 80 percent of abusive parents (Steele and Pollak 1974:128; Helfer 1975:41; Schmitt 1978). Other service programs claim to have helped the "majority of families" (Green 1976:27; Bean 1975:139; Galdston 1975:380). These optimistic estimates are backed by little in the way of specific detail.

In contrast to these general evaluation statements, research findings of projects focused more specifically on evaluating outcomes of abuse treatment programs tend to be considerably more reserved. Using a repetition of abuse subsequent to agency intervention as a measure of success, Morse, Sahler and Friedman (1970) and Skinner and Castle (1969) found high rates of recidivism.

Johnson provides a detailed study of recidivism based on a careful analysis of the records of all families offered protective services in two cities (Nashville, Tennesse; Savannah, Georgia) between August 1971 and April 1974. The records were reviewed for reincidence of maltreatment, length of time between repeated events of maltreatment, the severity of subsequent injury as compared with the first injury, and the action taken by the agency. The study concluded that approximately 60 percent of the reported children had been reabused; the more recent incidents had a relatively high probability of being more serious in nature than previous incidents; reentry into the system occurred in a short period of time in a high percentage of the cases. The report notes that "there is no question that efforts to rehabilitate parents and prevent further neglect and/or abuse have generally failed" (1977:162).

In a follow-up study of 58 abused children completed by Martin and Beezley, "the children were evaluated at a mean of 4.5 years after abuse had first been documented. It was disheartening to note the current behavior of the parents toward the previously abused child. Parents of 21 of the children had had psychotherapy as part of their treatment program; 90 percent of the children of these parents were still in the biologic home. Even though the children were no longer being battered in the technical or legal sense, 68 percent of them at follow-up were still experiencing hostile rejection and/or excessive physical punishment. It should be noted however that these children were faring much better than those whose parents had received no formal treatment" (1976:256).

The Office of Comptroller General conducted a study of protective service outcomes. Selecting ten public welfare agencies in six states, they drew a sample of records in each location for each of three periods between June 1972 and June 1973 for a total of 724 cases overall. Case records were examined and some evaluation was made as to whether the child's care-giving arrangement was either (a) "critical" (child in imminent personal danger); (b) "serious" (child provided minimal care); (c) "fragile" (potential for danger but not actual danger); or (d) "satisfactory" (suitable parental and social supports are being provided to the child).

Similar levels of assessment were made from the record material on the child's physical and emotional well-being.

Analysis of the information from the 714 usable records of child-protective services showed that a child was generally in a "serious" or "critical" situation at case opening and that the child's situation generally improved after case opening, the percentage of younger children achieving improvement being significantly greater than that of older children (1976:17). At opening, only 36 percent of the children were in "fragile" or "satisfactory" situations. At the end of the study, 73 percent were in a "fragile" or "satisfactory" situation, indicating improvement in the situation for some 37 percent of the children served.

Baher et al. reports on the effects of an intensive-relationship approach to 23 families with the history of abuse of a child under four. Workers were in contact with the family for at least 18 months, and during the first three months of the contact scheduled two interviews a week with the client. Detailed process recordings were kept of all contacts as well as of the results of decision-making conferences regarding clients. Workers had a very limited case load and in every instance were professionally qualified. Outcome evaluations were formulated by workers in contact with the client by comparing the recorded details of their first contact with the client with their functioning at the end of 18 months of service.

The results . . . relating primarily to the interaction between the mothers and the battered children were disappointing. Only slight positive changes were noted in most aspects of these relationships, leaving many doubts about the effectiveness of our treatment service in improving the quality of mothering. . . . The majority of mothers could not be termed even fairly accepting of the battered children after twenty-one months of treatment. (1976:171)

Tracy, Ballard, and Clark (1975) provide evaluation outcome data on families with whom behavior-modification approaches to child management procedures were attempted. The interventions were provided by "family health workers" whose professional background is not given in the report. "The parents' verbal report was used to assess behavioral changes," although this was further augmented by "direct observation in the home, clinical reports and verbal reports of others." Forty-one treated families provided a pool of 129 behavioral concerns which needed changing. "Of these, 84 percent were rated improved or very improved, while 9 percent were rated worse or the same." Rating of changes was made by the health workers and project coordinator on the basis of some observable indicator. The group studied was composed of families of abused children and families at high risk for abuse. The results are not disaggregated, so it is impossible to tell outcomes for the abused families alone. A few single-case reports of progress through the use of behavior-modification procedures are also available in the literature (Polakow and Peabody, 1975).

The Berkeley Planning Associates recently completed the first large-scale comparative child abuse and neglect treatment-outcome study available. It covered 1,724 parents treated in eleven different protective-service demonstration projects throughout the nation. Despite the care and detail with which the study was conducted, the study itself notes its principal research deficiencies—namely, there is no control group, the workers provided the data used in studying outcome, clients were neither observed nor contacted directly, and there was no provision for follow-up.

The workers in most direct contact with the client at the demonstration project filled out a series of forms developed by the researchers in consultation with practitioners. Data was collected from the time of intake to service termination for 1,724 adult clients during 1975 and 1976. The forms completed included an intake form, goals of treatment form, and client follow-up form. A form listing services provided to the client and a client-functioning form were completed at the end of each calendar month. A client-impact form provided information on the client at the start of service and the same form was completed at termination of service.

Using reincidence as an outcome measure, it was found that 30 percent of the clients served by the demonstration projects engaged in severe abuse or neglect while in treatment. Evaluation of changes in specific client behaviors, client attitudes, or situational changes found that in every instance, fewer than 30 percent of the clients exhibited significant improvement. Less than 40 percent of the clients improved in at least one-third of those areas identified as problems at intake (1977:58).

Treatment interventions which seemed to provide a greater measure of success included lay-therapy programs, group parent-education programs, and self-help programs such as Parents Anonymous, although this may be partly a function of the fact that such services were more frequently used on a voluntary basis by motivated clients capable of making effective use of the service. Clients in treatment for longer periods of time showed greater positive change, suggesting the value of treatment.

Shapiro studied the consequences of agency intervention in the case of 171 families for whom an allegation of maltreatment was sustained. Twenty-seven percent of the families, 46 families, were identified as abusers. Data was obtained through interviews with the families during 1975 to 1977 supplemented by a review of the records.

Based on data from agency records and research interviews, the research staff "made a series of seven judgments on problem areas and the extent to which they had or had not improved" (1979:56). "Most families were judged to have shown some improvement in child rearing, but improvement in other problem areas was not common. Indicators of improvement in child rearing focused on physical care rather than on the more subtle psychological changes" (p. 61).

Both the Berkeley evaluation study (1977) and the Shapiro Child Welfare League study found that length of time in treatment was a factor associated with client improvement—little improvement could be expected unless contact was maintained with the client for a prolonged period. However, the Berkeley study concludes by noting that there is a need to "recognize the limitations of current approaches to treatment. Designs for treatment programs that can be predicted to benefit the majority of abusive or neglectful families in need of treatment have not yet been developed. The challenge of identifying truly effective approaches to treating child abuse and neglect remains" (Cohn 1979:519)—a conclusion that is clearly seconded by Shapiro in summarizing the results of the Child Welfare League study (1979:112).

A limited number of outcome evaluation reports are available on special approaches to maltreating families—group therapy, day care, coordinated services, self-help groups, foster care. Justice and Justice used Goal Attainment Scaling procedures in determining the outcome of their group therapy programs with abusive parents. Goal Attainment Scaling involves specifying a series of explicit, behaviorally objectifiable goals and then determining the level at which the goal has been achieved in therapy, for which a change score is computed.

Average length of group treatment was four or five months for 1½ hours once a week. The last report available, in 1976, showed that "abuse has not recurred among the 15 couples who have completed group therapy since May, 1973. Furthermore, six month follow-ups show that expected levels of outcome . . . are holding up" (1976:119).

Change scores are based on reports, presented by the parents, of changed behavior. Treated parents had a considerable investment in pre-senting themselves as changed. Three-quarters of the couples in the pro-gram had their child in a substitute care placement and return of the child was contingent upon the parents' improved functioning.

Stephenson describes the results of a preschool enrichment program for abused children and their families, preschool teachers acting as the primary therapists. There was considerable turnover and only 10 families appear to have remained in the program for more than a year. The children in the program for more than a year "showed a mean IQ in-crease of 14 compared to a mean gain of 2 for children less than a year and control children. In 55 percent of the one year plus families, a parent had moved from social assistance, usually via educational upgrading, to permanent employment" (1977:133).

The Bowen project conducted between 1965 and 1971 by the Juve-nile Protective Association of Chicago attempted to provide, under the auspices of a single agency, a comprehensive package of treatment inter-ventions to a limited number of abusive and neglectful families. Over the five-year period, an average of 25 workers delivered an average of 10 dif-ferent services to a total of 35 disorganized families, which included 162 children. The final report of the project notes that it is possible to de-scribe the treatment but difficult to provide any research evidence on out-comes. "The question of results must of necessity be answered in terms of clinical judgment and case description" (Juvenile Protective Assn. 1975:88). The report goes on to note that

by the time the project terminated, most of the parents were functioning at an improved level and the nature and amount of services needed had changed. They had more security, self-esteem and the neglecting symptoms had been ame-liorated to some degree. However they were still somewhat shaky in independent functioning. (p. 160)

A measure of the success of the project may be given by the fact that removal of children by the court had to be initiated for 8 of the Bowen Center's 35 families.

Lieber and Baker obtained evaluation self-reports from 613 members of Parents Anonymous from chapters across the country. Of the respon-dents, 50 percent reported that since joining the organization there had been a "great deal of improvement in their ability to handle the prob-lem." People who had been in the program for a longer period of time were more likely to feel there had been improvement. It might be noted that there was no validation of the self-report assessment and that only 53 percent of the respondents reported that they had ever actually physically abused their children (1977:140–41).

The successful use of foster family care to remove the child from any possibility of danger, and the subsequent healthy development of children placed in such substitute care, is reported by Kent. He studied the physical and emotional development of 219 abused and neglected children. Obtaining data from the schools and the social workers assigned to the case, he compared the child's functioning at the point of the agency's first contact with the child and a year later. In each agency, intervention had resulted in the placement of the child in substitute care, most frequently in a foster-family home. During the year in placement, the child made substantial gains in weight and height and "improved on nearly all the problem behaviors" (1976:28), and in I.Q. score, academic performance, and school peer relationships (p. 29). Kent concludes that "intervention in the form of removal of the child from the abusive environment had beneficial results" (p. 28). Kent's finding is supported by de Castro, Rolfe, and Hippe, who, in a longitudinal study of abused children, found greatest improvement in the limited number of children who had been placed in foster care (1978:52).

Attempts have been made at early identification of parents who are high risk for maltreatment of their children (Lynch and Roberts 1977; Knight, Disbrow, and Doerr 1978). A treatment program is then offered such parents as a primary prevention procedure, and the effects of such intervention are subsequently evaluated. On the basis of interviews, a questionnaire administered before and after the birth of the child, and observation by hospital staff of the mother's reaction and handling of the infant, 100 mothers were identified as high risk for abuse (Gray et al. 1978). Fifty of the mothers were randomly assigned to a program of intervention services consisting of frequent contacts by a pediatrician assigned to the family whenever indicated. The other 50 high-risk mothers were offered routine service.

In addition, there was a control group of fifty "low-risk-for-abuse" mothers identified by the interview, questionnaire, and observation procedures. At the end of seventeen months, the children in twenty-five families in each of the three groups—high risk, special service; high risk, routine service; and low-risk controls—were randomly selected for analysis. "There were no significant statistical differences on the basis of Central Child Abuse Registry, indications of 'abnormal parenting practices,' accidents, immunizations or Denver Developmental Screening Test scores" between the high-risk special-treatment group and the high-risk routine treatment group (1978:249).

However, no child in the high-risk special-treatment group "suffered an injury . . . that was serious enough to require hospitalization." On the other hand, five children in the high-risk routine treatment group required in-patient treatment for serious injuries thought to be associated with "abnormal parenting practices." The differences between the two groups with regard to this is statistically significant (p. 250).

Fitch studied 140 infants hospitalized in Denver because of child abuse. The families were randomly assigned to a control group and two experimental groups. The first was provided with a limited treatment program; other groups were provided with more extensive treatment programs. In addition, families of a matched group of nonabused children were studied. All children were given a variety of intelligence and physical and social developmental tests at various intervals. Mothers were given a standard questionnaire to determine changes in their perception of the child and his behavior. The treatment program, offered one of the experimental groups, consisted of close medical and child counseling service by a group of three pediatricians assigned to the family on a 24-hour on-call basis and of other services by community agencies who were involved in helping the family with its problems. These included marital, educational, and financial counseling; family-planning services; individual psychotherapy; anticipatory guidance; role modeling; assertiveness training; socialization group programs; and foster care.

Impact of intervention was measured by comparative changes in child development and by recurrence of abuse over a 30-month period of testing and retesting. The child development scores of the abused nontreated children and those of the treated group were the same (1977:64–66). However, although 8.7 percent of the previously abused but untreated group had been reabused, only 2.7 percent of the abused and treated group had been reabused (p. 169).

The available evaluation studies suggest that the agencies have apparently achieved some limited success. The amount of change one might expect the agencies to effect must be assessed against the great social and personal deprivation characteristic of the families who are the clients of such agencies. In addition the resources available to treat abusive families are limited and the technology available to the worker in trying to effect change in such families is blunt and imprecise. The low level of confidence in the technology available to treat effectively problems of child maltreatment is indicated by the fact that 39 percent of some 1,700 human-services personnel interviewed by Nagi agreed that "we just don't know enough to deal effectively with problems of child mistreatment" (1977:15). Scarce resources backed by a weak technology applied to a group of involuntary, disturbed clients, resistive to change and living in seriously deprived circumstances, would seem to guarantee the likelihood of limited success.

In summary, while Smith's conclusion that "No study has convincingly shown that any treatment of battering parents is effective" (1975:218) may be harsh and unwarranted, the conservative estimate of success by the Berkeley Planning Associates is perhaps closer to a reasonably valid expectation. They conclude their evaluation research study by saying that, overall, "most child abuse and neglect cases can probably not expect to have much more than a 40–50 percent success rate" (1977: p. XIV, vol. 11, final report).

Evaluation studies suggest that the social agencies and other professional interventions have apparently achieved some modest level of success in effecting positive change. The amount of change the community might expect as a consequence of such interventions must be assessed against the social and personal deprivations characteristic of the families who are the clients of such services. Even the modest success achieved may be more than could have been expected initially.

REFERENCES

Allen, Letitia S. 1978. "Child Abuse: A Critical Review of the Research and Theory." In J. P. Martin, ed., *Violence and the Family*, pp. 43–79. New York: Wiley.

Altemeier, William A. et al. 1979. "Prediction of Child Maltreatment During Pregnancy." *Journal of the American Academy of Child Psychiatry* (Spring), 18(2):205–18.

AHA (American Humane Association). 1978. *National Analysis of Official Child Neglect and Abuse Reporting*. Englewood, Colo.: American Humane Association.

——1979a. *Annual Statistical Report: National Analysis of Child Nelgect and Abuse Reporting 1977.* Englewood, Colo.: American Humane Association, February.

——1979b. *Annual Statistical Report: National Analysis of Official Child Neglect and Abuse Reporting 1978.* Englewood, Colo.: American Humane Association, October.

Antler, Joyce and Stephen Antler. 1979. "Child Rescue to Family Protection: The Evolution of the Child Protective Movement in the United States." *Children and Youth Services Review,* 1(2):177–204.

Antler, Stephen. 1978. "Child Abuse: An Emerging Social Priority." *Social Work* (January), 23(1):58–61.

Arnold, Mildred. 1962. *Termination of Parental Rights.* Denver: American Humane Association.

Baher, Edwina et al. 1976. *At Risk: An Account of the Work of the Battered Child Research Department. National Society for Prevention of Cruelty to Children.* Boston: Routledge, Kegan Paul.

Bean, Shirley L. 1975. "Use of Specialized Day Care in Preventing Child Abuse." In Nancy B. Ebeling and Deborah A. Hill (Editors), *Child Abuse: Treatment and Intervention,* pp. 37–42. Acton, Massachusetts: Publishing Services Group.

Bedger, Jean et al. 1976. *Child Abuse and Neglect: An Explanatory Study of Factors Related to the Mistreatment of Children.* Chicago: Council for Community Services.

Berkeley Planning Associates. 1977. *Evaluation: National Demonstration Program in Child Abuse and Neglect.* Berkeley, Calif.: Berkeley Planning Associates.

Better Homes and Gardens. 1978. "What's Happening to the American Family— Attitudes and Opinions of 302,602 Respondents." New York: Meredith Corporation. April.

Billingsley, Andrew and Jeanne M. Giovannoni. 1964. "Child Neglect Among the Poor: A Study of Parental Adequacy in Families of Three Ethnic Groups." *Child Welfare* (November), 43:196–204.

Blumenthal, Monica D. et al. 1975. *More about Justifying Violence: Methodological Studies of Attitudes and Behavior.* Ann Arbor: University of Michigan Institute for Social Research.

Boehm, Bernice. 1964. "The Community and the Social Agency Define Neglect." *Child Welfare* (November), 43:456–64.

Bourke, William. 1963. "The Overview Study: Purpose, Method, and Basic Findings." In *An Intensive Casework Project in Child Protective Services.* Denver: American Humane Association.

Burgess, Robert L. 1979. "Project Interact: A Study of Patterns of Interaction in Abusive, Neglectful and Control Families." *Child Abuse and Neglect: The International Journal,* 3:781–91.

Burgess, Robert L. and Rand D. Conger. 1978. "Family Interaction in Abusive, Neglectful and Normal Families." *Child Development,* 49:1163–73.

Burt, Marvin and Ralph R. Balyeat. 1977. A Comprehensive Emergency Services System for Neglected and Abused Children. New York: Vantage Press.

Caulfield, Barbara. 1978. The Legal Aspects of Protective Services for Abused and Neglected Children. Washington, D.C.: Government Printing Office

Cohen, Stephen S. and Alan Sussman. 1975. "The Incidence of Child Abuse in the United States." Child Welfare (June), 44:432–43.

Cohn, Anne. 1979. "Effective Treatment—Child Abuse and Neglect." Social Work (November), 24(6):513–19.

Collins, Marilyn C. 1978. Child Abuser: A Study of Child Abusers in Self-Help Group Therapy. Littleton, Mass.: PSG Publishing Co.

Creighton, S. J. "An Epidemiological Study of Child Abuse." Child Abuse and Neglect: The International Journal, 3(2):601–5.

Daniel, Jessica H., Eli H. Newberger, Robert B. Reed, and Milton Kotelchuck. 1978. "Child Abuse Screening: Implications of the Limited Predictive Power of Abuse Discriminants from a Controlled Family Study of Pediatric Social Illness." Child Abuse and Neglect: The International Journal, 2:249–59.

Davoren, Elizabeth. "The Role of the Social Worker." In Ray E. Helfer and C. Henry Kempe, eds., The Battered Child, pp. 153–68. Chicago: University of Chicago Press.

de Castro, Fernando, Ursala T. Rolfe, and Mark Heppe. 1978. "Child Abuse: An Operational Longitudinal Study." Child Abuse and Neglect: The International Journal, 2:51–55.

Delsordo, James. 1963. "Protective Casework for Abused Children." Children (November–December), 10(6):213–18.

De Mause, Lloyd, ed. 1974. The History of Childhood. New York: Psychohistory Press.

Disbrow, M. A., H. Doerr, and C. Caulfield. 1977. "Measuring the Components of Parents' Potential for Child Abuse and Neglect." Child Abuse and Neglect: The International Journal, 1:279–96.

Egeland, Byron and Don Brunnquell. 1979. "An At-Risk Approach to the Study of Child Abuse: Some Preliminary Findings." Journal of the American Academy of Child Psychiatry (Spring), 18(2):219–35.

Elmer, Elizabeth. 1977. Fragile Families, Troubled Children: The Aftermath of Infant Trauma. Pittsburgh: University of Pittsburgh Press.

——1979. "Abuse and Family Stress." Journal of Social Issues, 35:60–71.

Erlanger, Howard S. 1974. "Social Class Differences in Parents' Use of Physical Punishment." In Suzanne K. Steinmetz and Murry A. Strauss, eds., Violence in the Family, pp. 150–58. New York: Dodd, Mead.

Fitch, Michael J. 1977. Prospective Study in Child Abuse: The Child Study Program. Denver: Developmental Evaluation Center.

Folks, Homer. 1902. The Care of Destitute, Neglected, and Delinquent Children. New York: Macmillan.

Fontana, Vincent. 1973. The Maltreated Child. New York: Macmillan.

Fontana, Vincent and Esther Robeson. 1976. "A Multidisciplinary Approach to the Treatment of Child Abuse." Pediatrics (May), 57(5):760–64.

Foren, Robert and Roston Bailey. 1968. *Authority in Social Casework.* New York: Pergamon Press.

Galdston, Richard. 1975. "Preventing the Abuse of Little Children: The Parents Center Project for the Study and Prevention of Child Abuse." *American Journal of Orthopsychiatry,* 45:372–80.

Galdston, Richard. 1971. "Violence Begins at Home: The Parents' Center for the Study and Prevention of Child Abuse." *Journal of the American Academy of Child Psychiatry* (April), 10(2):336–50.

Garbarino, S. 1976. "Some Ecological Correlates of Child Abuse: The Impact of Socioeconomic Stress on Mothers." *Child Development,* 47:178–85.

Geddis, D. C., S. M. Monghan, R. C. Muir, and C. J. Jones. 1979. "Early Prediction in the Maternity Hospital." *Child Abuse and Neglect: The International Journal,* 3(2):757–66.

Gelles, Richard J. 1973. "Child Abuse as Psychopathology: A Sociological Critique and Reformulation." *American Journal of Orthopsychiatry* (July), 43(4):611–21.

Gelles, Richard J. 1978. "Violence toward Children in the United States." *American Journal of Orthopsychiatry* (October), 48(4):580–92.

Gelles, Richard J. and Murray A. Straus. 1979. "Violence in the American Family." *Journal of Social Issues,* 35:15–39.

Gil, David G. 1970. *Violence Against Children: Physical Abuse in the United States.* Cambridge: Harvard University Press.

Gil, David G. 1979. "Societal Violence and Violence in Families." In David G. Gil, ed., *Child Abuse and Violence,* pp. 357–85. New York City: A.M.S. Press.

Giovannoni, Jeanne M. and Rosina M. Becerra. 1979. *Defining Child Abuse.* New York: Free Press.

Gray, Jane, Christy Cutler, Janet Dean, and C. Henry Kempe. 1976. "Perinatal Assessment of Mother-Baby Interaction." In R. E. Helfer and C. H. Kempe, eds., *Child Abuse and Neglect: The Family and the Community,* pp. 377–88. Cambridge, Mass.: Ballinger.

Gray, Jane D., Christy A. Cutler, Janet G. Dean and C. Henry Kempe. "Prediction and Prevention of Child Abuse and Neglect." In *Proceedings of the 2nd National Conference on Child Abuse and Neglect,* 1978 vol. I, pp. 346–54. Wash. D.C.: Children's Bureau.

Gray, Charlene. 1978. "Empathy and Stress As Mediators in Child Abuse: Theory, Research and Practice Implications." Ph.d. dissertation, University of Maryland, August.

Green, Arthur. 1976. "A Psychodynamic Approach to the Study and Treatment of Child Abusing Parents." *Journal of the American Academy of Child Psychiatry* (Summer), 15:414–29.

Helfer, Ray E. 1975. *Diagnostic Process and Treatment Program.* Washington, D.C.: U.S. Children's Bureau.

Herrenkohl, Roy C. et al. 1980. "The Repetition of Child Abuse: How Frequently Does It Occur?" *Journal of Child Abuse and Neglect: The International Journal,* 3:67–72.

Holmes, Monica. 1977. *Child Abuse and Neglect Programs: Practice and Theory.* Rockville, Md.: National Institute of Mental Health.

Horowitz, Bernard and Wendy Wintermute. 1978. "Use of an Emergency Fund in Protective Services Casework." *Child Welfare* (July–August), 57(7):432–37.

Hunter, Rosemary, Nancy Kilstrom, Ernest Kraybill, and Frank Loda. 1978. "Antecedents of Child Abuse and Neglect in Premature Infants: A Prospective Study in a Newborn Intensive Unit." *Pediatrics* (April), 61(4):629–35.

Hyman, Irwin A. and James H. Wise. 1979. *Corporal Punishment in American Education.* Philadelphia: Temple University Press.

Jakobsson, Elizabeth, Dagmar Lagerberg, and Monica Ohlsson. 1989. "Early Signs and Symptoms in Neglected Children." *Child Abuse and Neglect: The International Journal,* 3(2):429–38.

Jameson, Phyllis A. and Cynthia Schellenbach. 1977. "Sociological and Psychological Factors in the Backgrounds of Male and Female Perpetrators of Child Abuse." *Child Abuse and Neglect: The International Journal,* 1:77–83.

Jayaratne, Srinika. 1977. "Child Abusers as Parents and Children: A Review." *Social Work* (January), 22(1):5–9.

Jobling, Megan. 1976. *The Abused Child: An Annotated Bibliography.* London: National Children's Bureau.

Johnson, Betty and Harold Morse. 1968. "Injured Children and Their Parents." *Children* (July–August), 15(4):147–52.

Johnson, Clara. 1977. *Two Community Protective Service Systems: Nature and Effectiveness of Service Intervention.* Athens, Ga.: Regional Institute of Social Welfare Research.

Justice, Blair and Rita Justice. 1976. *The Abusing Family.* New York: Human Services Press.

Juvenile Protective Association. 1975. *The Bowen Center Project: A Report of a Demonstration in Child Protective Services, 1965–1971.* Chicago: Juvenile Protective Association.

Kalisch, Beatrice J. 1978. *Child Abuse and Neglect: An Annotated Bibliography.* West Point, Conn.: Greenwood Press.

Kelly, Joseph B. 1959. "What Protective Services Can Do." *Child Welfare,* (April), 38:21–25.

Kempe, C. H. 1976. "Approaches to Preventing Child Abuse." *American Journal of Diseases of Children,* 130:941–47.

Kempe, C. H. and Ray E. Helfer, eds. 1968. *The Battered Child.* Chicago: University of Chicago Press. 2d ed., 1974.

Kempe, C. Henry et al. 1962. "The Battered Child Syndrome." *Journal of the American Medical Association* (July 7), 181:105–12.

Kempe, Henry C. and Ray E. Helfer. 1972. *Helping the Battered Child in His Family.* Philadelphia: Lippencott.

Kent, J. T. 1976. "A Followup Study of Abused Children." *Journal of Pediatric Psychology* (Spring), pp. 25–31.

Kinard, E. M. 1979. "The Psychological Consequences of Abuse for the Child." *Journal of Social Issues,* 35:82–100.

Knight, Mareen, Mildred Disbrow, and Hans Doerr. 1978. "Prediction of Child Abuse and Neglect Measures to Identify Parents' Potential." In *Proceedings of 2nd National Conference on Child Abuse and Neglect*, 2:259–69. Washington, D.C.: Government Printing Office.

Korbin, Jill. 1977. "Anthropological Contributions to the Study of Child Abuse." *International Child Welfare Review* (December), 35:23–31.

Korsch, Barbara, Jewell Christian, Ethel K. Gozzi, and Paul V. Carlson. 1965. "Infant Care and Punishment: A Pilot Study." *American Journal of Public Health* (December), 55(12):1880–88.

Lauer, Brian et al. 1974. "Battered Child Syndrome: A Review of 130 Patients with Controls." *Pediatrics* (July), 54(1):67–70.

Lefkowitz, M. M., R. L. Huesmann, and L. D. Eron. 1978. "Parental Punishment—A Longitudinal Analysis of Effects." *Archives of General Psychiatry.* (February), 35:186–91.

Lieber, Leonard and Jean M. Baker. 1977. "Parents Anonymous: Self Help Treatment for Child Abusing Parents. A Review and Evaluation." *Child Abuse and Neglect: The International Journal*, 1:133–48.

Light, R. 1973. "Abused and Neglected Children in America: A Study of Alternative Policies." *Harvard Educational Review* (November), 43:556–98.

Lynch, Margaret and Jacqueline Roberts. 1977. "Predicting Child Abuse, Signs of Bonding Failure in the Maternity Hospital. *British Medical Journal* (March 5), pp. 624–26.

MacFarlane, Kee and Leonard Lieber. 1978. "Parents Anonymous: The Growth of an Idea," In *Child Abuse and Neglect*. Washington, D.C.: National Center on Child Abuse and Neglect. June.

Maden, Marc F. and David W. Wrench. 1977. "Significant Findings on Child Abuse Research." *Victimology* (Summer), 2(2):196–224.

Mahomoud, Joyce. 1977. "Parents Anonymous in Minority Communities." *Protective Services Research Institute Report* (August–September), 2(7):5–6.

Martin, Harold, ed. 1976. *The Abused Child*. Cambridge, Mass: Ballinger Publishing Co.

Martin, Harold and Patricia Beezley. 1976. "Therapy for Abusive Parents: Its Effects on the Child." In Harold P. Martin, ed., *The Abused Child: A Multidisciplinary Approach to Developmental Issues and Treatment*. Cambridge, Mass.: Ballinger.

McCrea, Roswell. 1910. *The Humane Movement*. New York: Columbia University Press.

Melnick, Barry and John R. Hurley. 1969. "Distinctive Personality Attributes of Child-Abusing Mothers." *Journal of Consulting and Clinical Psychology* (March), 33(3):746–49.

Merrill, Edgar J. et al. 1962. *Protecting the Battered Child*. Denver: American Humane Association.

Morris, Marian and Robert Gould. 1963. "Role Reversal: A Necessary Concept in Dealing with the Neglected-Battered Child Syndrome." In *The Neglected Battered Child Syndrome*. New York: Child Welfare League of America, July.

Morse, Carol W., Olle Sahler, and Stanford B. Friedman. 1970. "A Three Year Followup Study of Abused and Neglected Children." *American Journal of Diseases of the Child* (November), 120:439–46.

Moss, Sidney. 1963. "Authority: An Enabling Factor in Casework with Neglectful Parents." *Child Welfare* (October), 42:385–91.

Nagi, Saad Z. 1975. "Child Abuse and Neglect Programs: A National Overview." *Children Today* (May), 4(3):13–18.

—— 1977. *Child Maltreatment in the United States.* New York: Columbia University Press.

Nelson, B. J. 1979. "The Politics of Child Abuse and Neglect." *Child Abuse and Neglect: The International Journal*, 3:99–105.

Nettler, Gwynne. 1958. *A Study of Opinions on Child Welfare in Harris County.* Houston, Tex.: Community Council of Houston and Harris County, October.

Oates, R. K., D. A. A. Davis, M. G. Ryan, and L. F. Stewart. 1979. "Risk Factors Associated with Child Abuse." *Child Abuse and Neglect: The International Journal*, 3(2):547–55.

Office of Comptroller General of the United States. 1976. *More Can Be Learned and Done About the Wellbeing of Children.* Washington, D.C.: Comptroller General's Office, April.

——1977. *Children in Foster Care Institutions: Steps Government Can Take to Improve Their Care.* Washington, D.C.: Comptroller General's Office.

Oliver, Jack. 1977. "Some Studies of Families in Which Children Suffer Maltreatment." In Alfred W. Franklin, ed., *The Challenge of Child Abuse*, pp. 16–37. New York: Grune & Stratton.

Paget, Norman K. 1967. "Emergency Parents: A Protective Service to Children in Crises." *Child Welfare* (July), 46(7):403–7.

Parke, Ross D. 1976. "Socialization into Child Abuse: A Social Interactional Perspective." In J. L. Tapp and F. J. Levine, eds., *Law, Justice, and the Individual in Society: Psychological and Legal Issues.* New York: Holt, Rinehart, Winston.

Parke, Ross D. and Candance W. Collmer. 1975. "Child Abuse: An Interdisciplinary Analysis." In E. Mavis Hetherington, ed., *Review of Child Development Research*, 5:509–90. Chicago: University of Chicago Press.

Paulson, Monrad. 1966. "Legal Protection Against Child Abuse." *Children*, 13:42–48.

Pelton, Leroy. 1978. "Child Abuse and Neglect: The Myth of Classlessness." *American Journal of Orthopsychiatry* (October), 48(4):608–16.

Pfohl, Stephen. 1977. "The 'Discovery' of Child Abuse." *Social Problems* (February), 24(3):310–23.

Pierce, Robert L. 1979. "Child Abuse: A Stress-Frustration-Aggression-Paradigm." Ph.D. dissertation, Washington University, May.

Polakow, Robert L. and Dixie L. Peabody. 1975. "Behavioral Treatment of Child Abuse." *International Journal of Offender Therapy and Comparative Criminology*, 19(1):100–13.

Polansky, Norman, Carolyn Hally, and Nancy F. Polansky. 1974. *Child Neglect:*

State of Knowledge. Athens, Ga.: Regional Institute of Social Welfare Research, July.

Polier, Justine W. and Kay McDonald. 1972. "The Family Court in an Urban Setting." In C. Henry Kempe and Ray E. Helfer, eds., *Helping the Battered Child and His Family*, pp. 208–24. Philadelphia: Lippincott.

Reavley, William and Marie Therese Gilbert. 1976. "The Behavioral Treatment Approach to Potential Child Abuse: Two Illustrative Case Reports." *Social Work Today*, 7(6):166–68.

Rein, Martin. 1963. *Child Protective Services in Massachusetts.* Papers in Social Welfare, No. 6. Waltham, Mass.: Florence Heller Graduate School for Advanced Studies in Social Welfare, November.

Robertson, B. A. and J. M. Juritz. 1979. "Characteristics of the Families of Abused Children." *Child Abuse and Neglect: The International Journal,* 3(2):857–62.

Scherer, Lorena. 1960. "Facilities and Services for Neglected Children in Missouri." *Crime and Delinquency* (January), 6(1):66–68.

Schmitt, Barton D. 1978. *The Child Protection Team Handbook: A Multidisciplinary Approach to Managing Child Abuse and Neglect.* New York: Garland STPM Press.

Schneider, Carol, Ray E. Helfer, and James Hoffmeister. 1976. "A Predictive Screening Questionnaire for Potential Problems in Mother-Child Interaction." In Ray E. Helfer and C. Henry Kempe, eds., *Child Abuse and Neglect: The Family and the Community*, pp. 393–407. Cambridge, Mass.: Ballinger.

Shapiro, Deborah. 1979. *Parents and Protectors: A Study in Child Abuse and Neglect.* New York: Child Welfare League of America.

Shorkey, Clayton T. 1979. "A Review of Methods Used in the Treatment of Abusing Parents." *Social Casework* (June), 60(b):360–67.

Skinner, Angela, and Raymond Castle. 1969. *Seventy-eight Battered Children: A Retrospective Study.* London: National Society for the Prevention of Cruelty to Children, September.

Smith, Selwyn M. 1975. *The Battered Child Syndrome.* London: Thornton Butterworth.

Spinetta, John J. and David Rigler. 1972. "The Child Abusing Parent: A Psychological Review." *Psychological Bulletin*, 77(4):296–304.

Stark, Rodney and James McEvoy. 1970. "Middleclass Violence." *Psychology Today* (November), 4:52–54, 111–12.

Starr, Raymond H. 1979. "Child Abuse." *American Psychologist* (October), 34:872–78.

Steele, Brandt F. 1975. *Working with Abusive Parents from a Psychiatric Point of View.* National Center on Child Abuse and Neglect. Washington, D.C.: Government Printing Office.

—— 1976. "Violence within the Family." In Ray E. Helfer and C. Henry Kempe, eds., *Child Abuse and Neglect: The Family and the Community*, pp. 3–23. Cambridge, Mass.: Ballinger.

Steele, Brandt F., and Carl B. Pollock. 1968. "A Psychiatric Study of Parents Who Abuse Infants and Small Children." In Ray E. Helfer and C. Henry Kempe, eds., *The Battered Child*, pp. 103–48. Chicago: University of Chicago Press.

Steinmetz, Suzanne K. 1977. *The Cycle of Violence: Assertive, Aggressive and Abusive Family Interaction.* New York: Prager.

Stephanson, P. Susan. 1977. "Reaching Child Abusers Through Target Toddlers." *Victimology* (Summer), 2(2):310–16.

Straus, Murray. 1979. "Family Patterns and Child Abuse in a Nationally Representative American Sample." *Child Abuse and Neglect: The International Journal*, 3:213–25.

Studt, Elliot. 1954. "An Outline for Study of Social Authority Factors in Casework." *Social Casework* (June), 35(6):231–37.

Ten Broek, Elsa. 1974. "The Extended Family Center: A House Away from Home for Abused Children and Their Parents." *Children Today* (March–April), 3:2–6.

Thomson, Ellen M. 1971. *Child Abuse: A Community Challenge.* Buffalo, N.Y.: Henry Stewart.

Tracy, James J., Carolyn Ballard, and Elizabeth H. Clark. 1975. "Child Abuse Project: A Followup." *Social Work* (September), 20:398–99.

Varon, Edith. 1964. "Communication: Client, Community and Agency." *Social Work* (April), 9:51–57.

Walters, David R. 1975. *Physical and Sexual Abuse of Children: Causes and Treatment.* Bloomington: Indiana University Press.

West, Joy E. and Eric D. West. 1979. "Child Abuse Treated in a Psychiatric Day Hospital." *Child Abuse and Neglect: The International Journal*, 3(2):699–703.

Wolock, Isabel and Bernard Horowitz. 1979. "Child Maltreatment and Maternal Deprivation Among AFDC Recipient Families." *Social Science Review* (June), 53(2):175–94.

Yelaja, Shan Kar. 1971. *Authority and Social Work: Concept and Use.* Toronto: University of Toronto Press.

Young, Leon R. 1966. "An Interim Report on an Experimental Program of Protective Service." *Child Welfare* (July), 45(7):373–81.

Young, Leontine. 1964. *Wednesday's Child.* New York: McGraw-Hill.

Zalba, Serapio R. 1967. "The Abused Child II—A Typology for Classification and Treatment." *Social Worker* (January), 12(1):70–79.

CHAPTER 2

CHILD ABUSE AS AN INTERACTIONAL EVENT

HAVING OUTLINED THE general problem of physical child abuse, the various procedures in dealing with the problem, and the extent to which these have apparently been successful in the first chapter, the focus in this chapter is on the particular aspects of physical child abuse which have been the concern of the research being reported.

This research attempted a detailed examination of the immediate parent-child interaction which culminated in physical abuse, with particular reference to child behavior as the stimulus for initiation of the interactional episode. The rationale for studying child abuse from such an orientation requires some explication.

Rationale: Bidirectionality of Parent-Child Relationships

Basic to the general hypothesis of the study being reported here is the concept of bidirectionality in parent-child relationships. Traditionally, and until quite recently, parent-child relationship research theorizing and prescriptive advice was based on the presupposition of unidirectionality. It was presumed that the parent is invariably the active agent, the child the passive recipient of influence efforts.

Traditional child guidance axioms exemplify the unidirectional orientation that the parent is always cause, the child always effect. "There are no problem children, there are only problem parents"; "emotional problems of children are the result of emotional problems of parents." "To know the child, we need to know the parent and knowing the parent, we know what's wrong with the child." Psychotherapists tend to see the child's behavior as symptoms of parent pathology (Weinberger 1972).

"Blaming" the parent, particularly the mother, as the primary "cause" of children's problems has been aptly characterized as the "mal de mére" syndrome (Chess 1964). Currently there is a greater recognition and appreciation of bidirectionality in parent-child relationships.

Parent-child relationships are more accurately characterized as the result of simultaneous, reciprocal, dynamic transactions. Both parties in the transaction act to stimulate response, and act in response to stimulation—both actively directing the course of events. The child is shaped by the behavior of others, while, at the same time, shaping the behavior of others. In doing so, the child modifies, regulates, and conditions parental behavior—creating, in some measure, his own environment. Bidirectionality, as opposed to a unidirectional orientation, views the child as an active partner in the process rather than merely the exclusively reactive object of parental interventions. The child and the parents are members of socio-psycho-biological systems engaged in an ongoing process of mutual modification.

Bidirectionality sensitizes us to the perception of child behavior as an antecedent to parents' behavior, not solely as a consequence of parent behavior. The dynamic aspect of the parent-child/child-parent interaction is aptly stated by Rosenthal, who talks of "the changing pattern of the mutual perceptions and behaviors of both infant and caretaker vis-á-vis each other as a result of their respective previous mutual perceptions and behavior vis-á-vis each other" (1973:302).

In contrast to a unidirectional perception of the socialization process, in which children are passively acted upon by parents, the view is that socialization is the result of "parent child interaction (which) occurs in a reciprocal social system and in which much of the progress toward cultural norms involves mutual adjustment and accommodations" (Bell and Harper 1977:109). Such an orientation suggests that while it is true that parents produce children, there may be much truth in the assertion that children produce parents.

The infant's characteristics shortly after birth—due to a combination of genetic, intrauterine, and perinatal influence—are determinants of children's reaction to their environment. Characteristic activity level, alertness, adaptability, distractability, persistence, reaction to distress, level of excitability and irritability, consolability (the amount and kind of intervention needed to comfort an infant) "affect the child's interaction with the environment (i.e., the mother primarily) in several ways: he reacts differently, he experiences the stresses and ministrations differently and last but not least, he influences the mother's emotions and behavior" (Alexandrowicz and Alexandrowicz 1975a:232).

Wolff (1971), who has done considerable observational research on neonatal behavior, concludes that "congenital differences in muscle tones, motility, duration of alertness, vigor of sucking, frequency of smiling, and stability of sleep-wake cycles certainly contribute as much to the mother-infant relations as the mother's individuality" (p. 96).

The child's behavior can selectively activate one or another of the variety of reactions which a parent is capable of emitting.

Children may respond to parent behavior in ways which gratify, and hence reinforce, some aspect of parent behavior; they may ignore or react negatively to other parent behaviors, which then tend to be discouraged or extinguished. Parent behavior is thus contingent on child behavior. The feedback from each party in the interaction has consequences for each, which, over a period of time, establishes the patterns of behavior which characterize the relationship.

Many responses on the part of the infant, for example smiling, vocalizing, and clinging are reinforcing to the mother and thus the infant reinforces the mother for reinforcing him with her smiles, vocalization, physical contact and kinesthetic stimulation. The phenomenon of attachment then becomes a characteristic of dyadic interaction, not a hypothetical state that resides inside one person. (Martin 1975:473)

Lamb reviews the research which indicates that children initiate efforts to elicit and sustain attention, using gaze and head aversion gestures to modulate and control adult response. He concludes that the research cited "lends scant support to the belief that infants are passive recipients of socializing stimulation. Infants direct the course of their development both by way of individual differences that are evident at birth and through the role they play in determining the nature of social interaction . . . all relevant studies point to one conclusion; that infants have the skills necessary to monitor the behavior of others and the ability to apply this information in modulating, terminating and initiating interaction with adults" (1978:149–50).

The infant "can indicate what it will or will not reject by swallowing or spitting out items that are given to it, by turning its head away from strong odors, by rejecting solids and forcing the mother to return to bottle or breast feedings and by falling asleep during overly rigid feeding schedules" (Bell and Harper 1977:132). These are simple examples of an extensive repertoire of behaviors available to, and controlled by, the child in regulating parental behaviors (Bell 1979).

In describing how the child's patterns of smiling, crying, eating, and sleeping make "fathers and mothers out of men and women," Rheingold concludes that "the child's behavior modifies the parent's behavior even as his behavior is being modified by theirs. As variables for analysis, they are completely confounded" (1969:789).

Concluding another review of the research regarding the infant's contribution to the parent-child relationship, Thoman notes:

It is now clear that from birth the human infant can process information and can differentially respond to sensory input. . . . . The earliest adaptation of the infant is toward the mother, while she, in a complementary fashion, must adapt to her baby, thus resulting in a dyadic feedback relationship. Since the newborn baby is able to discriminate perceptually and to learn simple responses, it would appear eminently reasonable to expect that the infant plays an active role, not simply a reactive one, from the beginning of this relationship. (1974:250)

Citing the relevant child-development research, Parke concludes that it is "clearly indicated that from an early age the infant was capable of a variety of perceptual and cognitive feats, making it a viable partner in an interaction context" (1978:69). The research demonstrates "the wide range of capacities as well as the readiness of the infant for social interaction" (p. 70).

Richmond, the Assistant Secretary of Health, Department of Health and Human Service, and Janice Juel attempted a summary recapitulation of the major findings of child development research during the 1970 decade. He noted a more visible, persistent interactionist theme in parent-child relationship studies. "The significant element in this theme is that the parents' behavior are no longer viewed as being solely responsible for the child's emotional development. Rather the unique individual capacities of the infant are seen as exerting a very direct influence on the parents' behavior" (1980:5).

Reciprocal influencing is in the service of mutual adaptation. Osofsky and Connors note that

Results from an increasing number of studies with neonates compel us to recognize infants as complex organisms with individualized patterns of reactivity and activity preferences at birth that coincide with, impinge upon and affect maternal interests . . . Actions, characteristics and styles of behavior exhibited by the infant play an important role in determining the stimulation he or she receives. (1980:523–24)

Mothers and infants interact through a complex process of mutual adoption or synchrony rather than a simple unidirectional relationship. It is necessary to conceptualize how the infant may influence the mother and the mother affect the infant through a reciprocal process. (*Ibid*:539)

The relationship which develops between infant and parents is the result of the extent to which their complementary needs and dispositions fit together to gratify or frustrate each other. "Goodness of fit," the extent to which parents and children share reciprocal temperamental predispositions, may initiate a pattern of interaction which spirals in a positive direction toward acceptance, or in a negative direction toward rejection and increased risk of abuse. Children, for instance, differ in their response to being held and cuddled, some apparently feeling discomfort in the restriction of movement this involves (Schaffer and Emerson 1964). A mother of such a child who looked forward to, and received gratification from, cuddling would be disappointed and feel rejected if her child responded negatively to being held. Children differ at birth in activity level (Thomas, Birch, and Chess 1963). An energetic mother would find it difficult to accept a slow-acting, lethargic child. What the parent brings to the parent-child relationship interacts with what the child, from the very start, brings to the relationship, creating "affinities or allergies." Depending on the "goodness of fit," the needs and temperamental predispositions of the respective partners in the relationship may be synchronous or asynchronous.

A "good" competent mother can compensate for a "difficult" baby or a "well-endowed" infant can overcome the shortcomings of less than "good" enough mothering (Alexandrowicz and Alexandrowicz 1975a:232). A "difficult" baby can evoke the negative mothering elements in an essentially competent, well-adjusted mother and an "easy" baby can activate the more limited positive mothering potential in a mother who has little aptitude or desire for the mothering role. A different kind of child makes a different kind of mother.

As Giovannoni, Conklin, and Iiyama note, the contribution of the child's endowment to "creating an environment" is integrally related to problems in mother child interaction. But, they say, problematic interaction must be reconceptualized as resulting not from noxious mothers but from noxious pairings, or at least of pairings with the potential for harmful effects on the child's development. . . . For example, a highly active infant may have a dissonant interaction with a mother who is more restrained and inhibited in her activity. . . . The child might bring to the relationship some attributes that are idiosyncratic and that may demand a caretaker who is more dedicated than usual. (p. 11) . . . and the mother, because of developmental problems or ideological preferences, may be only capable of, or have preference for, only a limited commitment to the demands of mothering. Once again, there is a dissonance in pairing between the individual child's greater than average demands and the mother unable or unwilling to provide this. (1978:12)

Advocating a bidirectional conceptualization of parent-child relationships, Bell (1964; 1968; 1971; 1975; 1979) points out that almost all of the child development research presumes, rather than establishes, unidirectionality of influence from parent to child. The preponderance of the research presents correlational findings which say nothing about antecedent-consequent causal relationships. They merely tell us that two variables are associated to a statistically significant degree but nothing about which has caused what. However, the results of the research have generally been interpreted so as to confirm the effects of parental behavior on the child, implying unidirectional causality.

In presenting the rationale for a bidirectional orientation toward parent-child interaction, interchange, and interdependency, Bell (1964; 1968) has reviewed and reinterpreted some of the child development research, demonstrating the validity of a bidirectional interpretation of the results obtained.

Almost every parent-child research finding might legitimately raise the question of bidirectionality in attributing causality. For instance, studying the impact of the cluster of behavior which is often labeled "hyperactivity," Waldrop, Pederson, and Bell note that "for hyperactive children, it would seem reasonable to think in terms of post-natal effects of the child on the parent as well as vice versa. A hypothetical scheme of stimulation and response between parent and child is suggested: A child who is unable to wait for gratification of his wishes may be so demanding and disruptive when frustrated that a parent would feel inclined to invoke punitive and restrictive responses; the punished child would react with hostility and thus stimulate further aggressive parental behavior. Thus the frequently observed relation between aggressive behavior in children and parental aggression could be due, at least in part, to congenital characteristics of the child" (1968:399).

There is a considerable literature which achieves some consensus showing that parental rejection of the child expressed in whatever forms—physical abuse, emotional abuse, or extreme neglect—is associated with hostility, aggression, passive aggression, or problems in management of hostility and aggression on the part of the child (Rohner 1975; Feshbach 1970). The association of the two variables appears to be incontrovertible. The direction of causation, once again, is open to some debate.

Reviewing the research associating child aggression and punitive parental responses, Feshbach noted that:

> Parents are not immune to their child's behavior and their response to a particular act may be influenced by the history of their interaction with the child. The parent who uses severe punishment may have begun by soft words which failed to achieve their objective of aggressive control. Children differ in their predisposition to aggression and in their docility. These variations in aggressiveness may evoke from the parent some portion of those very punitive behaviors which may be assumed to be their antecedents. Although one can exaggerate the influence of the child's aggression upon their parents' disciplinary practices, the possible contribution of the child's behavior to the parents-child interaction has been largely ignored and some attention to this dimension is required. (1970:228)

If almost from the very beginning of life, children evidence the capacity to initiate and regulate their interactions with their environment, this is progressively truer of the older child. Having achieved greater autonomy and independence, having developed, as a result of experience and learning a more varied repertoire of instigations which invite or require parent response, the component of the child's contribution to the parent-child interaction is necessarily more potent.

Child abuse is a manifestation of a particular kind of parent-child relationship. If parent-child interaction is generally bidirectional, this should be true of the child abuse interaction as well. This is the conceptualization of child abuse around which this research was oriented. We see the child abuse as an interactional event, in which the child's input is as significant as the parent's input. We turn now to the relevant research literature supporting the orientation presented above.

Research Regarding Bidirectionality—General Context

We will first review the literature pointing to the influence of the child in determining parents' behavior and then review the literature which is more directly focused on the child's contribution to the bidirectional interaction associated with physical abuse.

Observational studies of parent-child interaction in the home and under standardized laboratory conditions confirm the bidirectional nature of the relationship. Moss undertook an observational study of 30 firstborn children and their mothers over the first three months of life in the home. Specific, theoretically significant maternal and child behaviors were monitored during the period of extended observation. Moss concluded as a result of his analysis of the data that "the state of the infant affects the quantity and quality of maternal behavior and this in turn would seem to influence the course of future social learning" (1967:90). Both mother and child were found to emit behaviors which sought to influence the behavior of the reciprocal and to reinforce that behavior which is desired and satisfying.

On the basis of extended tape-recorded interviews with 54 primiparous mothers, Robson and Moss (1970) found that mothers were very responsive to the "social behavior" initiated by the child, i.e., smiling, eye contact, visual fixation, and following. It was more difficult for mothers to feel positive toward those infants who failed to initiate such behaviors.

The absence of such responses, ordinarily initiated by the child, makes it very difficult for parents to develop a positive relationship with the child. This is most poignantly detailed by Fraiberg (1974) in her study of parents and their blind children.

Having made detailed assessment under standardized conditions of healthy, full-term neonates when they were two to four days old, Korner demonstrated individual differences in frequency and duration of spontaneous crying, in irritability, soothability, and postural adjustments to adults holding them. Her observations lead to the conclusion that "the newborn is neither the unorganized nor the passive, receptive organism he is commonly believed to be" (1971:611).

Not only does the infant's general arousal and particularly his irritability have an effect on his caregiver, his relative soothability does as well. The mother's capability in soothing her infant is one of the cardinal challenges she faces in the infant's earliest weeks of life and her success or failure connot help but have an impact on her feelings of effectiveness and competence as a mother. (Korner 1974:108)

Similar studies over two decades by Thomas, Chess, and Birch (1963; 1968) of children's temperament suggest, with some overlap, three groups of children identifiable very early in life—the easy child, the difficult child, the slow to warm child. The parent who is fortunate enough to be faced with the responsibility of rearing an easy child—responsive, adaptable, predictable, generally cheerful in disposition, regular in patterns of eating, sleeping, elimination—find parenting rewarding and enhancing to their self-esteem. Individuals parenting a difficult child—irritable, irregular, unresponsive, not adaptable—find the role of parenting unrewarding. They feel inadequate, impatient, and burdened.

Observing children characterized by different levels of distractibility interacting with their parents in a standard problem-solving situation, Bee (1971) found that mothers of distractible children provided significantly more direction and structuring. The nature of the child's behavior "required" and evoked different responses from parents. Campbell similarly found that mothers of hyperactive children, interacting with their children in laboratory set tasks, "provided significantly more direct physical help, encouragement and impulse/control suggestions during the difficult tasks. . . . One interpretation is that these mothers have learned to structure tasks in response to their hyperactive child's inability to focus attention, control impulsivity and persist" (1973:347).

Two observers spent two one-hour sessions observing the interactions of 24 middle-class mothers and their adopted infants (Beckwith). One observer focused on the mother, the other on the child. In summarizing their results, they say one of the most "impressive" findings "is the reciprocity that regulates the social system that mothers and infants establish. Despite our observations method which set out specifically to identify the initiator and responder in all interactions, it was extremely difficult to attribute responsibility to one or another of the pair. . . . The infant can choose to increase the stimulation by his own initiations (crying, smiling, etc.) or he can choose to diminish it by ignoring the mother. A correlational study such as ours makes more difficult the task of unraveling the influences of the mother on the infant and the infant's effects on the mother" (1972:408).

Observing and coding differences in social behavior in a research playschool nursery, Leach found that children identified as having problems in separation were less responsive to other children and less responsive to their mothers than were a group of normal children. Only a limited number of the many variables studied showed differences in mother-child interaction and "these all showed differences in the *children* (emphasis in the original) rather than the mother". The researchers go on to add, "this surprised us" (1972:265).

Kogan and Wimberger (1971) and Kogan and Tyler (1973) observed the interaction of mothers and children in laboratory situations in attempting to identify differences between mothers' responses to their physically handicapped or mentally disturbed children as compared with the interaction of mothers and nonhandicapped children. In general, mothers of handicapped children showed more frequent directing and controlling behavior, perhaps in response to the mother's recognition that their handicapped children needed this kind of help.

Terdal, Jackson, and Garner used standard laboratory situations for observation and coding of 42 mothers' interaction with developmentally delayed children as compared with 40 mothers interacting with normal children. "The finding of increased directiveness shown by mothers of the retarded children is interpreted as direct support of the hypothesis that mothers respond to inadequate responding on the part of their child by increased structure. The directionality of effect must be viewed, however, as an issue that is not resolved" (1976:259). There was less question, however, about the bidirectionality of interaction.

More recently, videotaped observations of limited interactional events confirm the idea of reciprocity in the mother-child relationship. Illustratively, one detailed report of such observations by Brazelton et al. concludes that mother-child interaction is a "mutually regulated system in which both partners modify their acting in response to the feedback provided by their partner. It is surprising how early the infant plays an active role" (1975:147). "Even in his earliest interactions with his environment, social and non-social, the infant is impressively self-regulated and intentional" (p. 148).

In one observational study of the often neglected father-child relationship, Greenberg and Morris (1974) have detailed the behaviors emitted by infants which have the effect of inducing an affectionate paternal response to the child. The child's behavior results in "capturing" the father and developing a bond between father and child.

Clinical data confirm bidirectionality. Studying foster mothers' relationships with a series of foster children, Yarrow (1963) found that the foster mother behaved quite differently with different children. Each child evoked different kinds of behavior from the foster mother in response to the unique individual differences the child brought to the relationship.

Prechtl conducted a longitudinal study concerned with the development of parent-child relationships of 8 neurologically damaged, hyperexcitable infants in comparison with 10 normal control children. By the end of the third month, mothers of 7 of the 8 handicapped children were either rejecting or overanxious, whereas such marked reactions were true of only 1 of the 10 mothers of normal children. Prechtl reports that both he and his assistant found themselves reacting negatively to the handicapped children (1963:56), illustrating the influence of the child's behavior on the responses of the caregiver.

Pemberton and Benady studied 12 "consciously rejected children" who had been referred to a mental health clinic for treatment. "Consciously rejected children" were defined as those children whose parents had "excluded them from the family." These children were compared with "the next patient referred to the clinic of the same age and sex" (1973:575). The "consciously rejected children" presented such behaviors as encopresis, stealing, lying, negative and aggressive behaviors and a rejecting attitude toward parents significantly more frequently than the control group. An analysis of the "consciously rejecting" mother's behavior indicated that she was emotionally unstable and unsure of her role and needed a scapegoat, but the reasons for choosing the particular child were obscure. "However, the child's behavior in every case served to strengthen the process of rejection" (p. 577). Parental pathology and a particular child's reaction pattern interacted to develop and sustain a negative parent-child relationship.

A young child's night-waking is disruptive of family routine, presenting a difficult problem for working parents. Maternal anxiety and sleep problems in children are associated. In studying 77 babies followed from birth to 14 months of age, Bernal attempted to determine whether maternal anxiety was the "cause" or the result of night-walking in infants. Interviews with mothers and a diary kept by mothers was the source of the data. Twenty-four of the 77 infants studied proved to have difficulty in sleeping. This subgroup was differentiated from the other infants studied. Length of labor and birth was significantly longer for this group, and during the first ten days they cried more frequently and for longer periods of time than the other children. An analysis of child behavior and maternal responses during the first 14 months of the two groups of children studied "tends to support the idea that whether a baby develops sleeping difficulties or not may be independent of the maternal response to a greater extent than had been realized" (1973:767).

The idea that mishandling a child causes sleep problems may have come from observing the different techniques parents are sometimes driven to use when faced with a child who persistently wakes at night. But our results strongly suggest that the parents' behavior is caused by the children's sleeplessness rather than the other way around. (Richards and Bernal 1974:510)

Studying the night waking habits of 60 children in his pediatric practice, Carey (1974), found that sleep disturbances in young infants were associated with temperamentally low sensory threshold.

Experimental studies confirm bidirectionality by deliberately varying child behavior. Changes in child behaviors stimulate changes in parental response patterns.

Osofsky trained four 10- to 12-year-old girls to act in three identifiably different ways in role-play sessions—dependently, independently and stubbornly. They were then randomly assigned to role-play some standard situation with 65 white, middle-class mothers. In different role-play situations, the role-playing children emitted one of the three behavioral approaches listed above. The focus of the experiment was to determine if deliberately changing the child's behavior influenced changes in the mother's behavior. The findings supported the hypothesis. "The major finding of differences in parental responses to the children's changing behavior lent support to the proposal that children influence parental behaviors, just as parents influence children's behaviors in the socialization process" (1971:168).

In an experimental analogue of a parent's attempts to modify a child's behavior, Berberich found that the child's "correct" response to the parent's intervention tended to reinforce that type of intervention. In discussing the implications of the findings, Berberich notes that "parents of emotionally disturbed children have been labeled 'cold' and 'rejecting.' Some have been tempted to conclude that a child is emotionally disturbed *because* [emphasis in original] the parent is cold. Another possibility exists. It is quite likely that emotionally disturbed, retarded and underachieving children do not deliver much positive reinforcement. . . . Perhaps 'coldness' and 'rejection' and, in general, decreased adult involvement with a child occur as functions of the schedules of reinforce-ment given by some children" (1971:96).

A study by Yarrow et al. shows that nursery-school caregivers, success-fully trained to offer high nurturant behavior, offered significantly more non-nurturant responses when interacting with boys "who sought help frequently and who resorted to clowning for attention" (1971:306). The children's behavior tended to negatively modify the nurturant role orien-tation of the caregiver.

Stevens-Long used actors in studying responses to different children's activity levels. Videotapes of children presenting different levels of activity were presented to 30 subjects, who were asked to select preferred discipli-nary responses. Results confirmed the fact that "the activity level of the child influences the use of discipline by the adult" (1973:482). Overactive children were disciplined more severely.

Frodi et al. (1978) monitored skin conductance and blood pressure of 48 father and mother pairs as they watched a videotape presentation of in-fants. In addition, mood scales were administered. Half of the subjects saw a smiling infant, half an infant crying. The different babies were labeled "normal," "difficult" and "premature." Unlike the smiling infant, the crying infant elicited decided changes in autonomic arousal and was perceived as aversive. Skin conductance increases were especially notice-able when the crying infant was labeled "premature."

Detailed single-case-history reports are an additional procedure in con-firming the transactional influence of children on parents. Alexandrowicz and Alexandrowicz (1975a; 1975b) collected data on children's behavior during the first month of life, using the Brazelton Neonatal Behavior As-sessment Scale. Selecting two children who had scored toward the ex-treme ends of the scales, they interviewed parents before the end of the second year.

One child, Carmel, consistently tested from the first day of life as highly irritable, excitable and difficult to quiet. Her behavior "made her an ungratifying and demanding baby who created for herself a very dif-ferent environment from the one a relaxed, alert and responsive infant would create" (Alexandrowicz and Alexandrowicz 1975a:238). A follow-up psychiatric study a year after birth indicated how family organization and parental role allocation has been influenced by Carmel's character-istic responses. It was clear that a different kind of child would have evoked a different pattern of responses from the parents.

A second case study (Alexandrowicz and Alexandrowicz 1975b) was concerned with another child who rated consistently high on favorable test characteristics throughout the first month of life. "Debbie was an infant with fair motor development, high ability to achieve relaxation (by herself or with help) and was highly resonsive to physical contact and to the human voice and face" (1975b:177). Psychiatric study follow-up at 22 months showed a well-adjusted, happy child, despite pathogenic features in the parental pair.

Included in their longitudinal-study sample of 120 children followed from the time of conception, Thomas et al. identified three women "who had clearly defined attitudes of rejection before their child's birth. This resulted from various problems and conflicts regarding their pregnancies." In the case of two of these mothers, their babies, immediately after birth, displayed characteristics and dispositions which made them very easy to care for. Their initial "rejecting attitude did not crystallize. The third child had more intense and negative, nonadaptive responses so that her care involved both much more work and effort and less apparent success. This mother developed definite reactions of rejection and tension" (1961:726).

Thoman reports the results of the intensive observation and objective recording of one infant's behavior from birth through the first weeks of life which risked initiation of a negative parent-child relationship. The infant showed avoidance responses to being picked up and held despite the fact that the "mother was judged by observers to be relatively gentle . . . stimulation being neither continuous nor vigorous" (1975:187). The infant's behavior was a source of frustration and confusion to the parents.

Research Regarding Bidirectionality—Physical Abuse

If, as Bell notes, child abuse "is most frequently a consequence of disciplinary action taken by parents or caretakers in response to a specific act of a child" (1975:417), then studies which point to the child's behavior in the instigation and modification of discipline provide a convenient transition from studies concerned with reciprocity in parent-child relationships generally to the reciprocity in the child-abuse interaction specifically.

Using the Fels Parent Behavior Rating Scale, Donnelly conducted an observational study, in the home, of parent behavior toward psychotic children and their siblings in 51 families. Family interaction was observed for an average of four hours per family. The principal hypothesis of the study that there was a "demonstrable difference between parental behavior toward the psychotic child and that toward its sibling" (1960:336) was confirmed. As compared with their relationship with siblings, parents showed significantly less ability to understand the psychotic child's capacity and needs, and their relationship with the psychotic child was characterized by significantly less rapport and warmth:

The variables of 'understanding' and 'rapport' were closely related. . . . Parents understood more of the behavior and mental life of the siblings and thus their relationship with these children were closer and more mutually satisfying—the greater parent acceptance of the sibling was, understandably, closely related to the variable of 'warmth.' It is difficult to accept a person who is remote and difficult to understand. . . . Psychotic children behave in a manner that is more frustrating to their parents. This behavior may often be characterized as unresponsive, socially unacceptable or inappropriate for their age. Such problem behavior tends to initiate a circular interaction. (p. 356)

Disciplinary control procedures employed by the parent toward the psychotic child was more restrictive, more severe, less democratic than that employed with siblings. Parents were less "ready to explain the rationale of policies" (p. 257) with the psychotic child. In discussing this, Donnelly notes the interactional aspects in determining discipline:

The psychotic child, compared with his siblings, was less predictable and was often imperative in his behavior. Many of the parents said that they could not reason with such a child and arbitrarily placed restrictions on him. . . . The unresponsiveness of the psychotic child to the parent's explanations may have been a deterrent for explanation. Some of the children repeatedly asked the same questions. It was noted that many of these parents had low levels of frustration tolerance. The incessant questioning might have been 'just too much.' The siblings were more responsive and more readily understood the parent's explanations so the rewards were greater. Problems of discipline loomed larger in the case of the psychotic children. Parents often cease to punish a child when a child 'responds.' The psychotic children did not respond as readily as the siblings. (p. 358)

Patterson (1974) made a detailed, systematic observational study of the behavior of one 6½-year-old boy, Karl. The focus of the observation was the antecedents, concommitants and consequences of noxious, hostile stimuli, the initiation and persistence of such responses, and the network of stimuli controlling disciplinary interaction relating to noxious, hostile behavior.

The child was observed in the home interacting with other members of the family over a period of some 15 days, four hours each day scattered during the course of the day. One principal study conclusion of relevance to our concern here is that "in extended interchange, both members of a dyad affect each other's behavior. . . . The illustrative analysis strongly suggests that while the parents influenced Karl in these extended interactions, he also altered their behavior" (p. 919).

Patterson subsequently reported on an observational study of the noxious behaviors of 27 problem and 27 matched nonproblem boys. "The data supported the notion that many boys labeled as Conduct Problems do indeed perform disruptive behaviors at higher rates than their normal counterparts" (1976:305). "In general, it seemed that the identified child both resided in *and* contributed to an aggressive system [emphasis in original]. . . . In such interchanges, the deviant child gave and recieved increasing amounts of aversive events and was thus both a victim and architect of the system" (p. 268).

The child's reaction to being disciplined acts as a stimulus affecting the parent's subsequent intervention and further illustrating the child's influence in determining parent behavior. This sequence was experimentally tested by Sawin et al. Adults watched an aggressive act by a child on a television monitor. Discipline was administered and the child reacted to the punishment in one of four different ways, by pleading, making reparation, ignoring the punishment or by defiance. Adults reacted to each of the child's responses by additional discipline which varied with the nature of the child's response. The child who reacted to the initial attempt at discipline by apologizing and promising to behave was generally rewarded by the adult experimental subjects. The child who reacted to discipline by defiance was most harshly punished. The researchers' concluding note is that "not only do children's reactions serve to modify adult disciplinary behavior but they may serve to maintain adult punitiveness. These findings provide additional support for a bidirectional model of adult-child interaction in which the role of the child in controlling adult behavior is recognized" (1975:7).

Moving more directly to the child component in the child-abuse event, a number of factors can be cited which might conceivably make the child high risk for abuse. Some of these may be attributes of the child assigned by fate over which no one has control, but which, nevertheless, make for a difficulty in the interaction.

The child's sex might be a disappointment to the parents and may stimulate negative parental response. The child may be orthopedically handicapped and this may contribute to abuse. The child may have impaired hearing or sight. The child may be mentally retarded or autistic so that he does not, or cannot, understand. In these cases, the parent may be frustrated by a child's unresponsiveness, apathy, inability to learn, feel a sense of inadequacy as a parent and be additionally burdened with the extra care disability generally requires. Parenting has a greater probability of being an aversive experience.

About 7.5 percent of 134 battered infants studied by Smith et al. had serious congenital deficits, as compared with a 1.75 percent incidence of such deficits in the general population (1975:124). Reporting abused and neglected children together as a group, Soeffing (1975) noted the high frequency of "special" characteristics in the maltreated group, 1,680 of the 14,083 (12 percent) children reviewed having "special" difficulties, i.e., mental retardation, congenital defects, physical handicaps, premature birth, chronic illness, etc.

Both the 1977 and 1978 Annual National Statistical Report, collated by the National Study on Child Neglect and Abuse Reporting, indicate that children reported as abused manifested special characteristics in a similar limited percentage of the cases. In 1979, 12 percent of the children were reported as presenting special characteristics that might be regarded as high risk for abuse. In 1978 this was true of 14.4 percent of the children reported. In both years the largest percent of "special characteristics" children were identified as "emotionally disturbed" followed by children diagnosed as mentally retarded. Only a small percentage of the children were listed as prematures, physically handicapped, or chronically ill (AHA 1979a:50, 1979b:37).

One of the more persistent research findings however is the disproportionate number of premature and/or low birth-weight children who are abused. Stern (1973) found prematurity to be a factor in a study of child abuse of 12 children. Prematurity dictated a need to maintain the child in the hospital following the mother's return home. As a consequence, early interpersonal relationship between mother and child was altered in an undesirable direction. The development of any early close attachment was delayed. Klein and Stern (1971) found that 23.5 percent of 51 battered infants studied were low birth-weight infants. Low birth weight was associated with an increased risk of abuse.

Castle and Skinner, in a study of 78 abused English children, "noted a high incidence of babies described as 'premature' . . . double the national average." (1969:5)

This is confirmed in Elmer's study of 22 abused children, "a third of whom weighed less than 5.5 pounds at birth indicating prematurity." Furthermore "the abused children had twice the incidence of neurological signs as was true for the rest of the group." Slightly more than 50 percent of the group had I.Q.s under 80 and 8 of the 22 children "had marked difficulty in impulse control." (1971:350)

Smith et al. found that the prevalence of low birth weight among the study sample of 134 abused children was "four times greater than the national rate" (1975:124). Fomufod, Sinkford and Louy (1975) provide additional restrospective evidence of the relationship between low birth weight and child abuse. The factor is further analyzed by Fomufod (1976).

Holman and Kanwar (1975) found prematurity and low birth weight, and consequent early mother-child separation, as factors associated with child abuse in a study of 28 abused children. Similar findings are reported by Baldwin and Oliver (1975) in a study of 38 abused children and by Martin et al. (1974).

Maden and Wrench (1977:202), recapitulating, in tabular form, the results of 20 studies relating to low birth weight, congenital defects, and birth complications as associated with child abuse, show a statistically significant relationship in at least 7 studies.

A variety of reasons have been advanced explaining the relationship between child abuse and prematurity. The fact that the child may have to receive special care which limits contact with the mother immediately after birth reduces the possibility of effective bonding between mother and child, supposedly critical for initiating a positive mother-child relationship. Premature children require more care and hence are apt to be perceived as more demanding. Prematurity and low birth weight are associated with poor prenatal care, with out-of-wedlock conception and with birth to adolescent mothers, who may not be ready for, and are impatient with, parenthood. Martin and Beezley (1974) further suggest that subtle or mild neurological dysfunctions in infants' central nervous systems may result from difficult or atypical birth experiences, presenting the parent with greater difficulties in parenting.

Lamb suggests that the "characteristics of premature infants (their high-pitched cry, their distorted head-to-body ratio, their fragility and size, their wizened appearance) make them less effective elicitors of the 'cute response' " (1978:155) which reinforces positive parental responses to the child. Comparing the maternity hospital records of 50 abused children with 50 nonabused children, Lynch and Roberts (1977) found that abused children were significantly more likely to have been referred to a special care unit after birth, suggesting some atypicality in the child's birth experience.

A prospective study by Fitch et al. (1978) provides evidence of differences between abused and nonabused children shortly after birth. Data was obtained on a group of children and mothers before, and immediately after, birth. On follow-up, subjects were sorted into abuse and nonabuse groups only after these events occurred. Examination of APGAR scores relating to appearance, pulse, grimace, activity, and respiration obtained four minutes after birth showed that 96 percent of the nonabused children had the preferred scores of 9 or 10, while this was true of only 76.3 percent of the children subsequently abused.

Egeland also conducted a prospective study of child abuse. Detailed records were obtained on 275 mothers and children prior to and at birth. Follow-up over a 20-month period following birth resulted in identification of 26 infants who were abused or neglected, 5 having suffered physical abuse. The previously collected data was used in defining differences between the mothers and children involved in maltreatment as compared with their nonmaltreatment peers. Data relating to infant characteristics indicated that differences in levels of irritability did provide a modest increment to the variance between the two groups. The researcher notes that "the condition of the baby cannot in itself predict abuse and neglect within a mother child pair although the trends indicate that baby variables are involved. The importance of the baby's behavior in determining the quality of care he/she receives is noted in the results of the discriminant analysis involving the combination of mother infant and interaction variables when it was found that the Brazelton Factor 1, 'baby's orientation,' is the third best predictor of group membership" (1979:275).

Hunter et al. followed up 282 infants who had been admitted to the intensive care unit of a hospital and subsequently discharged to their families. Detailed data was obtained on the children and families at the time of admission. By the end of the first year, 10 children were reported as suffering from maltreatment. Background data on these children indicated that maltreated infants were less mature at birth and had more congenital defects than their nonmaltreated nursery mates. "It is probable that these neonates provided very few positive responses to their parents" (1978:634).

Comparing 25 abused children with their nonabused siblings, Lynch found that the abused children showed significantly greater health problems during their first year of life (1975:315). These involved serious or recurrent illness that made heavy demands on parents for child care.

Sandgrund, Gains and Green (1974) used standard intelligence tests in studying 60 abused children as compared with 30 nonabused controls. Of the abused group of children, 25 percent had scores below seventy. In contrast, only 3 percent of the nonabused children were found to be retarded.

A child's atypical social status, like atypical physical or mental status, may make the child high risk for abuse. Adapting to the birth of the child and making the necessary inevitable adjustments to the role of becoming a parent is made more difficult under a number of circumstances which consequently increase the risk of abuse, i.e., when the child is born out-of-wedlock, at a time when the marriage or the father-mother relationship is problematic, too soon after a previous birth.

A difficult beginning risks inauguration of a negative relationship between mother and child. The child is unplanned, the pregnancy is unwanted, the child is unwelcome and the child's parent-child interaction is off to a bad start. The child's very existence imposes a burden on the parent(s) for which they are unprepared, makes demands which can be met only with considerable difficulty, and interferes with the possibility of achieving alternative life goals and expectations. The child is, of course, not to blame for the inconvenience and the punishments which an unplanned pregnancy might impose; for the physical pain of a frequently difficult delivery; or the financial, social, and emotional sacrifice demanded by the need to involuntarily accept the role responsibilities of parenthood. Nevertheless, it is because of the child that the parent encounters all of this, so that while it is unjust, it is understandable that the parent attributes the source of a sequence of problems to the child.

In line with the suppositions which follow from this, scales developed to identify—for preventative intervention—mothers who are high risk for abuse include questions regarding the pregnancy and delivery experience, and the response of the parent to the presentation of the child immediately upon birth. Such programs further attempt to obtain observational data on labor and delivery room behaviors, post partum handling of the child, etc. (Gray et al. 1979).

Research findings consistently tend to show that the abused child, as compared with nonabused children, was more frequently an unplanned child, more often conceived out-of-wedlock, that a higher percentage of abusing parents were very young as compared with nonabusive controls (Smith et al. 1975:197), and pregnancy and delivery experience with the abused was more frequently problematic for abusive mothers (Lynch 1975:318; see also Baher et al. 1976:36–49).

The child who is the result of an unwanted pregnancy, illegitimacy, or "forced" marriage is noted a high risk for abuse in a number of different studies (Elmer 1971; Lukianowicz 1971; Nurse 1964). A comprehensive study of child abuse in New Zealand found that "the number of illegitimate abused children were two to three times greater than the expected number based on the population estimate" (Fergusson, Fleming, and O'Neill 1972:78).

Comparing abusive and nonabusive mothers with reference to whether or not the child was planned, Green (1976) found that 80 percent of the abused children were unplanned as compared with 55 percent of the children in the nonabused group. In recapitulation, the premature child, the child with a disability, the child born out of wedlock, or at the wrong time, or of the wrong sex, presents the parent, however unwittingly, with a stimulus which is aversive and which then risks potentiating whatever predispositions the parent may have toward child abuse.

More actively, certain patterns of child behavior are apt to be high risk for abuse. The irritable child; the negativistic child; the demanding, overly dependent child; the hyperactive child; the unresponsive child impose greater burdens on, and offer fewer satisfactions to, the parent.

Studies of temperamental differences in children, as evidenced immediately after birth, confirm every parent's observation that some children provoke more negative reactions than others. Researchers who have done detailed studies of infant temperamental differences conclude that

these findings raise several questions about the interaction of general parental attitudes and child characteristics in the evaluation of the parent-child relationships. Given any degree of ambivalence (incomplete acceptance and therefore partial rejection) of the parental role, the characteristics of the child may foster and reinforce a specific direction of parental attitudes and practices. It is easy to mother a normally active, positively responsive, highly adaptive, routine-accepting child whose mood is predominantly cheerful. It is quite another matter to maintain the same positive maternal responses to a highly active, poorly responsive, nonadaptive arrhythmic child whose mood is expressed by a preponderance of crying. (Thomas 1963)

A study of 71 cases of abused children led Milowe and Lourie to a 4-category grouping of abuse etiology. Two of the categories point to the child's contribution to the abusive event—i.e. (1) "defects in the child as a precipitating factor (particularly those defects which lead to lack of responsiveness or other irritating reaction creating frustration in the parent); (2) factors in personality development leading to the child's inviting others to hurt it or hurting itself" (Milowe and Lourie 1964:1079). The researchers report that "our studies of family interactions at the time of battering indicate that the chronic crying and irritability of the infant are often involved in the long downhill struggle of the parent to control his or her impulses" (Milowe and Lourie 1964:1081).

Descriptions of abused children tend to show them as presenting characteristics which are likely to make for difficulty in parent-child interaction. They tend to be depressive, hyperactive, destructive, fearful, withdrawn (Zalba 1967); presenting behavioral symptoms such as sleep difficulties and bed-wetting (Lewis 1969), and being listless, apathetic and fearful (Lukianowicz 1971), violent and aggressive (Galdston 1975).

Gil's report of the nationwide survey of abuse in 1967 and 1968 notes that in 34.1 percent of the incidents, according to the social worker most knowledgeable about the case, abuse was related to "a general attitude of resentment and rejection on the part of the perpetrator toward a child. In these cases not a specific act but the 'whole person' or a specific quality in the person such as his sex, his looks, his capacities, the status and circumstances of his birth is the object of his rejection." In 24.5 percent of the cases the workers indicated that abuse was associated with "persistent behavioral atypicality of the child, e.g. hyperactivity, high annoyance potential etc. Cases positively checked on this item may be considered child-initiated or child provoked abuse" (Gil 1970:127).

In a collection of 545 cases of abuse studied by the Erie County Children's Aid and Society for Prevention of Cruelty to Children a listing of circumstances associated with abuse showed "immediate or delayed response to specific acts of the child" in 142 instances, "misconduct of child by community standards" in 27 instances, and "persistent behavioral atypicality of child" in 32 instances (Paget, 1971:123).

Libbey and Bybee studied 25 cases of physical abuse of adolescents reported to a county department of public welfare. In 91 percent of the cases, "abusive incidents were immediately preceded by the adolescent disobeying or arguing with the parent" (1979:111). In 50 percent of the cases, parents further reported that "the adolescent had been 'generally difficult' recently; that is, truant, stealing or running away. The majority of the adolescents were categorized as having shown 'difficult to handle,' or serious, behavior problems (chronic truancy, stealing, running away) either previous to or immediately preceding the abusive incident" (p. 118). "This mild or severe acting-out behavior by the adolescent is frequently an antecedent to the abusive incident" (p. 124).

A study by the Denver Department of Public Welfare of 101 abused children highlighted the contribution the children made to the abusive interaction. A finding the Division considers significant is that nearly 70 percent of the children had shown physical or developmental deviation before the injury was reported.

The child welfare workers considered about 20 of the children to be

uncontrollable and subject to severe temper tantrums. In their opinion about 17 were below normal in speech development, 17 were mentally retarded, 16 had toilet training problems, 14 had feeding problems, 8 had physical handicaps or deformities and 2 suffered from brain damage.

The child welfare workers described the 52 children under 5 years of age as whiny, fussy, listless, chronically crying, restless, demanding, stubborn, resistive, negativistic, unresponsive, pallid, sickly, emaciated, fearful, panicky, unsmiling. . . . The children 5 years old or over typically appeared to the child welfare workers as gloomy, unhappy and depressed. They tended to be selfish and inconsiderate or unassertive and self-sacrificing. (Johnson and Morse 1968:149–50)

A study by Morse et al. of 25 abused children notes that

retrospectively the high frequency of retardation and of children perceived by their parents as 'problems' was impressive. . . . Fifteen of the 25 children were considered to be 'different'. Though this information was obtained during the initial hospitalization after the diagnosis of abuse, our follow up data supported those previous impressions of retarded and problem children preceding the abuse or neglect. (Morse et al. 1970:445)

Eight of ten abused children studied by Terr displayed hostile behavior which was interpreted as being retaliatory to the abusive parent. "This angry behavior worsened the already strained relationship between the parent and the child" (1970:669).

A study comparing 255 abused children with 108 nonabused children from similar kinds of families found the abused children to be more frequently below average in intelligence, less physically attractive, and more likely to be either "extremely sluggish" or "overactive" (Fergusson, Fleming, and O'Neill 1972:284–85).

A detailed study of 60 abuse cases at the Downstate Medical Center, Brooklyn, New York, noted that "abused children manifested major psychological, neurological and cognitive defects when compared with nonabused, normal controls. Abused children were reported by mothers to be more self-destructive and more aggressive, both at home and in school. A larger number of abused children required more attention than their siblings—the mother's perception of the abused child as the most aggressive and demanding of her offspring made this child vulnerable to scapegoating" (Green 1975:170).

Listed among children's characteristics which contribute to the abuse incident are "pathological traits creating extra burdens" for parenting, "poor response to nurturance," "difficulty with impulse control," "normal or accidental traits which . . . have special significance for parents" such as feminine behavior in a male child which triggers anxiety about latent homosexuality in the parent (Green 1975:172–73).

The finding of a lack of mutuality and reciprocity in abusive mothers' responses to their children is indicated in a videotaped study of interactional sequences between abused children–abusive mother pairs as compared with matched experimental nonabusive groups. Robison and Solomon found that abusive mothers were more "insensitive to the moods and signals" of their children than nonabusive mothers. Abused children are less responsive to their mother. "The major picture which emerges is of a dyad 'out of sync' " (1979:249).

George and Main arranged for trained observers to code the day care center behavior of 10 physically abused children one to three years of age and 10 matched non-abused controls. The abused children responded negatively to friendly overtures from other children and caregivers and engaged in aggressive behaviors significantly more frequently than the matched controls. In interpreting the findings, the researchers consider the hypothesis that the abused children's atypical avoidance and aggressive responses were a consequence of the abuse they had suffered. Alternatively, however, they note that since the children "were not only more aggressive, but also responded more negatively to friendly overtures, they may readily be termed more 'difficult'—Our study was not addressed to the question of how these particular children come to be selected for parental abuse. It does affirm, however, that even this early in childhood the infant who has been abused can be 'difficult' " (1979:316).

Ried and Taplin conducted systematic observations of interaction of 27 families where there was evidence of child abuse and compared these observations with the observations of 27 nonabusive families. Observations were made of 14 categories of carefully defined aversive behaviors emitted by family members. Observations indicated that "abusive families are characterized by a high overall level of aversive behavior significantly higher than that demonstrated by families in which there was no evidence of child abuse. Further, the highest level of aversive behavior was exhibited by the abused children themselves" (1978:7). The researchers further conclude that "the results of the present study strongly suggest that the child is not a passive participant in the abuse process. Rather, the abused children observed in this study were, because of constitutional defect, temperament or ineffective parenting, extremely difficult to handle" (p. 18).

An observational study of patterns of parent-child interaction in 17 abusive families, as compared with a matched group of 19 non-abusive control families, concluded that there was "little to suggest that children in abuse families behave in a fashion remarkably different from controls". The researchers note, however, that while "rate differentials" did not reach statistical significance, "the rates of negative behaviors by youngsters in abuse families do suggest more aversive conduct by these children than controls." (Burgess and Conger 1978:1171). Children from abuse households displayed almost 50 percent more negative behavior than did their counterparts from control families.

In an interview and record review study of 87 abused children from six public welfare agencies in different parts of the country, Shapiro found that in "most instances the problems described involved some very provocative behavior, lending support to the now increasingly common observation that children are not necessarily passive recipients' of parental violence but are involved in a circular process in which they often provoke the parent's response" (1979:91–92).

Research findings not only indicate that abused children, as compared with nonabused children, are different in some significant ways, but further, as contrasted with their nonabused siblings or with nonabused children in other families, the abused child is perceived by his mother as "different"—more difficult to rear, more troublesome. Ounsted et al. (1974) obtained descriptions of abused children by abusive mothers which indicated perceptions of the children as clingy, aggressive, disobedient—in general, hard to mother.

In comparing the behavior of 134 abused children with a control group of 53 nonabused children, Smith et al. found that a significantly greater percentage of abusive mothers compared with control mothers considered their child difficult (1975:125). While difficulties such as crying or clinging behavior were more often encountered by the abusive parent, it might be noted that the researchers indicate that "the results do not support the suggestions that these children necessarily invite physical abuse since after being in the hospital for some time, they were not observed to be more irritable than the controls" (p. 196).

Green compared the attitude of 60 abusive mothers toward their child with that of 30 nonabusive control mothers. Mothers in the abused group more frequently reported their children to be problems at home and in school. "The mother's perception of the abused child as the most aggressive, difficult and demanding of her offspring made this child vulnerable to scapegoating" (1976:419). Morse, Sahl and Friedman (1970) found that 60 percent of the 25 battered children whom they studied were considered to be "difficult" by their parents.

Personal interviews with 39 members of Parents Anonymous in five different cities resulted in the finding that "58 percent reported that at least one of their children had some form of handicap or special problem and 33 percent reported that at least one of their children was hyperactive. Ninety-two percent reported that one of their children was the focus of their abuse" (Lieber and Baker 177:140).

Fitch et al. used a standard Child Behavior Characteristic Scale in comparing the perception of the child by 64 mothers who had abused their children and 34 mothers who had not. Nonabusive mothers perceived their children as "being easier to quiet, less difficult to care for and more easily pacified" and having a "more agreeable disposition" than did the abusive mothers. On the other hand, mothers of the abused group viewed their children as being "less sulky, less sad looking and less moody" (1978:58).

De Lissovoy presents a preliminary analysis of social work interviews with 34 abusive mothers in which they were asked to describe the abused child as compared with their other children. In general, the abused child was perceived as different—"model descriptions included 'never slept,' 'cries a lot,' 'always sick,' 'does not stay well,' 'follows me around,' 'gets into everything' (1979:345). The research was prompted by de Lissovoy's attempt to define the "abuse provoking child." He concludes by noting that "as an active member of the family transactional system, the child's behavior, innocent in terms of motivation and in some cases instigation, may serve as the abuse provoking stimulus" (p. 341).

Herrenkohl and Herrenkohl collected data on some 580 children in families referred for abuse. Data were obtained from agency and hospital records, and from interviews with parents. A comparison was made between the abused child and a nonabused sibling. More of the abused children were born prematurely and significantly more had lower APGAR scores in early infancy, indicating less adequate development. Children who were targets for abuse, as contrasted with the nonabused sibling, were more often described by their mother as presenting difficulties in "excessive eating or refusal to eat, eating bizarre material, frequent temper tantrums, sleeping problems, head banging, behavior problems, moodiness" (1979:265). Mothers perceived themselves as having less influence or control over these children as compared with nonabused siblings.

On balance, then, the general picture suggests that the abused children are perceived by their mothers as being more difficult to care for than the nonabused child. One might argue that such subjective perceptions are distortions which permit the abusive mother to resolve problems of guilt in abuse by "blaming" the abused child. This would, however, need to be established, rather than merely asserted. Until that is done, one must respect as valid the mother's perception of the level of difficulty in dealing with the child.

In support of the contention that parents perceived the abused child as different and more difficult is the fact that in families with a number of children, often, although not invariably, one particular child is involved in abuse. Whatever general predispositions toward abuse the parent may bring to the situation, these are not indiscriminately discharged. While many children in contact with such parents are potential abusees, actually some particular children seem to attract abuse. Delsardo notes that in

"33 cases, all multiple child families, only one child in each family was being abused" (1963:218). Burland reports that in the "majority of abusive families studied (28) only one child was abused" (1973:585). In a study of 115 cases of abuse, Bryant concludes that "normally one child in the family was selected to be abused and once the abuse began there was a tendency for it to be repeated on the selected child" (1963:129). (See also Boardman, 1962).

This general finding does not preclude the fact that in some more limited percentage of cases, more than one sibling in the family has been found to be the target of abuse (Gil 1970; Lauer et al. 1974; Herrenkohl and Herrenkohl 1979).

Child-abuse practitioners are aware of the significance of the child's behavior as this impacts on the development of abuse events. Some 80 practitioners, from a variety of professions providing services in child-abuse situations, were asked to list the factors which, in their experience, they perceived to be causally related to child abuse (Gillespie, Seaberg, and Berlin). A rank order importance of the 32 variables identified was obtained. Four of the highest variables, rated in order of importance, related to behaviors emitted by the child: "child defiant of caretakers," "excessive demands of child on caretakers," "hyperactive child," "child unresponsive to caretakers" (1977:346).

Discussion: The Child's Contribution to Abuse

Having reviewed the general literature and the more specific child-abuse literature which gives emphasis to, and validates, a bidirectional orientation to child abuse, some additional comments need to be made.

The concept of bidirectionality as applied to child abuse would suggest that a child-abuse incident is a complex concatenation of interactive elements denoting some reciprocity between abuser and abused. The abuse event is not the product of the exclusive input of the abuser but is rather the result of the inputs of both parties involved in the incident. Neither is totally responsible nor is either totally innocent.

There is increasing acceptance of the parent⇆child interactional equation in incidents of abuse.

The changing focus from a one-sided emphasis on what parents do in abusing their children to a bidirectional, interactional view is exemplified by the following change in the definition of child abuse by prominent child abuse researchers. Previously, Kempe and Helfer had defined abuse in terms of "any child who received nonaccidental physical injury (or injuries) as a result of acts (or omissions) on the part of his parents or guardians." (1972:1) More recently, Helfer (in B. Kalisch 1978) modified this definition as follows: "Any *interaction* or *lack of interaction* between a *caregiver* and *child* which results in *non-accidental* harm to the child's *physical* and/or *developmental* state" (p. xxi, emphasis in original). Elaborating on this definition, Helfer states that

the problems children get into are indeed the results of an interaction or lack of interaction between a caregiver and child. The concept of the interaction is important since it is the input of *both* the caregiver and the child that must be considered. (p. xxi)

A frequently cited comprehensive review of the child-abuse literature by Parke and Collmer likewise stresses the need for such a reorientation. They note that

a serious shortcoming in both the psychiatric and sociological models [of child abuse] is their *failure to give adequate recognition to the interactive nature of child abuse. It is insufficient to view abuse from a unidirectional viewpoint*, whereby the main cause is located in either the parent or in external social circumstances. One important feature of the social-situational approach is the recognition that both partners, the child victim as well as the parent, need to be considered if child abuse is to be fully understood. In particular, the role that the child himself may play in eliciting abuse needs to be more closely examined. (1975:545; emphasis added)

Two recent reviews of the literature, focussing on the child's contribution to the abuse event, is further evidence of a growing appreciation of bidirectionality in child abuse (Roberts 1979; Friedrich and Boriskin 1976).

Belsky (1980) notes, in formulating an ecological model of child abuse, that "more recently we have come to recognize that within the family, abused children have to be considered as potential contributors to their own maltreatment: available models no longer view the child exclusively as an unwitting victim but also as a causative agent in the abuse process." (p. 324)

While a more comprehensive listing of the variables associated with child abuse has given recognition to the child component in the child abuse event, the various determinants are accorded different emphases in the research and the literature. As is true of the parent-child general research and literature, there is a decided overemphasis on the parent variable and a decided underemphasis on the child. The impact of the child in explaining and understanding child abuse has received little actual attention.

The relative neglect of the child's role is confirmed in reviewing the listings in a comprehensive bibliography on child abuse and neglect (Kalisch, 1978), covering the literature on this topic from the late 1880s to 1977. The bibliography lists 77 references dealing with the individual characteristics of abusive parents and only 11 that refer to the "child's role in provoking abuse." Furthermore, of 118 references listed under family dysfunction (in the causation of abuse and neglect), only the same 11 entries refer to the child's role.

A detailed review of the child abuse and neglect literature through 1977 concludes that

> there has been little attention directed to a study of the interaction, under a variety of circumstances, between abused children and their parents. Efforts at developing typologies which can be useful for prevention and treatment are primarily centered on the dynamics of the parents rather than on the kinds of interaction which may be causing abuse. (Holmes 1977:158)

The deliberate selective focus here on the child's contribution is designed to give heightened visibility to this component of the interaction. It is, in effect, a deliberate effort to correct the previously noted overemphasis on parent variables so as to achieve a more balanced perspective.

It would be clearly erroneous however to substitute one unidirectional orientation with another unidirectional orientation—namely, child as change agent, parent as target of change.

The integrity of the transactional nature of the parent-child relationship needs to be clearly recognized. Both are important as contributing to the interaction; at some point the child component in the interaction may have greater valence for determining the resultant vector, at another point the parent's component may be the more significant component.

Nor does the suggested reorientation in the conceptualization of the child abuse event imply, beyond this, that we ignore the validated and decided influence of cultural prescriptions and situational imperatives in determining abuse. It merely calls for a more explicit recognition of the fact that the child-related variables are determinants in the specific response employed by a particular parent in interacting with a particular child.

The explanation for the imbalance and the decided ambivalence about acceptance of a more pronounced bidirectional perspective is, hypothetically, ideological. In discussing this, Korner says:

It is surprising, although historically understandable, that for so long there has been an almost exclusive emphasis on the parent's effect on child development without considering what the child represents as a stimulus to the caregiver. This emphasis on parent effects has been especially strong in the United States. There are many reasons for this, one of which is the strong emphasis on environmental factors as being almost exclusively responsible for shaping the development of children. This undoubtedly stems in part from a repudiation of Old World tenets, some of which are based on the assumption that there are inequalities of birth and class. The thought that there might be genetic or biological differences among individuals which could influence development was too close to Old World dogma and had to be rejected until recently. Besides, there was some comfort in the thought that parental actions determine outcome, in spite of the guilt-producing aspects of this stance. At least it implied a degree of control over the developmental process. . . . (1974:118)

Bell (1975) likewise notes that the strong environmental bias in American psychology and sociology militated against comfortable acceptance of bidirectionality because it was equated with heavier emphasis on biological determinants. In addition, this point of view was consonant with the ideologies and conceptualizations that were most potent in determining the prevalent child-rearing prescriptions during the immediate past decades. The orientation of both psychoanalytic psychology and its derivatives, ego-psychology, Rogerianism, etc. and behavioral modification place the stress on the parent and parental inputs in determining the outcome of parent-child relationships.

Reinforcing this orientation toward parent-child interaction is the widely accepted conception of the child as "tabula rasa." The image of the tabula rasa child waiting to be molded by his social and parental environment is "nourished by two powerful forces—the Watsonian optimism about the infinite malleability of personality, which has permeated learning theory, and the American rendition of Freud, which emphasizes interpersonal factors and underplays physiology, constitution and fate" (Wenar and Wenar 1963:704).

An hypothesis in contradiction to the more traditional statement of the direction of cause and effect is rarely considered. Even when explicitly stated it is given little consideration in interpreting results. For instance, Timberlake compared the behavior of 30 physically abused children and a matched group of 30 physically non-abused children in foster care. One of the findings indicated that physically abused children attributed reasons for their placement to their own objectionable behavior significantly more often than did the non-abused children. The explanation offered for this correlation of abuse experience and self-definition is that "physically abused children were more likely than non-abused children to assume the bad-guy role with its negative self-image . . ." (1979:285).

The explanation derives from theoretical considerations regarding the effects on self-identification of labeling imposed by others. An alternative hypothesis is offered relating to this and other findings in the study which is then implicitly rejected and not further pursued. Thus Timberlake notes that non-abused children actually do come into foster care primarily as a consequence of situational reasons rather than as a consequence of behavior on the part of the child. "Therefore their perception of the situational reason for their placement appears accurate. Following the same line of reasoning the abused children may have accurately perceived that they were placed in care more as a result of their own provocative behavior than as a result of life threatening behavior of their parents" (ibid:285). The same correlational finding is thus quite differently explained as a result of an accurate perception by the child of his contribution to the decision rather than as a result of distorted perceptions imposed by labeling. The second explanation, permitted by the same correlation and possibly as valid as the labeling hypothesis, is considerably less acceptable ideologically.

The general tendency to disregard the child as an active actor in the abuse event is additionally reinforced by two related perceptions, both of which are erroneous. One is that very young children are incapable of autonomous, self-directed behavior and two, that most physically abused children are very young. The fact is that the largest percentage of physically abused children are decidedly well beyond infancy. This age group of children is clearly recognized as having the capacity for self-directed behavior, capable of making autonomous decisions.

But even this is truer than had been previously supposed for the minority of abused children who are in infancy. Current research has more and more firmly established, as noted, the fact that even young children are selectively responsive to stimuli and initiate behaviors designed to selectively stimulate behavior in caretakers.

To some extent, this view of the child as an innocent, passive victim in the abuse event is in contradiction to another view of the child frequently espoused by professionals concerned with child welfare. In foster care, adoptions, institutional care, and divorce proceedings, the child is precieved as capable of making, and entitled to make, decisions in matters which affect him. Here the child is seen as a competent, responsible, active participant in what transpires. If the objection is raised that the two apparently inconsistent perceptions of the child relate to different age groups of children, we need to be reminded once again that the very largest percentage of abused children are over five years of age.

One might add that to deny the child's contribution to the abuse event, to see the child as only a passive cipher acted upon in a consequential event, is a profound disrespect to the child. It denies the child's individuality, his desire and capacity for autonomy, his ability to assertively and effectively contend with his interpersonal environment.

Some of the predisposition to reject the notion of bidirectionality results from the feeling that it suggests something we have come to abhor—it suggests "blaming the victim." With "contribution" of behavior comes "responsibility" for behavior and the implication for "blame." Admittedly, it is very difficult to suggest a need for a more balanced perspective by giving greater visibility to, and focusing on, child variables, without at the same time suggesting that we are "blaming" the child. This is decidedly not our intent.

We wholeheartedly agree with Steele and Pollack when they say that "despite the contributions which infants make toward the disappointments and burdens of their parents, they can hardly be used as an excuse or adequate cause for child abuse" (1974:115). But while not excusing the parent for abuse, we cannot, if we want to fully understand the abuse event, dismiss the child's contribution as an inconsequential factor.

Perhaps a distinction needs to be made between control and intentionality. It is true that parents are more consciously deliberate than infants or very young children in selecting a particular intervention designed to control for the expressed purpose of achieving certain specific results. However, while the infant or young child may have considerably less capacity and experience for such "intentional" behavior, while less consciously deliberate, his or her behavior is no less effective in control—in determining the behavior of others. Bell and Harper note, in discussing the attachment behavior of infants, that the "signal and executive aspects of a child's attachment repertoire affect parents in such a way as to achieve and maintain proximity. It is not necessary that the child 'plan' or have the 'intention' of keeping the parent nearby. It is only necessary that the child's behavior be effective. And there is little doubt that young children are very competent" in effecting and maintaining parental proximity (1977:64).

Deliberate intentionality is not necessarily implied in identifying the factors which determine the interaction. The child may not consciously and deliberately intend to affect parents' behavior in a particular way, yet responding to his own bio-psycho-social needs leads to certain behavior which has a strong probability of evoking certain parental behaviors.

Nor is there any suggestion in this that the child consciously "invites" abuse or deliberately "provokes" abuse. This may be a factor in a small percentage of cases where the child might be motivated by guilt to invite punishment in making restitution or where a child acting provocatively risks abuse to obtain attention from otherwise indifferent parents. In the more typical situation, however, abuse is the unintended consequence of the child's attributes and/or child behaviors as a stimulus to parent response.

There is no suggestion in what has been said that while the child actively participates in the abuse event and contributes to shaping its ultimate outcome, he is a coacting equal. Clearly the parent, by virtue of his greater maturity and experience, has, or should have, a greater repertoire of benign responses and greater responsibility in determining that abuse should not occur.

In response to much of the research presented in this chapter, it might be argued that the child's hyperactivity, or aggressiveness, or apathy, or mental deficiency, etc., was the result of abuse rather than an initial contributory element to abuse. One might say, along with Bakan, that "the abuse of a child creates a child who invites abuse" (1971:111). Child abuse researchers find it difficult, if not impossible, to determine whether or not the disabilities and/or characteristic aversive behavior of the abused child antedated the abuse or are a consequence of abuse. Generally the child becomes available for study after the abuse event. In the absence of the longitudinal study which provides detailed data on children before they are abused as compared with post-abuse functioning of the same child, we are left with some residuals of nagging doubt as to the cause and effect sequence. The research does suggest, however, that certain kinds of child characteristics and behavior, whatever the "cause" of their genesis, are likely to be associated with the instigation of abuse whenever they are manifested.

REFERENCES

Alexandrowicz, Malca K. and Dov Alexandrowicz. 1975a. "The Case History of a Happy Child." *Child Psychiatry and Human Development* (Spring), 5:174–81.
—— 1975b. "The Molding of Personality: The Newborn's Innate Characteristics in Interaction with Parents' Personalities." *Child Psychiatry and Human Development* (Summer), 5:231–41.
AHA (American Humane Association). 1979a. *Annual Statistical Report—National Analysis of Child Neglect and Abuse Reporting—1977.* Englewood, Colo.: American Humane Association (February).
—— 1979b. *Annual Statistical Report—National Analysis of Official Child Neglect and Abuse Reporting.* Englewood, Colo.: American Humane Association (October).
Baher, Edwina et al. 1976. *At Risk: An Account of the Work of the Battered Child Research Department, Society for the Prevention of Cruelty to Children.* Boston: Routledge and Kegan Paul.
Bakan, David. 1971. *Slaughter of the Innocents.* San Francisco: Jossey-Bass.
Baldwin, J. A. and J. E. Oliver. 1975. "Epidemiology and Family Characteristics of Severely Abused Children." *British Journal of Preventive and Social Medicine* (December), 29:205–21.
Beckwith, Leila. 1972. "Relationships between Infants' Social Behavior and their Mothers' Behavior." *Child Development,* 43:397–411.
Bee, H. L. 1967. "Parent Child Interaction and Distractability on 9 Year Old Children." *Merrill-Palmer Quarterly,* 13:175–90.
Bell, Richard Q. 1964. "The Effect on the Family of a Limitation in Coping Ability in the Child: A Research Approach and a Finding." *Merrill-Palmer Quarterly,* 10:129–42.
—— 1968. "A Reinterpretation of the Direction of Effects in Studies of Socialization." *Psychological Review,* 75:81–95.
—— 1971. "Stimulus Control of Parent or Caretaker Behavior by Offspring." *Developmental Psychology,* 4:63–72.
—— 1975. "Reduction of the Stress in Child Rearing." In L. Levi, ed., *Society, Stress, and Disease: Vol. 2. Childhood and Adolescence,* pp. 416–21. New York: Oxford University Press.

—— 1979. "Parent-Child and Reciprocal Influence." *American Psychologist* (October), 34(10):821–25.

Bell, Richard Q. and Lawrence V. Harper. 1977. *Child Effects on Adults.* New York: Wiley.

Belsky, Jay. 1980. "Child Maltreatment—An Ecological Integration." *American Psychologist* (April), 35(4):320–331.

Berberich, John P. 1971. "Do the Child's Responses Shape the Teaching Behavior of Adults?" *Journal of Experimental Research in Personality*, 5:92–97.

Berkowitz, Leonard. 1962. *Aggression: A Social Psychological Analysis.* New York: McGraw-Hill.

—— 1973. "Control of Aggression." In B. M. Caldwell and H. R. Ricciuti, eds., *Review of Child Development Research*, 3:95–140. Chicago: University of Chicago Press.

Bernal, J. L. 1973. "Night Waking in Infants During the First 14 Months." *Developmental Medical Child Neurology*, 15:760–69.

Boardman, Helen E. 1962. "A Project to Rescue Children from Inflicted Injuries." *Social Work* (January), 7:43–51.

Brazelton, T. Berry. 1975. "Early Mother Reciprocity." In *Parent Infant Interaction*, pp. 137–54. CIBA Foundation Symposium 33. New York: Associated Scientific Publishers.

Brown, A. and R. Daniels. 1968. "Some Observations on Abusive Parents." *Child Welfare* (February), 47:89–94.

Bryant, Harold D. 1963. "Physical Abuse of Children: An Agency Study." *Child Welfare* (March), 42(3):125–30.

Burgess, R. L. and R. D. Conger. 1978. "Family Interaction in Abusive Neglectful and Normal Families." *Child Development*, 49:1163–1173.

Burgess, R. L. and R. D. Conger. 1977. "Family Interaction Patterns Related to Child Abuse and Neglect: Some Preliminary Findings." *Child Abuse and Neglect: The International Journal*, 1:269–77.

Burland, Alexis, Roberta Andrews, and Sally Headston. 1973. "Child Abuse: One Tree in the Forest." *Child Welfare* (November), 52:585–92.

Cameron, James R. 1977. "Parental Treatment, Children's Temperament and the Risk of Childhood Behavioral Problems: 1. Relationship between Parental Characteristics and Changes in Children's Temperament over Time." *American Journal of Orthopsychiatry* (October), 47:568–76.

Campbell, Susan B. 1973. "Mother Child Interaction in Reflective, Impulsive and Hyperactive Children." *Developmental Psychology*, 8:341–49.

Carey, William. 1974. "Night Waking and Temperament in Infancy." *Journal of Pediatrics*, 84(5):756–58.

Castle, R. L. and A. Skinner. 1969. *78 Battered Children: A Retrospective Study.* London: National Society for the Prevention of Cruelty to Children.

Chess, S. C. 1964. "Mal de Mere." *American Journal of Orthopsychiatry*, 34:613.

de Lissovoy, Vladimir. 1979. "Toward the Definition of 'Abuse Provoking Child.' " *Child Abuse and Neglect: The International Journal*, 3:341–50.

Delsardo, J. D. 1963. "Protective Casework for Abused Children." *Children*, 10:213–18.

Donnelly, Ellen M. 1960. "The Quantitative Analysis of Parent Behavior toward Psychotic Children and their Siblings." *Genetic Psychology Monographs*, 62:331–76.

Egeland, Byron. 1979. "Preliminary Results of a Prospective Study of the Antecedents of Child Abuse." *Child Abuse and Neglect: The International Journal*, 3:269–78.

Elmer, E. and G. Gregg. 1967. "Developmental Characteristics of Abused Children." *Pediatrics*, 40:596–602.

Elmer, E. et al. 1971. "Studies of Child Abuse and Infant Accidents." In J. Segal, ed., *Mental Health of the Child*. Rockville, Md: National Institute of Mental Health, June.

Fergusson, David M., Joan Fleming, and David P. O'Neill. 1972. *Child Abuse in New Zealand*. Wellington: Research Division Department of Social Welfare.

Feshbach, Seymour. 1970. "Aggression." In P. H. Museen, ed. *Charmichael's Manual of Child Psychology*, 2:159–260. 3d ed. New York: Wiley.

Fitch, Michael et al. 1978. *Prospective Study in Child Abuse: The Child Study Program*. Denver, Colorado: Department of Health and Hospitals, Mimeo.

Fomufod, Antoine K. 1976. "Low Birth Weight and Early Neonatal Separation." *Journal of the National Medical Association* (March), 68:106–9.

Fomufod, Antoine K., Stanley M. Sinkford, and Vicki E. Loug. 1975. "Mother Child Separation at Birth; A Contributing Factor in Child Abuse." *Lancet* (September 20), 2(7934):549–50.

Fraiberg, Selma. 1974. "Blind Infants and Their Mothers: An Examination of the Sign System." In M. Lewis and L. A. Rosenblum, eds., *The Effect of the Infant on its Caregiver*, pp. 215–32. New York: Wiley.

Friedrich, William N. and Jerry A. Boriskin. 1976. "The Role of the Child in Abuse: A Review of the Literature." *American Journal of Orthopsychiatry* (October), 46:580–90.

Frodi, Ann M., Michael Lamb, Lewis A. Leavitt, and Wilberta L. Donovan. 1978. *Fathers and Mothers Response to Infant Signals: Possible Contributions of Children to Their Own Abuse*. Madison: University of Wisconsin Press, mimeo.

Galdston, Richard. 1975. "The Parenting Center Project for the Study and Prevention of Child Abuse." *American Journal of Orthopsychiatry* (April), 45:372–81.

George, Carol and Wang Main. 1979. "Social Interaction of Young Abused Children: Approach, Avoidance and Aggression." *Child Development*, Vol. 50:306–18.

Gil, D. G. 1970. *Violence Against Children, Physical Child Abuse in the United States*. Cambridge: Harvard University Press.

Gillespie, David F., James R. Seaberg, and Sharon Berlin. 1977. "Observed Causes of Child Abuse." *Victimology: An International Journal* (Summer), 2:342–49.

Giovannoni, Jeanne M., Jonathan Conklin, Patti Iiama. 1978. *Child Abuse and Nelgect: An Examination from the Perspective of Child Development Knowledge.* San Francisco: Rand Research Associates.

Gray, Jane D., Christy Cutler, Janet Dean, and Henry Kempe. 1979. "Prediction and Prevention of Child Abuse." *Seminars in Perinatology* (January), 3:85–90.

Green, Arthur H. 1976. "A Psychodynamic Approach to the Study and Treatment of Child Abusing Parents." *Journal of American Academy of Child Psychiatry* (Summer), 15:414–29.

Green, Arthur H. 1975. "The Child Abuse Syndrome and the Treatment of Abusing Parents." In Stefan A. Pasternak, Ed., *Violence and Victims,* pp. 167–79. New York: Spectrum Publications.

Green Arthur H., Richard W. Gaines, and Alice Sandgrund. 1974. "Child Abuse: Pathological Syndrome of Family Interaction." *American Journal of Psychiatry,* 131:882–86.

Greenberg, Martin and Norman Morris. 1974. "Engrossment: The Newborn's Inpact upon the Father." *American Journal of Orthopsychiatry* (July), 44:520–31.

Harper, L. 1971. "The Young As a Source of Stimuli Controlling Caretaker Behavior." *Developmental Psychology,* 4:73–88.

Helfer, Ray. 1973. "The Etiology of Child Abuse." *Pediatrics* (April), 51:777–79.

Herrenkohl, Ellen C. and Roy C. Herrenkohl. 1979. "A Comparison of Abused Children and Their Non-abused Siblings." *Journal of the American Academy of Child Psychiatry* (Spring), 18(2):260–70.

Holman, R. R. and S. Kanwar. 1975. "Early Life of the Battered Child." *Archives of Disease in Childhood* (January), 50:78–80.

Holmes, Monica. 1977. *Child Abuse and Neglect Program: Practice and Theory.* Washington, D.C.: Government Printing Office.

Hunter, Rosemary, Nancy Kilstrom, Ernest Kraybill, and Frank Loda. 1978. "Antecedents of Child Abuse and Neglect in Premature Infants: A Prospective Study in a Newborn Intensive Care Unit." *Pediatrics* (April), 61:629–35.

Hyman, Clare A., Robert Parr, and Kevin Browne. 1979. "An Observational Study of Mother-Infant Interaction in Abusing Families." *Child Abuse and Neglect: The International Journal,* 3:241–46.

Johnson, Clara. 1974. *Child Abuse in the Southeast: Analysis of 1172 Reported Cases.* Athens: Regional Institute of Social Welfare Research, University of Georgia.

Johnson, B. and H. A. Morse. 1968. "Injured Children and their Parents." *Children,* 15:14752.

Kalisch, Beatrice J. 1978. *Child Abuse and Neglect: An Annotated Bibliography.* Westport, Conn.: Greenwood Press.

Kempe, C. Henry and Ray E. Helfer. 1972. *Helping the Battered Child and His Family.* Philadelphia: Lippincott.

Kempe, C. Henry and Ruth Kempe. 1978. *Child Abuse.* Cambridge: Harvard University Press.

Klein, M. and L. Stern. 1971. "Low Birthweight and the Battered Child Syndrome." *American Journal of Diseases of Children,* 122:15–18.

Kogan, Kate L. and Herbert C. Wineberger. 1971. "Behavior Transactions between Disturbed Children and Their Mothers." *Psychological Reports*, 28:395–404.

Kogan, Kate L. and Nancy Tyler. 1973. "Mother Child Interaction in Physically Handicapped Children." *American Journal of Mental Deficiency*, 77(5):492–97.

Korner, Anneliese. 1971. "Individual Differences at Birth: Implications for Early Experience and Later Development." *American Journal of Orthopsychiatry* (July), 4:608–19.

—— 1974. "The Effect of the Infant's State, Level of Arousal, Sex and Ontogenetic State on the Caregiver." In Michael Lewis, Leonard A. Rosenblum, eds., *The Effect of the Infant on its Caregiver*, pp. 105–21. New York: Wiley.

Lamb, Michael E. 1978. "Influence of the Child on Marital Quality and Family Interaction During the Prenatal, Perinatal and Infancy Periods." In Richard M. Lerner and Graham B. Spanier, eds., *Child Influences on Marital and Family Interaction: A Life-Space Perspective*, pp. 137–64. New York: Academic Press.

Lauer, B. et al. 1974. "Battered Child Syndrome: A Review of 130 Patients with Controls." *Pediatrics*, 54:67–70.

Leach, Gill M. 1972. "A Comparison of the Social Behavior of Normal and Problem Children." In N. B. Jones, ed., *Ethological Studies of Child Behavior*, pp. 249–84. Cambridge, England: Cambridge University Press.

Lewis, Harold. 1969. "Parental and Community Neglect: Twin Responsibilities of Protective Services." *Children*, 16:114–18.

Lewis, M. and L. Rosenblum, eds. 1974. *The Effect of the Infant on Its Caregivers*. New York: Wiley.

Libbey, Patricia and Rodger Bybee. 1979. "Physical Abuse of Adolescents." *Journal of Social Issues*, 35(2):101–25.

Lieber, Leonard and Jean M. Baker. 1977. "Parents Anonymous: Self-Help Treatment for Child Abusing Parents—A Review and Evaluation." *Child Abuse and Neglect: The International Journal*, 1:133–48.

Lukianowcz, Nancy. 1971. "Battered Children." *Psychiatria Clinica*, 4:257–80.

Lynch, Margaret A. 1975. "Ill Health and Child Abuse." *The Lancet* (August 16), 2(7928):317–19.

Lynch, M. A. and J. Roberts. 1977. "Predicting Child Abuse: Signs of Bonding Failure in the Maternity Hospital." *Child Abuse and Neglect: The International Journal*, 1:491–92.

Maden, Marc F. and David F. Wrench. 1977. "Significant Findings on Child Abuse Research." *Victimology* (Summer), 212:196–224.

Martin, Barclay. 1975. "Parent-Child Relations." In Frances D. Horowitz, ed., *Reviews of Child Development Research*, 4:463–540. Chicago: University of Chicago Press.

Martin, Harold and Patricia Beezley. 1974. "Preventions and Consequences of Child Abuse." *Journal of Operational Psychiatry* (Fall–Winter), 6:68–76.

Martin, H. et al. 1974. "The Development of Abused Children: A Review of the Literature." *Advances in Pediatrics*, 21:25–73.

Milowe, I. D. and R. S. Lourie. 1964. "The Child's Role in the Battered Child Syndrome." *Journal of Pediatrics*, 65:1079–81.

Morse, C., J. Sahler, and S. Friedman. 1970. "A Three-Year Follow Up Study of Abused and Neglected Children." *American Journal of Diseases of Children*, 120:439–46.

Moss, Howard A. 1967. "Sex, Age and State as Determinants of Mother-Infant Interaction." *Merrill-Palmer Quarterly*, 13:19–36.

Nurse, Shirley N. 1964. "Familial Patterns of Parents Who Abuse Their Children." *Smith College Studies in Social Work* (October), 35(1):1–25.

Osofsky, Joy D. 1971. "Children's Influences Upon Parental Behavior: An Attempt to Define the Relationship with the Use of Laboratory Tasks." *Genetic Psychology Monographs*, 83:147–69.

Osofsky, Joy D. and Karen Connors. 1980. "Mother Infant Interaction: An Integrative View of a Complex System." In Joy D. Osofsky, ed., *Handbook of Infant Development*, pp. 519–39. New York: Wiley.

Ounsted, Christopher, Rhoda Oppenheimer, and Joral Lindsey. 1974. "Aspects of Bonding Failure: The Psychopathology and Psychotherapeutic Treatment of Battered Children." *Developmental Medicine and Child Neurology* (August), 16(4):447–56.

Paget, N. 1971. *Child Abuse: A Community Challenge*. East Aurora, N.Y.: Henry Stewart.

Parke, Ross D. 1978. "Parent-Infant Interaction: Progress, Paradigms and Problems." In Gene P. Sackett, ed., *Observing Behavior, Vol. 1: Theory and Applications in Mental Retardation*, pp. 69–94. Baltimore: University Park Press.

Parke, R. D. and C. W. Collmer. 1975. "Child Abuse: An Interdisciplinary Review." In E. Mavis Hetherington, ed., *Review of Child Development Research*, 5:509–90. Chicago: University of Chicago Press.

Parke, R. D., D. B. Sawin, and G. Kreling. 1974. "The Effect of Child Feedback on Adult Disciplinary Choices." Unpublished manuscript.

Patterson, Gerald. 1976. "The Aggressive Child: Victim and Architect of a Coercive System." In E. Mash, L. Hamerlynck, and L. Handy, eds., *Behavior Modification and Families*, pp. 267–316. New York: Brunner-Mazel.

Patterson, Gerald R. 1974. "A Basis for Identifying Stimuli Which Control Behaviors in Natural Settings." *Child Development*, 45:900–911.

Patterson, Gerald and J. A. Cobb. 1973. "Stimulus Control for Classes of Noxious Behaviors." In J. F. Knutson, ed., *The Control of Aggression: Implications from Basic Research*, pp. 145–99. Chicago: Aldine-Atherton.

Patterson, Gerald, R. A. Littman, and W. Bricker. 1967. "Assertive Behavior in Children: A Step Toward a Theory of Aggression." *Monographs of Society for Research in Child Development*, 32:1–43.

Pemberton, D. A. and D. R. Benady. 1973. "Consciously Rejected Children." *British Journal of Psychiatry*, 123:575–78.

Prechtl, H. F. R. 1963. "The Mother-Child Interaction in Babies with Minimal Brain Damage." In B. M. Foss, ed., *Determinants of Infant Behavior*, 2:56–66. New York: Wiley.

Rheingold, Harriet L. 1969. "The Social and Socializing Infant." David A. Goslin, ed., *Handbook of Social Theory and Research*, pp. 779–90. Chicago: Rand McNally.

Richards, Martin and Judith Bernal. 1974. "Why Some Babies Don't Sleep." *New Society* (February 28), 33:509–11.

Richmond, Julius and Janis Juel. 1980. "A Perspective on Primary Prevention in the Earliest Years." *Children Today* (May–June), 9(3):2–6.

Ried, John and Paul S. Taplin. 1978. "A Social Interactional Approach to the Treatment of Abusive Families." Portland: Oregon Research Institute, mimeo.

Roberts, Maria. 1979. "Reciprocal Nature of Parent-Infant Interaction: Implications for Child Maltreatment." *Child Welfare* (June), 58:383–92.

Robison, Esther and Frances Solomon. 1979. "Some Further Findings on the Treatment of the Mother-Child Dyad in Child Abuse." *Child Abuse and Neglect: The International Journal*, 3:247–51.

Robson, K. S. and H. A. Moss. 1970. "Patterns and Determinants of Maternal Attachment." *Journal of Pediatrics*, 77:976–85.

Rohner, Ronald P. 1975. *They Love Me, They Love Me Not: A Worldwide Study of the Effects of Parental Acceptance and Rejection.* New Haven: HRAF Press.

Rosenthal, Miriam K. 1973. "The Study of Infant-Environment Interaction: Some Comments on Trends and Methodologies." *Journal of Child Psychiatry and Psychology*, 14:301–17.

Sameroff, Arnold J. and Michael J. Chandler. 1975. "Reproductive Risk and the Continuum of Caretaking Casualty." In Frances D. Horowitz, ed., *Review of Child Development Research*, 4:187–244. Chicago: University of Chicago Press.

Sandgrand, A., R. W. Gains, and A. H. Green. 1974. "Child Abuse and Mental Retardation: A Problem of Cause and Effect." *American Journal of Mental Deficiency*, 3:327–30.

Sawin, Douglas, Ross D. Parke, A. Neil Harrison, and Barbara Freling. 1975. *The Child's Role in Sparing the Rod.* Yellowsprings, Ohio: Fells Research Institute.

Schaffer, H. and P. Emerson. 1964. "Patterns of Response in Physical Contact in Early Human Development." *Journal of Child Psychology and Psychiatry*, 5:1–14.

Schneider, Carol, James K. Hoffmeister, and Ray E. Helfer. 1976. "A Predictive Screening Questionnaire for Potential Problems in Mother-Child Interaction." In Ray E. Helfer and C. Henry Kempe, eds., *Child Abuse and Neglect—The Family and the Community*, pp. 393–406. Cambridge, Mass: Ballinger.

Shapiro, Deborah. 1979. *Parents and Protectors: A Study in Child Abuse and Neglect.* New York: Child Welfare League of America.

Silver, L., C. Dublin, and R. Lauril. 1971. "Agency Action and Interaction in Cases of Child Abuse." *Social Casework*, 52:164–71.

Smith, Solwyn, R. Hanson, and S. Noble. 1975. *The Battered Child Syndrome.* London: Butterworths.

Soeffing, M. 1975. "Abused Children and Exceptional Children." *Exceptional Children*, 42:126–33.

Steele, B. and C. Pollak. 1974. "A Psychiatric Study of Parents Who Abuse Infants and Small Children." In R. Helfer and C. Kempe, eds., *The Battered Child*. Chicago: University of Chicago Press.

Stern, L. 1973. "Prematurity As a Factor in Child Abuse." *Hospital Practice* (May), 8(5):117–23.

Stevens-Long, Judith. 1973. "The Effect of Behavioral Context on Some Aspects of Adult Disciplinary Practice and Affect." *Child Development*, 44:476–84.

Tapp, J. L. and L. Kohlberg. 1977. "Developing Senses of Law and Legal Justice." In J. L. Tapp and F. S. Levine, eds., *Law, Justice, and the Individual in Society*. New York: Holt, Rinehart and Winston.

Terdal, Leif, Russell H. Jackson, and Ann M. Garner. 1976. "Mother Child Interactions: A Comparison between Normal and Developmentally Delayed Groups." In E. Mash, L. Hamerlynck, and L. Handy, eds., *Behavior Modification and Families*. New York: Bruner-Mazel.

Terr, L. 1970. "A Family Study of Child Abuse." *American Journal of Psychiatry*, 127:665–71.

Thomas, A., H. G. Birch, and S. Chess. 1963. *Behavioral Individuality in Early Childhood*. New York: New York University Press.

Thomas, Alexander, Herbert Birch, Stella Chess, and Margaret E. Hertzig. 1961. "The Developmental Dynamics of Primary Reaction Characteristics in Children." *Proceedings Third World Congress of Psychiatry*, 1:722–26.

Thomas, Alexander and Stella Chess. 1977. *Temperament and Development*. New York: Brunner-Mazel.

Thomas, Alexander, Stella Chess, and H. G. Birch. 1968. *Temperament and Behavior Disorders in Children*. New York: New York University Press.

Thomas, Evelyn B. 1974. "Some Consequences of Early Infant-Mother Relationships." *Early Child Development and Care*, 3:249–61.

—— 1975. "How a Rejecting Baby Affects Mother-Infant Synchrony." In *Parent Infant Interaction*. CIBA Foundation Symposium 33. New York: Associated Scientific Publishers.

Timberlake, Elizabeth M. 1979. "Aggression and Depression Among Abused and Non-Abused Children in Foster Care." *Children and Youth Services Review*, 1:279–91.

Waldrop, Mary F., Frank Pederson, and Richard Q. Bell. 1968. "Minor Physical Anomalies and Behavior in Preschool Child." *Child Development*, 39:391–400.

Weinberger, Gerald. 1972. "Some Common Assumptions Underlying Traditional Child Psychotherapy." *Psychotherapy: Theory, Research and Practice* (Summer), 9:849–52.

Wenar, Charles and Solveig C. Wenar. 1963. "The Short Term Perspective Model, the Illusion of Time and the Tabula Rasa Child." *Child Development*, 34:697–708.

Weston, J. T. 1968. "The Pathology of Child Abuse." In R. Heifer and C. Henry Kempe, eds., *The Battered Child*. pp. 77–102. Chicago: University of Chicago Press.

Wolff, P. H. 1971. "Mother-Infant Relations at Birth." In John G. Howells, ed., *Modern Perspectives in International Child Psychiatry*, pp. 80–97. New York: Brunner-Mazel, 1971.

Yarrow, L. J. 1963. "Research in Dimensions of Early Maternal Care." *Merrill-Palmer Quarterly*, 9:101–14.

Yarrow, M. R., C. Z. Waxler, and P. M. Scott. 1971. "Child Effects on Adult Behavior." *Developmental Psychology*, 5:300–311.

Zalba, S. 1967. "The Abused Child: II. Typology for Classification and Treatment." *Social Work* (January), 12:70–79.

CHAPTER 3

METHODOLOGY

The Study Design

THIS RESEARCH COULD BE classified as a hypothesis-generating field study which describes and analyzes incidents of child abuse in terms of the child-parent interaction which culminates in physical abuse. The study is based on the assumption that parents who abuse their children are partly reacting to their children's behavior; that the abuse results from a chain of parent-child interactions that are related, in part, to the child's behavior and its meaning to the parent. This perspective on child abuse relies on the bi-directionality of parent-child interaction, emphasizing that such interaction cannot be understood without reference to the contribution of the child. The aim of this study, then, is to clarify the child's contribution to child abuse as manifested in parent-child interaction which culminates in physical abuse of the child.

We locate the concerns of this study at one limited point in the total ecological configuration which needs to be taken into consideration for the broadest approach to child abuse. A comprehensive orientation to child abuse would take into account the microsystem—the immediate psycho-socio-economic situation of the family and the developmental history and current personality functioning of immediate members of the family in the marital, parent-child and sibling-sibling sub-systems; the ecosystem—the variables operating in the larger social system in which the family is embedded and which impact on the family; the macrosystem— cultural beliefs and values in society at large which affect the organization of and behavior in the micro and ecosystems. The concern of the study lies within the microsystem and even more narrowly within that system at one point in time and place. In the conflicting foci on dispositional elements and situational elements in abuse the focus here is on situational variables.

The study was designed to proceed in two stages. The first stage consists of an analysis of confirmed reports of child abuse received by the Wisconsin Department of Health and Social Services during 1974–1975. The purpose in studying these reports was to identify, explicate, and statistically describe any distinctive patterns of child behavior associated with abusive incidents.

The second stage of the research consists of extended interviews with parents who were identified as abusive by county departments of social services (CDSS) following their investigation of reports of alleged abuse. Interviews were taped, transcribed, summarized both statistically and clinically, and analyzed in terms of the parent-child interaction and the child's contribution. Furthermore, in a random sample of these cases, the interviews were supplemented by a review of related agency records, as a check on the reliability of data collected in the interviews.

Our choice of indirect and ex post facto methods of inquiry through an interview was in response to the limited choices available to us. Child abuse and other forms of injurious behavior do not lend themselves to direct, in vivo study by either naturalistic observation or experimentation (Megargee 1969:1040–42). Hence it was necessary to study incidents which had already occurred.

The generally recognized entitlement of families to privacy regarding the details of intimate family functioning explains the fact that "the majority of all social scientific research on the family involves the use of interviews or questionnaires. Less than one percent of current research on the family employs observational techniques" (Gelles 1978:409). The constraints of privacy are intensified with regard to the more sensitive family problems such as child abuse. Selecting incidents which had been identified, and confirmed, by protective social service agencies was a matter of feasibility, but it was also consistent with our effort to understand, in particular, child abuse in families served by social service agencies so as to contribute, through our research, to current protective service practice.

Accepting the agencies' definition of abuse as the basis for identifying a study group may do an injustice to those people selected for study. Despite the ambiguity regarding definitions of abuse, we settled the question administratively. In another time, in another place, these same people engaging in the same behavior may not have been defined as abusive. While the procedure we followed may have involved this possibility of error, it does have the advantage of reflecting the realities of protective service practice. These were the families which were actually reported, contacted, identified, designated as abusive with whom service was attempted.

Reviewing the report forms and other agency records provided accounts of the abusive incidents which had been prepared by the social workers involved. In our interviews, the principal or sole informant was the parent who admitted having abused the child; we interviewed few spouses and no children. Reconstructing an incident involving two or more people on the basis of information obtained, retrospectively, from only one of the participants is no doubt questionable. In this case, however, it seems to have been the best choice we had. Originally, we had planned extensive, separate interviews with second parents whenever possible. However, there were a limited number of intact families in our sample; many were single parents. Where second parents were available and interested, we invited them to join us informally—with their spouse's consent—and to participate as they saw fit. We chose not to interview the abused children or their siblings. We expected a wide age range among the children. Some would be too young to be effectively interviewed. We were reluctant to impose—even on the older children—the burden of retrospectively reexperiencing the abusive incident. Furthermore, we anticipated greater resistance to participation in the research by both parents and protective agencies if the children were to be involved.

Attempting to reconstruct the abusive incident by interviewing the abusive parent may be open to further question because it not only relies on an untrained participant-observer but on one who may need to distort the account of what happened in order to justify his behavior (Megargee 1969:1041). This problem of unreliability is classically illustrated in the Japanese movie *Roshomon*, in which several people participate in an incident and give quite different accounts of it, based on their respective needs and wishes.

Admittedly, the procedure imposes a considerable burden for sophisticated observation on the part of the respondent. The presumption is that a parent who is an active participant in the abuse event can be simultaneously aware of the multiple complex aspects of the unfolding event. Furthermore in reconstructing the event verbally, there is a tendency to impose a greater degree of rationality and logic than might have been operative in the enactment of the event itself. And yet, until it is possible to have neutral objective uninvolved observers available from initiation to termination of an abuse event, it would seem that persistent sensitive probing of the perception of informed participants may be the only feasible alternative.

Furthermore, the potency of the interview itself as an instrument for generating valid information regarding a child's behavior and patterns of parent-child interaction is open to dispute. Some studies indicate discrepancies between such content obtained through interviewing and by direct observation (Smith 1958; McCord and McCord 1961; Weller and Luchterhand 1969; Cotler and Shoemaker 1969). Such discrepancies, however, may result, in some measure, from deficiencies in the interviewing approach and hence may not reflect on the interview itself as a valid data-gathering technique. For instance, Graham, Rutter, and George (1973) used the interview to obtain from mothers a valid picture of the temperamental characteristics of children. The interview guide was specific and clear as to the kinds of information the interviewer sought. Information was obtained on seven categories of behavior: mood, intensity of emotional expression, activity, regularity, malleability, fastidiousness and approach-withdrawal to new people. Inter-rater reliability of ratings of these categories of behavior on the basis of the tape recordings of the interview was uniformly high, and the profiles obtained were accurately predictive of the difficulties in behavior which the children manifested in school a year later, as shown by teacher behavior ratings.

Lytton, moreover, concludes in his methodological review of parent-child interaction studies, that

with the modifications introduced recently which mean that the information input is more strictly controlled, the interview has shown reasonable agreement with other data and will have a useful role to play, particularly in obtaining data that are inaccessible to direct observation and for information about internal cues. (1971:677)

It may be, then, that the effectiveness of the interview as a valid data-gathering technique is highly dependent on organization of the interview and skill in interviewing. With these considerations in mind, we arranged for all of our interviews to be conducted by two skilled, experienced interviewers, who helped to develop the data-gathering instruments, and who participated fully in all phases of the study. Both interviewers were graduates of a professional degree program in social work and each had at least two years of experience in a social agency subsequent to achieving the M.S.W.

The interviews were based on a structured interview schedule of closed and open questions which were used with appropriate probes and accompanied by a self-administered checklist, designed to measure whether the parent tends to evaluate the abused child negatively or positively. The interview schedule, moreover, was pretested on volunteers from Parents Anonymous and revised to minimize ambiguities and inadequate wording.

As noted in the above discussion, this is an ex post facto or retrospective study, which relies on interviews with parents to reconstruct incidents in which they had physically abused one of their children. As such, it is an example of data collection by naturalistic observation with the use of informants—one of the principal techniques used by behavioral scientists in their research (Megargee 1969:1040–41). Such an approach does not permit experimental manipulation of independent variables and random assignment of subjects to experimental groups. Its relative lack of control over the various independent variables that may be involved means that relations between variables cannot be established with the kind of definiteness that is possible with experimental methods. There is a high risk of erroneous interpretation of one's findings, and alternative explanations can usually be found, based on uncontrolled factors (Kerlinger 1973:390–91). This lack of control over possible independent variables is a weakness in the study design which could not have been offset by the addition of a 'control' or comparison group. The impossibility of random assignment of subjects to groups makes it likely that other uncontrolled variables will be present in even the best possible match. Hence we concluded that any slight gains in control obtained by the addition of a comparison group would be heavily outweighed by the practical difficulties involved in finding and studying a comparable group.

Report Form Review

Having received a report of possible abuse, and having made some assessment of the situation, the social worker assigned to the case is required to complete a standard report form (appendix B). A copy of this form is then filed in the state office of the Wisconsin Division of Health and Social Services.

We reviewed all of such forms on file at the state office for the years 1974–1975, selecting out only those forms which met the following delimitations: (1) The report of abuse was substantiated; (2) The abuser was the child's natural or surrogate parent; (3) The abuse was not sexual abuse. Eight hundred and thirty report forms of substantiated nonsexual abuse by parents were found for the years 1974–1975. File report forms were identified before review by the research team. Structured, precoded form items include information on the source of the abuse report referral; the demography of the family, the abuser, and the abused child; the nature of the abusive action, and the injury sustained; the stresses impinging on the family at the time of the incident; the disposition of the case and the services offered.

Our principal focus of concern in reviewing the state reports was to attempt a clarification of child behaviors associated with substantiated abuse. There was planned continuity between the report review phase of our project and the subsequent interviews with abusers. In both instances, we were interested in the abuse incident itself, with particular orientation to the child's behavior, which might have initiated or precipitated the series of parent-child interactions eventuating in abuse. The report forms were studied as a source of information, in and of themselves, regarding the child's behavior relating to the abuse incident. They were studied further for their heuristic value. As a result of the study of the report forms, we became sensitized to patterns of children's behavior recurrently associated with abuse. This enabled us to develop the interview form for use in our subsequent interview with abusive parents and to provide a preliminary categorization of child behaviors associated with abuse.

The report form, completed by the protective service worker responsible for working with the family, provided two sets of relevant data. A series of structured precoded items provided the worker's assessment of stresses immediately associated with the abuse incident and the assessment of the child's role in the incident. A second source of data was provided by the worker's unstructured summarized account of the incident in response to an open-ended request on the report form. This asked for a short statement regarding the abuse incident and the factors precipitating the abuse incident. Workers generally included a two to four sentence paragraph in providing these details.

The findings of this first stage of the study, involving 830 incidents, will be presented in detail in chapter 4 and compared with other findings reported in the child abuse literature. Questions regarding the representativeness of the sample of records reviewed and the representativeness of the group of clients interviewed will be dealt with in the separate specific chapters concerned with the record review data and the interview data.

Interviews

SAMPLE SELECTION

Our original proposal for this unit of the study called for a sample of 100 abusive parents. In order to sharpen our focus on the child-parent interaction as an independent variable in child abuse, we wished to control for other factors generally found to contribute to physical abuse. We consequently had originally intended limiting interviewee selection to middle-income intact families of abused children 12 years of age or younger, to screen out the contaminating effects of low-income stress, single-parent stress and adolescent change. We saw the selection of such delimiting criteria regarding family income, family structure, and the nonadolescent child as means of isolating and highlighting the role of the child and child-parent interaction in physical abuse. Study of Wisconsin abuse reports in the first stage of our study, however, emphasized the impracticality of attempting to collect such a restrictive sample among a protective-services client population.

Hence we finally chose to include all protective service cases in which (1) a recent physical, nonsexual abuse of a child was indicated; (2) the identified abuser was a parent, stepparent, or adoptive parent (later expanded to include foster parent, of which there is one in our sample); and (3) the identified abuser acknowledged having injured the child.

OBTAINING RESPONDENTS

Protecting subject confidentiality, anonymity, and right to a voluntary decision on whether or not to participate in this sensitive-area research precluded direct access by our research group to recently substantiated cases of abuse. Hence, with the approval and cooperation of the Wisconsin Department of Health and Social Services we arranged early in 1977 to gain access to subjects through first three, and then six, county departments of social services. These six counties—Milwaukee, Kenosha, Racine, Rock, Waukesha, and Dane—were within the vicinity of our home base in Madison and accounted for more than 50 percent of the reports of alleged abuse filed by Wisconsin's 72 counties in 1975 and 1976. Milwaukee County alone, on which we were depending for 70 to 80 percent of our planned 100 interviews, accounted for more than a third of Wisconsin's 4,130 abuse reports in 1975 and 1976 (Oghalai 1977). Eventually five of these counties contributed to our final sample of 66 cases as follows: Milwaukee County Department of Public Welfare, 51 cases (77 percent of the sample); Rock County CDSS, 8 cases (12 percent); Dane, 3 cases (five percent); Waukesha, 2 cases (three percent); and Kenosha, 2 cases (three percent).

Our procedure for safeguarding the identity of the abusing parents and their freedom to refuse an interview was to request that the social workers in direct contact with such clients give or mail to them a letter from our research group inviting their participation and offering them the incentive of a $25 honorarium for consenting to an interview. A supporting cover letter from the cooperating social agency was also attached, along with a postcard addressed to the research group. (In appendix A, see letter from the research group and an example of the covering letters from one of the participating agencies.) If clients then chose to be interviewed, they could return the postcard with their name and telephone number. Hence client contact with us, and their identification to the research group, was initiated and controlled by the clients themselves.

Until such time as the client voluntarily made the decision to contact us, their identity and anonymity were safeguarded. While the names of the invitees were known to the agency, they become known to us only on receipt of the postcard sent by the parent. We subsequently modified this procedure to reduce the burden on the individual worker assigned to the case by having all of the letters to substantiated abusers sent by the Central Registry Office of the State Office of the Department of Health and Social Services. The mechanism for safeguarding the identity of the parent registered as abusive from the research group was maintained in this procedural change.

Wisconsin statistics had indicated that more than half of the abuse reports were substantiated and that in 73 percent of the cases the abuser was a parent or parent surrogate. We estimated that, based on state studies of 1975 and 1976 statistics (Oghalai 1977), the six counties cooperating in our study would generate about 1,000 abuse reports, some 550 of which would be confirmed. Three-quarters of these would have a parent or parent surrogate as the identified abuser, amounting to more than 400 appropriate referrals. Thus a response rate of 30 percent to 40 percent of the clients invited to participate in the study would yield 120 to 160 interview acceptances, apparently allowing us a reasonable margin of safety in aiming for 100 interviews in one year. Nevertheless, in practice we obtained drastically fewer cases than anticipated. Despite an adequate response rate of 35 percent, we had conducted only 38 of our expected 100 interviews by the end of the first year of interviewing, and 7 of these had to be excluded from the study because they were incomplete or had not identified a specific usable incident. Extending the data-collection phase of our study for another year yielded 39 more interviews, 4 of which were excluded from the study. Hence, at the end of two years, we had 66 usable interviews, even though our overall response rate over the 2 year period was in line with our anticipations—36 percent.

The shrinkage we experienced in the number of cases eligible for our study was consistent with that reported in a recent Child Welfare League of America (CWLA) study of a similar population yielding a similar response rate. The researchers encountered a similar "drastic shrinkage of the number of eligible cases anticipated by the participating agencies. From agency data it appeared it would be easy to obtain 250 cases from five agencies. In fact only 171 cases were secured despite the addition of a sixth agency" (Shapiro 1979:xi). In both the CWLA study and our own the difficulty in obtaining the sample size originally anticipated seems to have been related primarily to a fewer number of eligible cases than had been estimated from available statistics. Client unresponsiveness and unavailability were secondary, contributing factors.

THE INTERVIEW SCHEDULE

Our primary data collection instrument was an interview schedule,* developed to guide our interviews with the identified abusive parent. The interview was designed to be a focused, retrospective-introspective

---

* Copies of the interview guide are available on request to Professor Alfred Kadushin, School of Social Work, 425 Henry Mall, University of Wisconsin, Madison, Wisconsin, 53706.

recapitulation and analysis of the abusive incident. It also covered the longitudinal parent-child relationship from conception through the first year of life and currently. Particular emphasis was given to the child and the child's behavior as perceived by the abusive parent. The interview proceeded as follows. After a brief introduction to the study and to the interview procedure, we tried to obtain a brief picture of the family and living situation, including the names, ages, and grade in school of the children; the marital status; and the living, working and child-caring arrangements of the parent(s). This was followed by questions eliciting a description of the abused child and the time and place of the abuse event.

The next series of questions focused on the abuse incident itself, the behavior of the child immediately preceding the onset of the incident, the parent's initial behavior in response, the child's response to the parent's initial intervention, the parent's subsequent response, the thinking, feeling behavior of the participants throughout the process from initiation to termination. There were questions designed to give us a picture of the specific stresses faced by the parents and the child around the time of the abuse event. These were followed by questions regarding the nature of previous disciplinary problems with this child, as contrasted with other children in the family, and the support system available to the respondent. A series of questions probed for longitudinal data regarding the parent's own childhood experiences and the developmental relationship with the abused child from conception through current interaction.

Typescripts of the recorded interviews were coded by two researchers working independently. Coding a total of 127 items for the 66 respondents, the rate of agreement between the two coders was 95 percent. However, some items of greater subjectivity had lower rates of agreement. In no case, however, was the rate of agreement lower than 82 percent.

Respondent Reliability

To obtain some measure of the validity of the data obtained through our interviews, two steps were taken. First, immediately after each interview, the interviewer rated the subject's response and the data obtained, with the following results for the 66 cases included in the study. Response to the interview was considered "accepting, cooperative" in 56 cases (84.8 percent of the sample) and either "hostile, guarded, evasive" (1) or "somewhat hostile but questions answered" (9) in 10 cases (15.2 percent).

Furthermore, the data obtained was judged "somewhat unreliable" in 4 cases (6.1 percent) and "reliable" (55) or "somewhat reliable" (7) in 62 cases (93.9 percent). In effect, then, there were only 11 cases (16.7 percent) in which there was any question of doubtful reliability as judged by the interviewer, or 55 cases (83.3 percent) which were judged wholly reliable. We should note, however, that any case whose data had appeared grossly unreliable on the basis of the interview was eliminated from the study and hence would not be represented here. There were 2 cases eliminated for this reason.

Second, one of the two interviewers subsequently read a random sample of 35 percent of the case records of these 66 respondents. The records were maintained at five county departments of Social Services or Public Welfare, as follows:

	Cases Reviewed	Cases Contributed	
Milwaukee County	13 of 51 cases		(25%)
Rock County	4 of 8 cases		(50%)
Dane County	2 of 3 cases		(67%)
Kenosha County	2 of 2 cases		(100%)
Waukesha County	2 of 2 cases		(100%)
Total:	23 of 66 cases		(35%)

It might be noted that in every instance client permission was obtained for a review of agency record material.

In reading the case records, the investigator was mainly concerned with information that provided a check, or a second vantage point, on the data collected in our interviews. Of primary importance, then, were the overlapping areas of information, which were contained in both the records and the interviews. Of lesser interest were record data not in the interviews or interview data not in the records. For all of the eight categories of information addressed in the interviews, the investigator noted whether the record and interview material overlapped; if so, the investigation stated whether they were consistent or discrepant, and then specified any discrepancies. Following are the results:

A. *Identifying data* (number, age, and grade placement of children; age, occupation, income, education and marital and employment status of respondent and spouse; whether or not the abused child was placed in substitute care; age, gender, race, and ordinal position of the abused child). In this area there was no pattern of discrepancies in the 23 cases reviewed. The record and interview material overlapped substantially in every case. There were minor discrepancies but no sign of systematic bias in this area.

B. *Abusive incident* (time and location of incident; child and parent behavior, feelings, thoughts and intentions before, during, and after the incident; third-party involvement in the incident; subsequent thoughts about what was accomplished and what might be done differently). Of the 23 cases reviewed, the records of 17 (74 percent) mention the incident explored in our interview. In the other 5 cases, similar incidents are described in the records, and in every case the picture of the family interaction obtained in the interview is essentially the same as that contained in the records. In almost all cases, our interviews provided a more detailed picture of the abusive incident than did the agency records, but any overlapping data was quite consistent.

In summary, in 4 of the 23 cases reviewed (17 percent), the respondents apparently tried to put themselves in a more favorable light or make themselves more comfortable by avoiding or misrepresenting certain facts relating to the abusive incident: (1) misrepresenting the timing of the incident; (2) avoiding a recent serious incident and presenting a lesser, more remote one; (3) altering the facts to appear less culpable in a criminal case; and (4) minimizing difficulties with the children and the harshness with which they were handled.

C. *Situational factors—stress/support* (problems related to marital or other relationships; job, employment, care/control of children other than abused child; finances; housing; physical illness; substance abuse; how felt that day; whether drinking that day; available sources of emotional support). This is another area in which there was much overlap in relevant data between the interview and the case record, but in every case the data from the two sources were consistent. Any differences between record and interview material involved one or the other containing additional recent stresses, but no pattern was evident.

D. *Disciplinary interaction with abused child and nearest sibling* (previous disciplinary problems with the abused child; how handled; why handled differently; other behavior of abused child evoking discipline in recent months; whether nearest-age sibling showed similar behavior; how it was handled; if handled differently, why). This is another sensitive area, like that of the abusive incident, but surprisingly enough, there was little data of this sort in the case records. Overlapping data were present in only 4 of 23 cases (17 percent). In 2 of these 4 cases there were discrepancies: agency records indicate a pattern of harsher discipline toward all the children than the respondents admitted to in the interview.

E. *Childhood experience of respondent* (whether respondent experienced corporal punishment during childhood; whether relationship with own parents was primarily positive, negative, or ambivalent; whether separated from parents because of death, divorce, child abuse, or neglect). Here there were 7 of 23 cases (30 percent) with overlapping data, and among these there were no discrepancies.

F. *History of child in relation to respondent* (whether child was planned; whether abortion was considered; nature of the pregnancy and delivery; whether the baby was of low birth weight; whether child was born at a good or bad time and nature of the situation at the time; reaction to presentation of the child and the child's gender; whether the child was born in or out of wedlock; who the child was named after; effect of the child on the relationship with other parent and other children; child's health during the first year; amount of care the child needed and how difficult the child was during the first year; what the early problems with the child were; and the child's mental, emotional, physical disabilities or handicaps). Little overlapping data in this area, probably because our focus was on the earliest history, but all overlapping data was consistent.

G. *Impressions of the child now* (general description of the child now; who the child reminds the respondent of and whether the resemblance is positive or negative; what the respondent enjoys about the child; what about the child is bothersome or frustrating; and which child in the family is hardest and which is easiest to live with and why). Overlapping data in only one case in this area. No discrepancies.

By far the most discrepancies between interview and record material occurred in the area of the abusive incident. There is clearly a tendency for data in this area to be biased in the direction of putting the respondent in a more favorable light. Nevertheless, about 83 percent (19 of 23) of the cases reviewed were found to be free of major discrepancies in the area of the abusive incident. Note that this is quite comparable to the interviewer's postinterview assessment that 83.3 percent of the total cases included (55 of 66) were wholly reliable. Furthermore, the postinterview ratings by the interviewer for the 23 cases reviewed show that three of the four least reliable respondents were detected through the interview alone. In fact, they were the only three cases rated "somewhat unreliable."

Additional support may be derived from the comparable findings in a recent Child Welfare League of America study with a similar population (Shapiro 1979). A comparison of data obtained in the interviews and the data in the agency records which were reviewed with the client's permission indicated that discrepancies of any kind related to the abuse or neglect of the child occurred "in only 15 percent of the cases. In 9 percent of the cases the abuse or neglect charged was more severe in the records than had been noted by the client in the research interview" (p. 16).

REFERENCES

Cotler, Sheldon and Donald J. Shoemaker. 1969. "The Accuracy of Mothers' Reports." *Journal of Genetic Psychology*, 114:97–107.

Gelles, Richard J. 1978. "Methods for Studying Sensitive Family Topics." *American Journal of Orthopsychiatry* (July), 48(3):408–24.

Graham, Philip, Michael Rutter, and Sandra George. 1973. "Temperamental Characteristics as Predictors of Behavior Disorders in Children." *American Journal of Orthopsychiatry*, 43:328–39.

Kerlinger, Fred. 1973. *Foundation of Behavioral Research*. New York: Holt, Rinehart, and Winston.

Lytton, Hugh. 1971. "Observational Studies of Parent-Child Interaction." *Child Development* (September), 42(3):651–84.

McCord, Joan and William McCord. 1961. "Cultural Stereotypes and the Validity of Interviews in Child Development." *Child Development*, 32:171–85.

Megargee, Edwin I. 1969. "A Critical Review of Theories of Violence." In *Crimes of Violence: A Staff Report Submitted to the National Commission on the Causes and Prevention of Violence*, 13:1037–1116. Washington, D.C.: Government Printing Office, (December).

Oghalai, Karen. 1977. *Ten Year Summary of Child Abuse Reporting in Wisconsin*. Madison: Wisconsin Department of Health and Social Services.

Shapiro, Deborah. 1979. *Parents and Protectors: A Study of Child Abuse and Neglect*. New York: Child Welfare League of America.

Smith, Henrietta T. 1958. "A Comparison of Interview and Observation Measures of Mothers' Behavior." *Journal of Abnormal and Social Psychology*, 57:278–82.

Weller, Leonard and Elmer Luchterhand. 1969. "Comparing Overviews and Observations in Family Functioning." *Journal of Marriage and the Family*, 31:115–22.

CHAPTER 4

RECORD REVIEW OF ABUSE INCIDENTS

THE WISCONSIN BASED STUDY of interactive processes in abusive families involved both detailed interviews with family members and consideration of a representative sample of abuse incidents. To provide a preliminary picture of dynamics that occur in these families, a survey of statewide reports submitted by social workers was conducted. All abuse reports completed during 1974–1975 in Wisconsin describing confirmed cases in which the child's parents were the perpetrators were included in the study. Because sexual abuse is considered a category of abusive behavior distinctively different from physically assaultive actions, such cases were excluded from the survey. The 830 abuse reports which met these delimitations were examined.

It is estimated that during 1974 and 1975 there were a total of 1,284 substantiated cases of nonsexual physical abuse perpetrated by parents in Wisconsin. The sample of 830 cases examined represents 65 percent of the total number of possible eligible cases. The difference between the total number of eligible cases and the number actually examined resulted primarily from lack of availability of records being processed or in use at the time the files were being searched for the project. A copy of the report form is included in appendix B.

We will first present a general picture of the abuse family, the abused child, and the nature of abuse. We will throughout compare these findings with the relevant national data for a closely similar period to test the representativeness of this sample of abusers as against the larger national sample of abusers. We will then focus on our principal concern in reviewing this record material, namely, the reported abuse incident itself and the child's behavior relating to the incident.

Family Characteristics

Most of the abusers in the survey (83 percent) were the child's natural parents. Fifteen percent were stepparents, and a negligible number were adoptive parents of the abused child. Fathers were identified as the abuser in 59 percent of the cases, mothers in 41 percent. Mothers in our study were as likely as fathers to abuse children younger than thirteen, but fathers were more likely to be the perpetrators when adolescents were injured (appendix C, table 1).* Fathers abused three-quarters of the teenage girls and seven in ten teenage boys in the sample. Three-fifths of the abusive mothers and one-quarter of the abusive fathers were raising their children as single parents.

Although 15 percent of the abusive parents were younger than 25, 22 percent were 40 or older. The average age of these parents was 32. This wide age range is reflected in the children as well. While one-third were younger than 6, another third were adolescents. Their average age was 9.1 years, slightly older than the national average of 8 years for abused children reported by the American Humane Association (1978) for 1976.

This picture of the abusing family and the abused child as presented in the 1974–1975 Wisconsin State Report form is consistent in most respects with the findings of a national survey of abuse for 1976 (AHA 1978). The national study paralleled the Wisconsin picture in that natural parents were most frequently identified as the abusers and, as was true for our sample, fathers were identified more frequently than mothers (55 percent fathers, 45 percent mothers). The largest percentage of the parents were likewise over 30, although only 14 percent were over 40, as compared with the figure of 22 percent over 40 for the Wisconsin group.

Of the Wisconsin abusive families, 40 percent were single-parent families, and 35 percent of the national group were single-parent families, most frequently as a consequence of divorce, separation, or desertion.

While a larger percentage of the national survey families were receiving some form of public assistance—37 percent as compared with 23 percent of the families in the Wisconsin group—the fact that workers noted financial problems for 53 percent of the Wisconsin families indicated that both groups were economically deprived.

Many of the Wisconsin families were large, 43 percent caring for four

---

* Tables describing consequential findings are in the text itself. Tables describing sample characteristics and other tables are in appendix C.

or more children, while 44 percent of the national survey group had three or more children. As was true for the Wisconsin group, a little over 50 percent of the abusive fathers nationally had not completed high school, and many were unemployed and unskilled.

Age and sex of abused children in the Wisconsin group were comparable with the figures of the national sample. As was noted above, the average age of abused children in both groups was similar, the largest percentage of both groups being over five years of age. A larger percentage of females was abused nationally (54 percent), as compared with males (46 percent), which duplicates almost exactly the Wisconsin statistic (55 female, 45 male).

Differences between the race of the Wisconsin abused child and the national survey data reflect differences in the racial composition of the state. The national survey data for 1976 indicates that 61 percent of abused children were Caucasian, 20 percent black, 12 percent Hispanic, in addition to a small percentage of American Indians and Orientals. This compares with the larger percentage of whites in our sample (81 percent), a smaller percentage of blacks (14 percent), and an almost total absence of Hispanic children.

With regard to family composition and demographic characteristics of abused children and abusive parents, it can be said that the group of families whose reports we were studying were fairly representative of abusive parents and abused children nationwide.

In summary, the "typical" abused child in the sample was a white girl or boy nine years old. The "typical" abusive parent was the natural father of the child, white, and in his early thirties. However, abused children and their parents came from all age and racial groups. The parents were almost as likely to be mothers as fathers. The overwhelming majority of the families were poor. A substantial minority were single parents with more than the average number of children. (See appendix table C.1.)

The Abuse Incident

Most of the children in the sample (81 percent) were beaten by their parents, with the hand or an instrument. A smaller number of children were kicked, thrown, pushed, or dropped. Other forms of severe maltreatment (tying up, strangling, burning, shooting, or stabbing the child) occurred infrequently. Perhaps because of the difficulty in assessing the presence of such abuse, psychological mistreatment of the child was noted in only one of five cases (appendix table C.2).

Previously published surveys (AHA 1978; Gil 1970; Maden and Wrench 1977) report that most abused children sustain minor injuries as a result of the incident. Data from Wisconsin are in accord with this finding. Four out of five of the children had bruises, or welts; another 16 percent had sprains, lacerations, abrasions, or cuts. The more severe types of injury (fractures, suffocation, burns) were inflicted in 5 percent of the cases. Five of the 830 children died as a result of their injuries. The relatively minor nature of the physical harm done during most of the incidents explains why 86 percent of the children required no medical care. Children in the Wisconsin survey were less likely to require hospital treatment than abused children nationwide (AHA 1978:24).

Parents used different abuse methods to inflict injury on children of different ages. While the very young and adolescents were more likely to be beaten with the hand, parents were more likely to strike latency-age children with an instrument. Very young children were tied up or thrown more often, while those older than five were more apt to be kicked. Young children were also more likely to sustain severe injury as a result of this experience, a finding duplicated in other abuse studies (Maden and Wrench 1977). In the Wisconsin sample, preschool children were hospitalized more than seven times as frequently as their school-age counterparts.

Examination of the abuse incidents included in this sample suggests that parents usually use punitive methods more closely akin to forms of physical punishment generally accepted for use in child rearing in our society. The more extreme and unacceptable the method, the less likely it was to be used by abusers in the study. While the abuse literature tends to focus on maltreatment of very young children, they were in the minority in the sample we studied. Our findings suggest that more attention should be paid to abusive experiences of children older than 5 and especially of teenagers. However, the serious nature of the injuries sustained by the vulnerable very young also justified continued strong community and professional concern for their welfare.

The Abuse Context

The significance of environmental factors in the etiology of abusive parental behavior is outlined in what Parke and Collmer describe as the sociological model of child abuse. The model posits that "cultural attitudes towards violence and the use of physical force as a form of control in interpersonal relationships" (1975:11) and "the degree of stress and frustration encountered by individuals in different positions in the social structure" (p. 12) are key factors in the development of such behavior. We have already described the prevalence of one of these stress factors, poverty, among families in the Wisconsin survey. Results of a number of other studies offer evidence of the validity of these hypotheses (Gelles 1973, 1978; Parke and Collmer 1975). Applying the model to analysis of data from the Wisconsin sample led us to examine the extent to which violence had become an integral part of intimate interpersonal relationships in these families, and how they reacted to other noneconomic sources of stress with which they had to cope.

VIOLENCE PATTERNS IN THE FAMILIES

It has frequently been suggested that one particular child in the family is usually singled out as the target for abuse (de Lissovoy 1979; Helfer 1973). While evidence exists that more than one child may be subject to episodes of maltreatment (Gil 1970; Maden and Wrench 1977), many of these studies do not describe the proportion of cases in which only one child in the family is treated this way. In some research reports, sibling abuse is reported for a substantial number of families (Gil 1970; Lauer et al. 1974).

Protective service workers investigating the history of mistreatment in these Wisconsin cases found evidence that only one child had been previously abused in one-fifth of the incidents. Siblings had been subject to excessive punishment in another one-fifth of the cases. It appears, therefore, that two distinctly different patterns of violence towards children exists. In one, a single child is repeatedly maltreated; in the second, which is equally likely to occur, abuse of several children in the family is evident.

In the remaining cases, the structure of the question on the report form does not allow us to determine whether the worker was uncertain about the history of violence toward children in the family or had found no evidence of previous abuse. Because information was missing for more than one-half of the cases, the conclusion about distribution of abuse must be considered highly speculative, pending more detailed research.

Patterned interpersonal aggression may also appear in other forms in family relationships. Parke and Collmer note, "Closer examination of familial violence reveals striking degrees of interrelationships among marital conflict tactics, disciplinary techniques, and the methods employed by children in settling sibling conflicts" (1975:13). In research using a national sample of more than 2,000 American couples, Gelles (1978) also found that observation of marital violence by children was correlated with their subsequent use of parental violence when rearing their own offspring.

Reporters in Wisconsin were asked to describe abuse of adults that had occurred in study families. Again, the investigators provided no information for more than one-half of the incidents. In the remainder, evidence of such behavior was noted in one out of three cases. In almost all of these adult abuse cases (87 percent), fathers had maltreated family members. Only 19 of the 338 mothers in the sample were designated adult abusers.

Among the 830 abusive families in Wisconsin whose report forms we were reviewing, there appears to be a small but significant subgroup in which violence has become an established behavior pattern involving a number of family members. In the 393 cases where information is sufficient to examine such behaviors, one-quarter show evidence of both previous child abuse and mistreatment of adults. Two-thirds of the incidents for which prior abuse of adults is noted also give evidence of previous abuse of the young, while two-thirds of the cases where no adult abuse is noted have no such history of child abuse (table 4.1).

TABLE 4.1

Abuse of Adults and Previous Abuse to Children in the Family

Previous Child Abuse	Evidence of Adult Abuse	
	Yes	No
To child and/or siblings	62% (91)	35% (87)
No abuse or don't know	38% (55)	65% (160)
Total:	100% (146)	100% (247)

There are other indications that violence tends to generalize towards multiple targets in this special group of families. While in the sample as a whole, families are equally likely to have previously abused one child or siblings, parents in this special subgroup were twice as likely to have maltreated siblings of the abused child. For many of these 91 abusive adults, violence has become a well-established, repetitive response pattern, aimed at both one's spouse and a number of one's children; 81 of these 91 abusers were males. Because information on the history of violence is not available for more than one-half of the cases in the survey, caution is again required in extrapolating from this data (appendix table C.3).

The intergenerational theorem that abuse experienced in childhood is repeated as abuse inflicted in adulthood, discussed in chapter 2, is not confirmed in the report-form statistics. Abusive parents were listed as having been mistreated as children on only 25 percent of the report forms.

In summary, the Wisconsin study provides evidence that parents who abuse their children may adopt abusive response patterns and exhibit them repeatedly in interaction with other family members, adults as well as children. However, the relative number of families in which this occurs may be very small, and the forms which this violence takes will vary from family to family. In some cases, no prior abuse of any family member is indicated. Maltreatment of the child is, in such situations, a one-time occurrence that is rarely or never repeated.

STRESS FACTORS CONTRIBUTING TO ABUSE

In addition to problems already described, protective service investigators in Wisconsin evaluated individual, family, and community-related stresses affecting the alleged abuser (appendix table C.4). The stress category reporters found most applicable was that labeled personal emotional difficulties. More than two-thirds of the parents were perceived as having this type of problem. However, few of the parents were receiving inpatient care or mental health clinic treatment as a result. Only 13 had been recently discharged from a mental hospital, and 34 were clinic clients.

Very few of the abusers had other health/mental-health problems. Only 3 percent displayed "incapacitating mental deficiency". One in ten was physically ill or injured when the abuse occurred. In 13 percent of the cases, abusers were considered addicts, usually of alcohol rather than drugs.

There were no differences between male and female abusers in the number of physical or mental-health problems they experienced, but the parents did differ somewhat in the types of handicaps they faced. Mothers were more than twice as likely to be retarded to an extent considered incapacitating; fathers were twice as likely to be addicted to alcohol.

Stress in the marital sphere was the second most frequently cited problem category, experienced by two out of five families in the survey. Spouse conflict was cited more often for male abusers (47 percent) than for females (37 percent), but males were more likely to be living with their spouses than were women.

Other potential stress factors affecting family life included the loss of, or addition of, a member of the group. Despite the large number of single-parent homes in the sample, reporters felt absence of an essential family member was significant in only 9 percent of the cases. This was considered more important for abusive mothers than for fathers. Although the women were approximately twice as likely to be single parents, workers felt this loss affected them almost six times as often as it did the men. Addition of a new family member through the birth of a baby was reported in only 38 of the incidents studied.

In addition to personal and family problems, investigators were asked to note criminal activity on the part of the abuser. Other studies have noted "an extensive record of criminal activity, particularly among male abusers" (Maden and Wrench 1977:206). However, in Wisconsin, workers described such problems in only 8 percent of the cases. No differences were found between mothers and fathers in the extents to which they faced this type of stress.

In general, the families in this study were especially prone to exhibiting personal emotional and marital difficulties. Physical illness and alcohol addiction affected a small but important segment of the sample. Other specific individual and family stresses were present in very few instances, as were conflicts between the abusive parent and the community.

It is not possible within the scope of this research to determine the degree to which worker expectations affected judgments in this area. The predominance of psychological perspectives in the abuse literature may help explain why, for so many of these parents, major problems are perceived as intra and inter-personal rather than community-based. (Gillespie et al. 1977)

Agency Involvement

Of the families in the Wisconsin survey, 96 percent received some type of social services as a result of the investigation of the incident, a much higher proportion than the 54 percent receiving services nationwide (American Humane Association 1978:19). For nine out of ten of the families, casework was provided. One in four were referred to a guidance or counseling clinic, and one in ten received public medical care. Maternity care, day care and homemaker services were provided in few instances. Abusive mothers were offered more assistance with financial problems, despite the fact that male abusers were equally as likely to be unemployed. Results suggest that women were also given more public medical and homemaker services than men in the sample (appendix table C. 5).

Juvenile court proceedings were instituted in one-quarter of the cases and criminal proceedings in one-fifth of the incidents. For those families who went to juvenile court, the most likely decision was for transfer of custody. In only two instances had the parents' legal rights to the child been terminated at the time the data was collected.

Criminal court proceedings followed a similar path, with the most serious decisions occurring least often. In three out of five of the cases referred to the court, action terminated in the district attorney's office or the petition was dismissed. This figure probably indicated the difficulties workers face in providing adequate proof of criminal intent in such cases. In 14 instances, the court had sentenced the abuser at the time of data collection.

Abuse of young children was more likely to result in court proceedings than that of their older cohorts. Parents maltreating those of preschool age were twice as likely to find juvenile court or criminal court judges taking some action. Abusive fathers were much more likely to receive a criminal sentence. Thirteen of the fourteen abusers found guilty by this court were males. No differences were found between abusive men and women in the percentage involved in juvenile court procedures.

Placement of the child occurred much more often than the relatively minor form of the injuries sustained by many of the children would have led us to expect. One-third of the children in the sample were removed from the home. For 85 (10%), the placement was temporary, and they had been returned to the home by the time the report was filed. Among the children still in placement, half were in foster care and almost all of the rest resided with relatives. Seventeen of the children had been institutionalized. Siblings were also removed in 12 percent of the instances where the abused child had brothers and sisters.

Nationally, 18 percent of the children were placed out of the home in

1976, 6 percent being voluntary placements, 12 percent being court ordered placements (AHA 1978:table 4.4).

The decision to place the child outside the home varied, depending upon the age of the child who had been abused. In contrast to findings for court action, however, it was the oldest rather than the youngest child who was most likely to be removed. The nature of the data does not provide clues to the rationale used for these decisions, although one may speculate that the adolescent's greater independence and desire to separate from the family may be factors considered by the workers in these cases.

Removal of siblings occurred most often when the abused child was very young. This may occur because protective service workers respond to incidents in which serious injury is done to the preschool child by protecting brothers and sisters from parental contact as well. Concern about the advisability of continued child-rearing by the parent and the desire to obtain some legal jurisdiction in the case are both more clearly evident when parents abuse children who are younger than 6.

The Child's Involvement in Abuse Events

Child abuse, as a repetitive pattern of interaction in the family, is reinforced by the behavior of both the parent and the child. Data concerning the child's participation in abusive events is provided in the Wisconsin report form by the protective service worker who was asked to indicate stresses that served as precipitating factors in the abuse incident being reported. Family breakup, job loss, participation in an argument, excessive alcohol or drug intake, and overreaction to the child's behavior were the potential sources of stress listed on the report form. By far the most important stress source, according to these workers, was the activity of the child. Parents were described as overreacting to crying, disobedience, hostility or some other behavior of the child in more than nine out of ten of the incidents. In contrast, approximately one in ten were reacting to family or job difficulties, and 14 percent were under the influence of alcohol or drugs.

A second assessment of the child's role was provided by members of the research group who, after reading the worker's description of the incident on the report form, were asked to indicate whether the abuse was victim precipitated. The coders found this to be true for 77 percent of the cases.

This judgment can be questioned, since it is based on a limited amount of information about each case provided in the abuse report. However the size and consistency of the findings drawn from two different sources are impressive. Based on this preliminary information, it does seem that the child plays an active role in interaction with the parent that results in abuse.

Child's Behavior During Abusive Events

A basic question that arises when examining participation of the child in abuse is that which asks what activities he or she is engaged in when parents responded abusively. Reviews of previous research (Martin 1978:12–16) point out that this issue has not been adequately addressed. The literature describes some problematic characteristics of children and suggests these characteristics may play a role in the incident (Friedrich and Boroskin 1976; Martin and Beezley 1974; Parke and Collmer 1975), but the behavior of the children is not described in any detail.

An exploratory study of this issue was conducted, using data from the Wisconsin survey. On the report form, investigators were asked to write a paragraph on: "(1) what precipitated the alleged abuse; (2) the alleged abuse incident." Description of the activities of the child in this paragraph was then analyzed and behavior categories developed to describe actions of the child that occurred prior to the adult's abusive response.

There is, of course, only a very limited amount of information on the event available in these reports. It is difficult to determine whose perception of the incident is included—that of the parent, the child, the person reporting abuse had occurred, or the investigator. These limitations suggest the need for a much more detailed follow-up study analyzing interaction of parent and child during the event. This study has been carried out and its findings are discussed in the chapters that follow. During this report-form-review stage of the research, we were interested in analyzing the child behavior associated with an abuse incident, as described by the worker who made the assessment. We were also concerned with the development of a classification scheme to categorize abuse-related child behaviors for use in the second stage interview study. Results described here do not imply that children "cause" parental abusive behavior. The actions of the child provide only one of many sources of stimuli to the parent who ultimately responds with excessive discipline (de Lissovoy 1979).

The item asking for a statement of the incident which precipitated abuse was left blank by the worker in the case of 55 reports (6 percent). The overwhelming majority of the reports, where there was a summary (91 percent), mentioned some behavior of the child associated with the initiation of a parent-child interactional sequence culminating in reported, substantiated abuse. In 16 percent of the cases the child's behavior was not described in sufficient detail to permit categorization. The child was simply depicted as "misbehaving," "disobedient," or "acting up" preceding the abuse by the parent. More frequently, however, the short descriptive statements by the worker gave sufficient detail about the behavior so as to permit categorization by the researcher with some confidence.

In more than three quarters of these cases (571) interaction between parent and child occurred in the home. In another 48 incidents (6 percent) parent and child were outside the home when the abuse occurred. In 137 instances (eighteen percent), the behavior was enacted in the home but the initial interaction culminating in abuse most directly involved siblings or peers, rather than parents.

Behavior of the child inside and outside the home was sorted into a number of categories. Many of the reports in the study described more than one activity of the child during the abuse episode. In order to capture the range of these activities, we classified them in temporal order, first describing the behavior immediately preceding abuse (immediate precursor), then coding preceding activities (second precursor, third precursor, etc.): Table 4.2 lists the child's behaviors which were the immediate precursors of abuse, in order of frequency.

The largest single category, accounting for 21 percent of the incidents, involved aggressive behavior. Sometimes this was manifested as physical aggression. Of the 173 instances of aggression, 15 percent involved physical aggression, most often directed against parents, less frequently directed against siblings or peers (table 4.3).

The worker's verbatim statements on the report forms follow:

Child, 3, was held and struck with hands by father because she kicked her mother.

Kay, 17, can be very belligerent and defiant. She runs continuously without telling her parents where she will be. She was about to take off again when her father stopped her. Kay began kicking, hitting and screaming, and to subdue her, her father pulled her to the floor where they began to hassle. Father hit her with his hand.

TABLE 4.2

Child Behaviors: Immediate Precursors of Abuse

Behavior Category	Percent	Number
Aggressive behavior	21	173
Lying, stealing	9	73
Entrance/exit behavior	7	56
Behavior involving food, elimination, sleeping	7	56
Performance of household chores	5	39
Defiance of parental orders	4	35
Crying, whining	4	31
Disapproved habits	3	28
Dating, sexual behaviors, disapproved friends	3	27
School-related problems	3	27
Overactivity	3	25
Other and unspecified misbehavior	16	135
No misbehavior mentioned	15	125
Total	100	830

TABLE 4.3

Aggressive Behavior of Abused Children: Immediate Precursor of Abuse

	Percent	Number
Directed at people	75	129
Directed at objects	24	41
Unspecified aggression	2	3
Total	100	173

Mother requested that daughter, 13, stay at home. Daughter argued and swung at mother, missing mother, who then struck back at daughter, hitting her in the face and leaving bruise to her lower left cheek.

Aggressive interaction also involved fights with the child's siblings or peers:

The abuse incident was precipitated by conflict among siblings. Harry had been fighting with his brother. His sister attempted to stop the fight. Harry hit his sister. Father then hit Harry with a belt for hitting.

Hyperactive girl, 9, fighting with her friend while riding in parent's car. Parent became irritated and threatened child. Child did not stop. Mother dragged child by neck into house and slapped child on face.

Mrs. C says she had a "bad day" when Christopher, 6, tried to stick a straight pin in his younger brother's leg. She hit him quite hard on the face with her hands, without thinking, causing a bruise.

Verbal aggression is more frequently associated with abuse than is physical aggression. Of the cases categorized as involving aggression, 60 percent related to verbal aggression. Talking back, sassing, cussing, bad-mouthing parents initiated the interaction which culminated in abuse. Frequently, however, some other behavior of the child initiated the parent-child interaction. During the course of the interaction, verbal aggression on the part of the child intensified parental anger, escalating the interaction toward abuse. It is often the verbal aggression, rather than the initial behavior which initiated the interaction, which elicits the abusive response.

Ruth, 16, had been pouting because mother would not let her go ice skating. She became angry and refused to complete a craft project promised for school. Mother ordered her to do it. Ruth sassed her mother, who then grabbed her, shook her and slapped her, bruising cheek near eye.

Teacher called Mr. R, informing him that his daughter, Jennie, 14, had talked back and left the classroom without permission. Upon his questioning her about the incident when Jennie came home, she talked back with a wise guy attitude. There were bruises and welts as a result of Mr. R's throwing Jennie on the bed and choking her.

Father had been drinking. Family sat down to Thanksgiving dinner and had guest. Alice, 16, made a crack about wishing her father was dead. Fighting started and finally father and daughter decided to step outside and settle it. Girl alleges father struck first blow. Both were bruised.

Mother lost her temper after Johnie, 6, refused to get off his sister's back, literally. He sassed his mother when she asked him to do this and she slapped him across the eye.

Rosemarie, 13, was taping a song that was on the radio and told her mother to be quiet. When she wasn't, Rosemarie swore at her, which made Mrs. B angry. She threw her tea at Rosemarie, pushed her to the floor, kicked her in the back and hit her with a belt.

Dick, 15, and his stepfather became involved in an argument following Dick's apprehension for a number of burglaries in the community. Mr. W had been drinking. During the course of the discussion, Dick told him to shut up. Mr. W hit Dick in the right eye out of anger, which resulted in a black eye.

Mother found out that Kathy, 14, had skipped school when she found her in a restaurant and brought her home. Child talked back and mother beat her on face, hands and arms with a broom handle.

Harvey, 16, disobeyed his father by staying overnight at a friend's house and when he got home, his father started to yell at him. Harvey yelled back and swore at his father. Then his father hit him in the mouth with his fist. Mr. K had been drinking and became upset when the boy swore at him.

Mrs. F had left home for approximately two months prior to the incident. Her five-year-old son Larry resented her return home because of his feeling of being previously rejected. Larry kept calling his mother a "bitch." Mother whipped him with a belt, causing welts.

Wendy, 16, pushed her 12-year-old sister down the stairs and kicked her in the mouth with her bare foot. In response, Mr. O hit Wendy across her thighs with a belt. Wendy then swore at him and used much profanity as he was leaving the room. He became angry and came back and hit her harder across the thighs. Rather severe bruises and welts were made on the front of Wendy's thighs.

Margaret, 13, was fighting with her younger sister. Her mother came out to break up the fight, mother pushed Margaret from her sister with her foot, causing a bruise to her right knee. Margaret began hitting her mother. Younger sister ran in to tell father of Margaret's action. Father came out and grabbed her by the hair and pulled her to the house, slapping her in the face with his open hand. When Margaret talked back, he lost his temper and hit her with his fist, causing bruises to Margaret's left arm and right eye.

In 24 percent of the instances categorized as aggressive behavior on the part of the child, associated with the initiation of an interaction culminating in abuse, aggressiveness was in the form of destructive activity.

Ricky, 7, is very destructive. Mrs. V just recently had a dresser refinished because Ricky had scratched it. He maliciously marred it again. His mother gave him a whipping with a belt.

Andy, 9, jumped on a new bed and broke the box spring. His father hit him on the face with his hands, which left bruises.

[Child] threw the cat in the tub, almost drowning it. Mother disciplined her with a belt.

Sheldon, 9, is a very difficult child to control. Mrs. P asked him to come in out of the rain. He wouldn't and started banging his head against the house. She finally got him in and sent him to his room and he began to destroy it, chipping the paint off the newly painted walls in his room. Mrs. P became angry and picked up his bed while he was in it so that he fell off, hitting his head. She then took a wooden spoon and spanked him on his buttocks with black and blue marks resulting.

The father overreacted to child's misbehavior. David, 7, was running about the house, hit an end table and broke a lamp. The father, who was a strong disciplinarian, slapped the child with an open hand on the side of the face, which caused an obvious bruise and welt.

Norma, 5, made a mess with her mother's cosmetics. Parents held child down and beat her on the buttocks with a wooden paddle to the point of inflicting bruises.

The mother became angry and hit child, 3, on the face and arms after he took a part off the vacuum cleaner and broke it while she was trying to clean house.

William, 9, had proceeded to pull down the drapes, plus poured water on the TV. Mother became so angry she was going to whip him with a belt on the butt, but he crawled under the bed and the belt accidentally hit his face.

Saul, age 9, had been previously referred for care to an institution for emotionally disturbed children. On leave from the institution for a weekend at home, he was found breaking side-view mirrors off cars. On Saturday he had turned in a false alarm. Mrs. L then slapped the boy across the face and gave him a severe spanking, causing black and blue buttocks.

Steven, 8, threw a rock at a car. His mother used an extension cord to "get after him." She raised a welt near his right eye.

Lying or stealing was involved in 9 percent of the incidents, in or out of the home. Behavior was coded as lying or stealing when there was reasonable proof that it had occurred, or when parents suspected the child had engaged in such behavior.

Child, 8, wrote on siblings with a magic marker and then lied to father about it. Beaten with belt by father. Bruised and hospitalized for three days with an eye injury.

Doris, 14, had disobeyed her mother the previous evening by having others over when mother was gone, then lied about it, despite a neighbor seeing them. Doris became belligerent when faced with this. Her mother became angry and lost her temper, striking Doris on the face with her hands and fists, pulling her hair and causing her to bang her knees.

Mother has had to go to school repeatedly for child's [13] behavior—acting up in class, suspended, etc. When she returned home after suspension, mother learned that Leonard had received a refund on book he had "lost" but he had lied about. This mother used extension cord to beat him on legs and thighs.

Lisa, 10, did not bring home her report card, saying it had not been given out. Mrs. X phoned teacher, who said they had been given out, and Lisa said the teacher was lying. Mother used belt on Lisa's back and arms for lying.

Child, 8, did not come home from school on time and lied to mother about where he had been. Mother beat child with belt on buttocks, back, and left arm.

Mr. F. had been experiencing behavior problems with Eunice, 16. The girl responded to him in a very negative, hostile manner. They argued frequently and violently, with Mr. F usually losing the verbal battles. On this occasion Eunice left the steam iron plugged in after she finished using it. The father confronted her with this, which she denied, and he burned her with the iron in order to "teach her a lesson" for disobedience and lying.

Father says Anna, 13, has been stealing money at home for some time. He said he warned her that if she stole again, he would use his belt on her. She allegedly stole money again from mother's purse so that he hit her with his belt, leaving bruise on the right hip area. He also grabbed her wrist, damaging ligament.

Mr. D admitted to whipping his son Christopher, 9, with a belt because the child stole $30 worth of food stamps.

Debbie, 11, stole money from her mother and brought it to school. When Mrs. Y found out, she hit Debbie with a belt on the back of her legs and buttocks while Mr. Y held her down. They believe this was necessary punishment.

The abused 8-year-old boy had taken some money from his stepfather's room and spent it for candy and other treats at the neighborhood store. His mother and father asked him about the incident and he denied being involved. They overreacted to his disobedience and spanked him with a belt, leaving bruises and welts on his back, buttocks and upper arms.

Peter had been caught stealing several times and again on the morning of the abuse. His father had been trying to control this behavior and had become frustrated. He lost control and slapped Peter with his hand several times around his face.

Irwin, 11, has had school problems in terms of appropriate behavior for a long period of time. He had previously been assigned to special classes. A note was sent home concerning a stealing incident at the school involving Irwin. Mr. R was returning from third work shift when he saw the note and hit Irwin with a belt.

Child, 12, was brought home by police for shoplifting a bag of potato chips. Mother overreacted and strapped her daughter's knees with a belt, causing mild bruises.

Child, 7, had stolen some mints at school. Parents made her stand in the corner. Mr. R allegedly continuously beat her with hand and belt from 5:45 P.M. to 1 A.M. No medical attention given. Child died as a result of beating.

Entrance-exit behavior was the problem cited in 7 percent of the abusive incidents. This involved running away, coming home late, leaving the home or yard without parent's permission.

Girl, 17, disobeyed parents and attempted to sneak out of house to meet her boyfriend—a 28 year old divorced man. This father is physically ill and was angry about his daughter's behavior. He took a willow switch and caught her walking up the highway and switched her.

Child, 13, stayed out all night, mother thought with child's girlfriend. She was told that the child had spent the night with her boyfriend. Mother got into fight with child about this, admitted she lost her temper and beat child with her hands. Medical care was given to child as outpatient.

Randy, 16, came home about 12 midnight after she was supposed to have been home at 6 P.M. She gave a flimsy excuse for her lateness which infuriated her mother. Mrs. G pushed Randy to the floor, pulled her hair, banged her head on the floor and hit her with a purse.

Patrick, 14, ran away from home as he felt he had too much work at home and couldn't do it right to please his mother. When he was picked up and returned home by the police, mother overreacted and allegedly struck him with a flashlight on the head.

Helen, 15, was attempting to run away for the fourth time. Mrs. J "spanked" Helen with a stick to prevent her from running away again. Mrs. J says she cannot control her daughter unless she uses physical discipline methods. Helen says she runs away because of too many restrictions at home. Family appeared very upset about abuse complaint. Mr. and Mrs. J both insist that bruises from spanking are not child abuse.

Janice, 9, had made a habit of coming home late from school. She seldom talked to her mother. On this occasion, she came home at 10 P.M. Her mother slapped her and hit her with an extension cord, causing bruises and welts.

Child, 3, walked out onto the highway. Father got extremely upset and spanked the child with his hand in excess.

Jack stayed out till 9 P.M. without telling mother where he was or who he was with. When he came home mother used a belt to discipline him. She hit him on back and legs.

Problems of biological functioning—eating, sleeping, elimination—were the focus of contention in 7 percent of the incidents.

Janice, 5, refused to eat breakfast and father claims he spanked her with a wooden spoon as no other reward and/or punishment had proven workable in the past.

Mother overreacted to her two year old son's unwillingness to eat his dinner. She allegedly threw the child ten feet across a room and then beat him with her shoe on his head and on one side of his body. The child's cuts required outpatient medical treatment.

Alleged child abuse precipitated by Bruce's refusing to eat ice cream. This 15 year old child vomited after eating a couple of spoonfuls of ice cream. Mr. C, who had just been laid off from work when the incident occurred, hit Bruce with his hands, leaving a black and blue eye and other bruises on the face. Mr. C tried to force Bruce to eat his own vomit but at that point Mrs. C intervened.

Valerie, 1, would not eat, spit up food and threw it on the floor. Father slapped child across the face.

Jimmy, 5, urinates in and on his bed, on the floor and on the rug. Parents are sure it is deliberate. Mother hit him with hands and fists during this week and father did same on previous week. Parents admit being unable to handle him.

Karen, 8, is somewhat retarded. She soiled during the night. Mrs. T is very tense and tries to strictly adhere to a schedule she has set up for herself. The soiling created a disruption in her schedule and necessitated cleaning up.

Child, 2, dirtied her pants and father became upset because the child went in her pants. He feels strict discipline is needed to effect changes in child's behavior. Father hit child with hands and a belt.

Mr. R, who works nights, was awakened in the morning by his 3-year-old daughter, Leah. She had smeared feces in bed and elsewhere. He became angry and hit her with his hand and a "spanking board."

Mother had been awake and working for past 36 hours. Child, 2, mischievous and active, would not go to bed. Mother spanked him with a wooden spoon on butt, causing bruises and welts.

Crying and whining accounted for 4 percent of child behaviors associated with abuse.

Tammy, 2, kept crying after Mrs. A went to work and Mr. A, after a long day at work, could not cope and hit Tammy with his hands, causing a concussion which required outpatient treatment.

One year old Beth had been teething and on the day of the incident had been crying for four and a half hours. Nothing the mother could do could comfort her [walk, rock, feed, change, bathe, etc.]. Mrs. Y became extremely frustrated and spanked the baby on the buttocks, hit her on the shoulder, scratched her on the side and bit her. Child was hospitalized for two days.

Problems around performance of household chores and defiance of parental orders accounted for 5 percent and 4 percent respectively of the behaviors coded as associated with abuse.

Brenda, 14, was asked to do the supper dishes by her father. When she refused, her father began hitting her with hands and belt, leaving bruises and welts on Brenda's upper thighs. Her father believes in strong patriarchal rule of all the children. In view of father's attitude, Brenda has a tendency to provoke her father further.

Mrs. A hit Jane, 9, with a mustard jar on the head and also slapped her in the face and pulled out some of her hair because she didn't clean her room as she was told to do.

Mr. E returned home finding that his 15-year-old stepdaughter, Eve, was attempting to take the family car to school. She had done this once before and damaged the car. She does not have a license to drive. Mr. E pulled Eve out of the car and threw her on the ground. He pushed her face into the ground and kicked her. He pulled her into the house and cut a large portion of her long hair off.

Child, 10, was told to remain at home for a short time to watch his younger brother. He didn't, and left his brother alone while he went to a friend's house. He then lied to his mother when she asked about his absence. His mother then took a belt and hit him about the buttocks. The child then said something sassy to her and she made him put out his hands and she hit him on the palms of his hands.

Irving, 5, was blowing the car horn while father worked on the motor. Irving refused to stop doing this and father, who had been drinking, threw the child from the car to the ground, resulting in a bone fracture.

June, 16, was under psychiatric care for her very angry, hostile attitude at home. When she throws a tantrum, parents lock her in her room till she calms down. On this occasion, June refused to go to her room and the father felt he had to violently force her into her room. He struck June with his hands and a belt.

When Mr. and Mrs. P returned from taking one of their children to the doctor, they found that Roberta, 13, had disobeyed them and had left her younger siblings, for whom she was baby-sitting, alone. Mr. P "spanked" her with a doubled-over belt, causing bruises on the back of her upper thigh.

The child's behavior regarding school and schoolwork precipitated the abuse incidents in 3 percent of the cases.

The stepfather had warned Gabriel, 13, that if he was suspended from school once more he would kick him all the way back to school. This is exactly what happened.

Alleged abuse precipitated by Ruth's bringing home low grades from school. Mr. K was angry at Ruth for this and started yelling and hitting her. He threw dinner plates at her and table knives. Ruth received a cut on her arm about one inch in length. There was swelling and redness around the cut.

Henry, 14, was suspended from school for the third time this year. Mother reacted by whipping child with an extension cord as a disciplinary measure.

Vera, 15, was habitually truant from school. Father came home and found her in bed during school hours. He beat Vera with his hands, causing bruises.

Parental concern with habits of which they disapproved accounted for 3 percent of behaviors associated with abuse. This involved swearing, drinking, smoking, uncleanliness. An additional 3 percent of the incidents were related to dating and sexual behavior specifically.

Victor, 16, and friends were smoking marijuana in the attic when discovered by his father, who lost his temper and struck Victor near the right eye and ear, causing a black eye.

Mr. G has a fear of fire and overreacted when daughter, 17, refused to stop smoking in bed. She has also been absent from the house frequently, with her whereabouts unknown, and was also associating with older kids believed to be involved in drug usage. Mr. G hit his daughter with his hands in the face, causing a bruise about her eye.

Jonathan, 6, had been caught playing with matches on several occasions and his mother threatened that she would burn his fingers the next time he was caught. He was caught playing with matches under the family camper trailer and his mother held his hand over the gas-stove burner. This resulted in third degree burns to one of his fingers.

Mrs. W, a single parent, arrived home from a date slightly intoxicated. She found that her youngest daughter June, age 8, had been smoking cigarettes again after she had, on numerous occasions, been reprimanded for this. Mrs. W stated that the last time June was caught smoking, she told her she would beat her if she ever was caught again. When Mrs. W discovered that June had been smoking again, she was so infuriated that she decided to carry out her threat and teach her a lesson. She took off her shoe and started beating June, causing bruises on her thigh and back. June was also scratched near the eye from her mother's ring.

After repeated warnings, father found child 11 with cigarettes and beer in his bedroom. Beat him with his belt as punishment.

Mrs. S had discovered that Stephanie, 15, had been repeatedly disobedient in that she had been seeing her boyfriend in the family's home while Mrs. S was at work. Mrs. S confronted Stephanie with this accusation and an argument followed. Mrs. S slapped Stephanie about the head and face, cutting the inside of her mouth. Stephanie was seen by a doctor the next day and received two stitches.

Virginia, 14, had been dating a boyfriend who was black. Father came home and daughter was there with her boyfriend. Father had been drinking, got angry, hit his daughter and fought with her boyfriend.

Mother caught Gloria, 13, "messing around" in bed with a boy. Mother took electric cord and hit Gloria across arms and hands. Gloria experiments sexually with older and younger boys.

Betty, 14, returned to parental home after spending an evening with her peers. She was drunk and this, coupled with the fact that she had been out with an individual her parents had refused to allow her contact with, precipitated incident. Betty was struck several times with an open hand and knocked down by her father. This was done in a fit of anger on his part.

In 16 percent of the cases, while some behavior on the part of the child associated with the abuse incident was noted by workers, their description of the behavior was too brief or too ambiguous for categorization. We further included in this category of "other and unspecified misbehavior" those behaviors which did not fit in other categories but were cited too infrequently for a separate category. Included under these "other" behaviors were a scatter of instance of play activity at the wrong place, or the wrong time, or unacceptable methods of play; and some instances of general disobedience.

Sol pulled down the ladder to a backyard swimming pool and climed in. Her two-year-old brother also climbed up the ladder and jumped into the pool into water over his head. Mother says he almost drowned. She slapped Sol on the upper body. A red mark showed for a few hours.

A neighbor made a complaint to the stepfather that Tim was playing in the neighbor's garage. Tim and the other children had been warned repeatedly to avoid other neighbor's yard. The stepfather hit Tim with his fist in the face.

According to his mother, Richard 6, was supposed to get ready for school but continued playing with their air conditioner until it came out of the window and down onto himself. Mrs. H said Richard's misbehavior made her "so mad" she took after his buttocks with a belt but "had trouble because he squirmed so much." Richard has a bad nose bleed, welts across his left cheek and an abrasion and bruise on his flank.

These behavior categories depict typical activities of children that serve as immediate precursors to abusive acts on the part of their parents. Secondary precursors of abuse (appendix table C.6) were also noted in one in five cases in the sample. All twelve behavior categories were utilized to describe these more remote precipitants and the frequency with which they are cited tends to parallel that found for immediate precursors. Third precursors were described in only twenty cases (2.4 percent of the sample). Despite the restricted amount of data available to assess activities of the children, inclusion of second and third precursors in these abuse reports does suggest that children may engage in a series of behaviors perceived by their parents as unacceptable prior to being abused. The nature of this process is more appropriately explored in the extensive interviews with parents described in the following chapter.

In recapitulation, behavior related to abuse as noted on the report forms involved both physical and verbal aggression against parents, siblings, and peers in and out of the home; and destructive behavior directed at things as well as people. Children fought, hit, scratched, yelled, cursed, broke and smashed and destroyed, lied and stole. Children refused to eat, made a mess at the table, disrupted mealtime, wasted food, demanded the wrong kind of food or demanded food at the wrong time. They urinated or defecated in the wrong place or at the wrong time, played with feces; refused to go to bed, played and made noise in bed instead of sleeping, refused to get up; refused to dress or wash or wear clothing selected.

General disobedience includes hyperactivity, temper tantrums, general restlessness and irritability, and boisterousness. Disapproved habits and sexual activity included drinking, smoking, unacceptable hair styles, thumb-sucking, nail-biting, masturbation, sex play, and dating others unacceptable to parents.

There was concern with defiance, or failure in the performance of household chores such as baby-sitting, dishwashing, housecleaning, caring for pets, picking up toys or clothing, and cleaning one's room. School problems included persistent lateness, truancy, fighting in school, breaking school rules, failure to do schoolwork, and vandalism. Exit-entrance behavior involved running away, coming home late, and leaving home without permission.

This survey of the behaviors of children in Wisconsin points to the highly varied nature of their activities prior to being abused. Many of these activities are noted in descriptions of typical child-management problems in the literature of child rearing. A number of them are also included in the literature depicting more severe behavior difficulties of childhood. (See, for example, Spivack and Spotts 1966; Walker 1970). The degree to which abused children exhibit behaviors that are atypical, excessive, or especially problematic for parents is an issue that the limited nature of our data does not permit us to address.

Aggressive behavior of the child is repeatedly cited in cases included in this survey. There are a variety of possible explanations for the prevalence of such activity during abuse episodes. The parents may be unusually harsh in their response to moderate forms of aggression displayed by their children. The children themselves may be atypical in the degree they provoke parents through verbal taunting and physically aggressive acts. Modeling effects may also be operative here. Parental violence towards the child may be imitated by the child in subsequent interactions with the parent. Whatever the etiological processes involved, it is clear that protective service workers will find parental reaction to such behavior a common theme in the cases they investigate.

The Child's Behavior in Context

Information available on the Abuse Report Form permits examination of a number of contextual factors that may clarify some of the conditions under which children engage in one activity or another. The relationship between appearance of these behaviors and characteristics of the child (age, sex), the parent (sex), and the abuse incident (degree of injury and medical attention the child received, method used to abuse the child) are described below. The relationship between the child's activity and consequences of abuse (placement of the child, involvement in court procedures) are also discussed. This assessment explores correlations between these background factors and the type of activity the child engaged in. Limitations inherent in use of a survey research design do not permit analysis of causal relationships. Because data on the child's behavior that serves as an immediate precursor of abuse are more complete than those describing more remote precursors, they will be used in the assessments which follow. More detailed information on the abuse incident is required before further study of second and third precursors is undertaken.

One contextual factor, age of the child, was consistently linked with the type of behavior the child engaged in prior to being abused. Age was divided into three main categories: the preschool child (five years or younger), the latency-age child (six to twelve) and the adolescent (thirteen to seventeen). Correlations were significant for eight behavior categories ($p \leq 0.1$) and suggestive for two others ($.01 < p \leq .05$). (See appendix table C.7.)

Not surprisingly, almost all instances in which crying or whining on the part of the child preceded abuse involved the youngest children in the sample. Preschoolers were also more likely to be described as overactive or to engage in activities involving food, elimination, or sleeping. Latency-age children were distinguished by their participation in lying or stealing. Approximately two-thirds of the cases describing these behaviors occurred among children six to twelve. Adolescents participated in almost all of the dating or sex-related activities and in a disproportionate number of cases involving conflict with parents over going out of, or coming into, the house.

There was a direct correlation between age of the child and participation in aggressive behavior (with adolescents engaging in half of these cases), performance of household chores, and disapproved habits. Education-related problems were spread equally among the two school-age groups. The only activity category for which no significant differences were found based on age of the child is that designated as "other acts of defiance," a finding replicating that reported in another study using different measures of this behavior (Martin 1978). Table 4.4 describes the most typical behaviors engaged in by children in each age group.

There were age differences as well in the extent to which the protective service investigator noted any type of behavior of the child on the Abuse Report Form. Some behavior was cited in three out of four cases involving the youngest children but in more than 90 percent of the adolescent incidents. (Appendix table C.7.) This difference may reflect actual or perceived variations in the extent to which children of different ages can purposely misbehave or refuse to obey their parents.

Comparison of the activities of boys and girls in the sample yields far fewer significant differences. (Appendix table C.8.) The data suggests that boys are more likely to engage in behaviors involving food, elimination, and sleeping; while girls exhibit more entrance/exit behavior, dating behavior, and aggression (results suggestive) and are more likely to be in conflict with parents over performance of household tasks (results suggestive). However, control for age effects produces nonsignificant gender differences for all but one of these behavior categories. Because girls are overrepresented among adolescents in the sample, findings suggesting they are more likely to exhibit a behavior may actually reflect the fact that adolescents are more prone to engage in the behavior. This occurs when entrance/exit behavior, aggression, and performance of household tasks are reassessed within the teen-age subgroup. Gender differences in these activities disappear. Only in the area of conflict with parents over dating and other sex-related activities do these gender differences persist. Girls

TABLE 4.4
Most Prevalent Behaviors by Age

For the Preschool Child	Percent	Number
Behavior involving food, elimination, sleeping	15.0	35
Crying, whining	11.6	27
Aggressive behavior	11.2	26
Overactivity	6.0	14
Defiance of parental orders	4.3	10
Total	48.1	112
For the Latency-Age Child		
Aggressive behavior	16.9	48
Lying, stealing	16.9	48
Behavior involving food, elimination, sleeping	6.3	18
Defiance of parental orders	5.3	15
Entrance/exit behavior	4.6	13
Total	50.0	142
For the Adolescent		
Aggressive behavior	32.9	93
Entrance/exit behavior	12.4	35
Performance of household chores	7.4	21
Dating, sexual behaviors, disapproved friends	7.1	20
Lying, stealing	6.7	19
Total	66.5	188

are involved in all of these activities among the latency-age and adolescent children.

Because fathers in this survey are more likely to abuse adolescents, we would expect to find significant differences between mothers and fathers in the behaviors that their abused children exhibit. However, no such differences were found. Within each of the three age groups, this lack of differentiation between the responses of male and female parents persisted except in one instance. Fathers were more likely than mothers to abuse crying or whining preschool children. In 20 cases, male parents abused young children involved in this activity, while mothers did so in only seven instances (Chi-square = 5.69, d.f. = 1, p = .0171).

Assessment of the relationship between the behavior of the child and characteristics of the abuse incident may illuminate some activities of the child parents respond to most harshly. Methods parents used in abusing the child were classified as beating (with the hand or an instrument) or other methods (more serious and unacceptable disciplinary techniques, including throwing, stabbing, tying up, shooting, or strangulating the child). Four out of five children in the sample were beaten. In the case of only two behavior categories were there indications that children engaging in certain activities were treated differentially.

Results suggest that children who lied or stole were much more likely to be beaten (10.2 percent of the beaten children) than to be mistreated in other ways (3.9 percent of children treated more harshly) (Chi-square = 5.07, d.f. = 1, p = .0243). This was particularly true for latency-age children who most frequently engage in this behavior. In 46 cases, these children were beaten after being accused of lying or theft but were treated more severely in only two cases (Chi-square = 5.17, d.f. = 1, p = .0230).

Opposing results were obtained when defiant activity was examined. Parents dealing with children engaging in this type of behavior were more likely to utilize less acceptable abuse methods. In almost one in ten cases involving use of harsh methods (9.2 percent) the child was described as refusing to obey his or her parent, while this occurred in 3.2 percent of the incidents in which children were beaten (Chi-square = 9.17, d.f. = 1, p = .0025). Exploration of the age group in which this pattern is most likely to occur suggests young children are frequent targets of harsh treatment. Of the preschoolers whose parents used severe abuse methods, 10.6 percent were depicted as defiant, while only 2.9 percent of the young children who were beaten engaged in this behavior (Chi-square = 3.56, d.f. = 1, p = .0591).

This finding raises a number of questions concerning the role of defiant behavior of the child in abuse events. The limited amount of information describing these events available in this survey makes it impossible to determine whether abusive parents who severely mistreat children attempt to justify their behavior by emphasizing their belief that the child has purposefully chosen to disobey them. An alternative explanation for our findings suggests that these parents become severely frustrated and eventually lose control and severely mistreat the child after he or she has persisted in being disobedient.

Two indicators of severity of abuse are available in this survey. One, describing injury to the child, was differentiated into minor and major categories. Children experiencing minor injury received bruises, welts, sprains, dislocations, abrasions, or lacerations. Approximately nine in ten children were injured in this manner. Major injury to the child included fractures, suffocation, or burns. The second indicator of severe injury describes the amount and type of medical attention the child required: 60 percent of the children needed no medical care, and an additional 25 percent received care but did not need medical attention; 8.5 percent did receive outpatient care, and 5.7 percent were hospitalized.

In two behavior categories, results of the survey suggested that the activity of the child was associated with the degree of injury he or she sustained. When children acted aggressively, they were more likely to sustain minor injury and to require no medical attention. One-fifth of the minor injury cases involved aggression; 11.3 percent of the severely injured children and 8.5 percent of those hospitalized engaged in this behavior. The tendency to receive minor injury when exhibiting such behavior was especially pronounced among the younger children in the sample. In 25 of the 26 cases in which they behaved aggressively, injury was minor, and in 24 cases they received no medical care.

On the other hand, children in conflict with parents over issues involving eating, sleeping, or elimination are prone to be more severely injured. While only 7 percent of all the children engaged in this class of activity, 12.5 percent of the severely injured children and 17 percent of all hospitalized children did so. Children who cried during abuse episodes were also more likely to be hospitalized. Such children comprised 14.9 percent of all those who were hospitalized, although only one of them was severely injured. All seven of these hospitalized children were preschoolers.

Tables 4.5 and 4.6 depict those activities most frequently found among cases involving severe injury to, or hospitalization of, youngsters in the sample. The significance of conflict with parents over eating and related activities in terms of potential threat to the safety of younger children is evident in both of these tables. Latency-age and adolescent children were hospitalized more often after behaving aggressively. Younger school-age children were more likely to be severely injured after lying or stealing; while for their teen-age counterparts, entrance/exit activities were associated with severe harm. Activities for which children are severely in-

TABLE 4.5

*Most Typical Behaviors of Severely Injured
Children by Age*

Behavior Category	All Severely Injured Children	Identified Cases Among		
		Preschoolers	Latency-Age	Adolescents
Behavior involving food, sleeping, elimination	12.5% (10)	(7 cases)	(1 case)	(2 cases)
Aggressive behavior	11.3% (9)	(no cases)	(4 cases)	(5 cases)
Lying, stealing	5.0% (4)	(no cases)	(3 cases)	(1 case)
Entrance/exit behavior	5.0% (4)	(no cases)	(1 case)	(3 cases)
Defiance of parental orders	5.0% (4)	(1 case)	(1 case)	(2 cases)
Total	38.8% (31)			

jured reflect the relative frequency with which that behavior category was noted in each age group. The more likely a child of a given age is to engage in an activity prior to being abused, the more likely he or she is to be severely abused in the process.

Approximately one in three children in this study were placed outside their homes as a result of the abuse incident. Comparison of the activities of children who remained at home with those who were removed yields no distinct differences between the two groups. Other factors, especially the child's age, serve as more potent predictors of placement than the child's behavior during the abuse event.

There was only one activity of the child associated with initiation of both criminal court and juvenile court proceedings. Young children who cried were more likely to have parents involved in such court proceedings (table 4.7). This finding may reflect the fact that such children are more likely to be hospitalized subsequent to their abuse experience than are children engaging in other behaviors. In criminal court cases, it is interesting to note that fathers are especially prone to respond abusively to crying preschoolers and that they are also more likely to be prosecuted for criminal misconduct than are mothers in the sample.

TABLE 4.6

Most Typical Behaviors of Hospitalized
Children by Age

Behavior Category	All Hospitalized Children	Identified Cases Among		
		Preschoolers	Latency-Age	Adolescents
Behavior involving food, sleeping, elimination	17.0% (8)	(6 cases)	(2 cases)	(no cases)
Crying, whining	14.9% (7)	(7 cases)	(no cases)	(no cases)
Aggressive behavior	8.5% (4)	(1 case)	(2 cases)	(1 case)
Defiance of parental orders	4.3% (2)	(2 cases)	(no cases)	(no cases)
Total	44.7% (21)			

TABLE 4.7

Court Involvement of Families with Crying Preschoolers

Type of Court Action	Family Involved in Court Proceedings		
	No	Yes	
Criminal court involvement (N = 231)	8.8% [a] (15)	19.7% (12)	$X^2 = 4.12$ d.f. = 1 p = .0423
Juvenile court involvement (N = 233)	8.0% (13)	20.0% (14)	$X^2 = 5.79$ d.f. = 1 p = .0161

[a] Percentages reflect cases in which preschoolers cried.

In two other activity categories, there is an association among the child's behavior, the child's age, and initiation of court action. Cases referred to criminal court were twice as likely to involve incidents in which the child lied or stole (13.8 percent) than were noncourt cases (7.6 percent). This difference is significant for pre-adolescent children. Of the criminal court cases in which children were of latency age, 30.4 percent concerned incidents in which the children engaged in this behavior, while only 14.3 percent of the noncourt cases did so (Chi-square = 6.05, d.f. = 1, p = .0139). Performance of household chores was an activity linked with initiation of juvenile court proceedings, but only for adolescent children. Teen-agers were involved in conflict with their parents concerning chores in 14.8 percent of the juvenile court cases but only 5.5 percent of the noncourt cases (Chi-square = 4.70, d.f. = 1, p = .0301).

There does not appear to be any consistent link between the types of activities children engage in prior to abuse and consequences of the abuse episode in terms of placement of the child or initiation of court action. However, examination of these activities does suggest some special situations in which court action is more likely to take place. It is clear that the age of the child must be considered in future research on the consequences of abuse.

Summary

We have identified a number of major characteristics of abuse episodes in the Wisconsin Survey:

1. Abused children are as likely to be preschoolers as they are to be teen-agers, as likely to be boys as they are to be girls. Younger children are more often males and teen-agers more frequently females. Older children are more likely to be abused by fathers, while those who are younger are equally likely to be abused by their male or female parents.

2. Poverty is prevalent among these abusive families. This is reflected in the large number of lower social class families, the prevalence of large and single-parent families in the sample, and the number of parents who are unemployed and receiving some form of public assistance.

3. Most of the children in the study were beaten by their parents, and most sustained minor injuries and did not require medical treatment. Younger children were more likely to be seriously injured and to require medical care.

4. A number of factors depict the context in which these abuse incidents take place. Two patterns of child abuse were evident—one in which a single child was abused, a second in which several children in the family were mistreated. Intergenerational transmission of abuse was not evident in most families in the study. However, stress factors suggesting the negative impact of poverty, personal emotional difficulties, and marital conflict were frequently noted in these cases. In a small but important subgroup of cases,

described as violence-prone families, indication of multiple abuse of children and spouse abuse were noted. In most of these families, fathers were the abusive parent.

5. Most of the families in the Wisconsin Survey received some type of social services. Court proceedings were instigated in a minority of cases and were especially likely to begin when young children were abused. A number of children were placed outside the home. This resource was used most often for teen-agers and least often for children of latency age.

Study of the behavior of children during abuse episodes led to the following findings:

1. When describing the abuse episode and its precipitants, most abuse investigators describe some activity of the child. These activities can be classified in eleven major categories, with aggressive behavior the most frequently noted behavior category.
2. The child's age is a highly important predictor of the type of activity he or she will exhibit in abuse situations. Differences in the behavior of preschool, latency-age and teen-age children were found in ten of the eleven activity categories. In contrast, examination of gender of the parent and child produced few significant differences between the activities of males and females.
3. There were some discernible differences in the behavior of children who were harshly treated or seriously injured and those who were not. Children described as defiant were more likely to be harshly treated by their parents. Those involved in conflict with their parents over food, elimination, or sleeping, and crying children, were most severely injured. There was a direct link between the frequency with which children engaged in an activity and the likelihood that they would be severely injured or hospitalized as a result of the abuse incident.
4. Placement of the child was not associated with the type of activity he or she engaged in. However, involvement in court proceedings was more likely in cases where young children cried or whined, latency-age children lied or stole (criminal court only), and teen-agers were in conflict with parents over performance of household chores (juvenile court only).

Conclusion

This description of the behavior of children during abuse episodes highlights the importance of the study of the role of children in abuse situations for a clearer understanding of these episodes and their consequences for both the parents and the child. This preliminary examination points out the need for more detailed study of transactional processes that occur during abuse events—research that is described in the chapters which follow.

REFERENCES

AHA (American Humane Association). 1978. *National Analysis of Official Child Neglect and Abuse Reporting*. Denver: American Humane Association.

de Lissovoy, Vladimir. 1979. "Toward the Definition of 'Abuse Provoking Child.' " *Child Abuse and Neglect*, 3:341–50.

Friedrich, William N. and Jerry A. Boriskin. 1976. "The Role of the Child in Child Abuse: A Review of the Literature." *American Journal of Orthopsychiatry* (October), 46(4):580–90.

Gelles, Richard. 1978. "Profile of Violence Towards Children in the United States." Paper Presented at the Annenberg School of Communications Conference on Child Abuse. Philadelphia, November 20.

Gelles, Richard J. 1973. "Child Abuse as Psychopathology: A Sociological Critique and Reformulation." *American Journal of Ortho-psychiatry* (July), 43(4):611–21.

Gil, David. 1970. *Violence Against Children: Physical Child Abuse in the United States*. Cambridge: Harvard University Press.

Gillespie, David, James Seaberg and Sharon Berlin. 1977. "Observed Causes of Child Abuse." *Victimology* (Summer), 2:342–49.

Helfer, Ray. 1973. "Etiology of Child Abuse." *Pediatrics*, 51:777–79.

Herrenkohl, Roy C. and Ellen Herrenkohl. 1979. "A Comparison of Abused Children and Their Non-Abused Siblings." *Journal of the Academy of Child Psychiatry* (Spring), 18(2):260–70.

Lauer, Brian, Else Ten Broeck and Moses Grossman. 1974. "Battered Child Syndrome: Review of 130 Patients with Controls." *Pediatrics*, 54:67–70.

Laury, Gabriel. 1970. "The Battered-Child Syndrome: Parental Motivation, Clinical Aspects." *Bulletin of The New York Academy of Medicine* (September), 46(9):676–85.

Maden, Marc and David Wrench. 1977. "Significant Findings in Child Abuse Research." *Victimology*, 2:196–224.

Martin, Harold and Patricia Beezley. 1974. "Prevention and the Consequences of Child Abuse." *Journal of Operational Psychiatry* (Fall–Winter) 6:68–77.

Martin, Judith. 1978. "Gender-Related Behaviors of Children in Abusive Situations." Ph.D. dissertation, University of Wisconsin.

Parke, Ross and Candace Collmer. 1975. "Child Abuse: An Interdisciplinary Analysis." In E. Mavis Hetherington, ed., *Review of Child Development Research*, pp. 509–90. Chicago: University of Chicago Press.

Spivack, George and Jules Spotts. 1966. *Devereux Child Behavior (DCB) Rating Sclae*. Devon, Pa.: Devereux Foundation.
Walker, Hill. 1970. *Walker Problem Behavior Identification Checklist*. Los Angeles: Western Psychological Services.

CHAPTER 5

INTERVIEW STUDY OF ABUSE-
EVENT INTERACTION

T HIS CHAPTER IS CONCERNED WITH a detailed examination of abuse
events as described by the parents in a structured interview. The
parents interviewed had been identified as abusive and had voluntarily
agreed to be interviewed. What follows is primarily a descriptive study of
the sequence of events that culminated in an act labeled as abuse by
those community agents sanctioned to make such a decision.

The choice of analysis of the interview data was dictated by the considerable heterogeneity of the limited number of interviews. The age of
abused children ranged from early infancy to late adolescence and included children of both sexes. The children manifested a variety of
categories of discrete behaviors associated with abuse. They came from
racially diverse families which covered almost the total socioeconomic
spectrum and varied in family structure. Both fathers and mothers of a
wide age range were the perpetrators of abuse, and severity of injuries
inflicted ranged from mild bruises to serious brain damage. Correlational
analysis with limited subjects in almost every conceivable cell might have
been the more rigorously scholarly, but certainly the less productive, alternative—yielding speculative and perhaps misleading results. Instead,
we opted, as this chapter indicates, for a descriptive analysis of what happened as the abuse event unfolded.

Whatever the results of efforts to distinguish between abusers and nonabusers in their general characteristics, orientation, background, and patterns of family interaction, the factor which ultimately definitively identifies a family as abusive is a particular event—the event of abuse. The
nature of the event—the happening which gives substance to the label of

abuse—needs to be understood. The abuse event is viewed as a discrete instance of aggressive behavior limited in duration, happening at a particular time and place.

A detailed examination of the event itself gives us a better appreciation of the reality as perceived by the parent, of the parents' assessment of the situation with which they were faced, and of the rationale for their reaction to it. Without excusing the behavior, an analysis of these considerations may enable us to better understand where the parents were "coming from" when they acted in a particular (aggressive) manner toward a particular child at some specific point in time. Our focus is on a specific abuse event, happening, occurrence, and the parent-child interaction within the time-limited duration, from start to termination, of that incident.

The aim is a better understanding of the abuse event, derived from a more explicit focus on the parent's perception of the child's behavior relating to the abuse incident and the parent's explication of his own choice of responses.

The procedure used in the interview was one of retrospective introspection. A series of questions attempted to bring the interviewee back in his own mind to the specific abuse incident for which a substantiated agency report had been made. Then questions were introduced which solicited sequential, detailed information regarding the child's behavior as a stimulus to parent's behavior and parent's response as a stimulus to the child's behavior. In effect, we attempted to "walk" the parents through the incident in retrospect, getting as detailed a description as possible of what each of the participants in the abuse incident were doing, thinking, and feeling at each point in the process.

Focusing on the abuse event itself for a more detailed examination leaves one with the feeling that specific situations are highly individualized, highly idiosyncratic. Like fingerprint patterns, abuse eventuates from such a varied and fortuitous concatenation of interactions and contexts that no two instances are alike. Generalizing does violence to the specifics of each event and robs it of some of the rich nuances that make specific individual events understandable.

What does stand out, however, is that the abuse is—in every instance, as far as we could determine—the result of a sequence of interactional sub-units generally initiated by something the child does and subsequently affected by the reciprocal response of the participants once the events get under way. It is an interactional process in which both the parent and the child make a contribution to the way the event proceeds. The question of whether the action taken by participants is intentional, deliberate, planned, is secondary to the fact that the actions taken, the behavior manifested, by each of the principal participants (and sometimes the peripheral participants) contribute to the determination of what happens. The process has a beginning, a middle, and an end, and it generally begins before it starts—previous experiences between parent and child impacting to affect the interaction in this specific incident.

Attempting to follow the process from beginning to end imposes a linear, sequential pattern on the interaction. Actually, like all significant human communications, the interaction itself is more accurately circular or simultaneously reciprocal.

In an interlocking ongoing interactive system, cause and effect, stimulus and response, dependent and independent variables can only be artificially and arbitrarily separated and identified. Each behavioral item is simultaneously both a response to a previous stimulus and a stimulus for a subsequent response, an uninterrupted sequence of interchanges.

The abuse event is one incident in a long history of interactive incidents between parent and child. The event itself is part of a long chain of incidents. It is therefore embedded in the ongoing interaction. Extracting the abuse event from the configuration of ongoing interactions is an arbitrary selection of a point of entry into the chain of ongoing system interactions. The point of entry—the abuse event—is affected by the whole series of prior incidents and will affect the subsequent series of interactions.

In studying immediate sequential interactions, it is difficult, and somewhat erroneous, to say that one "caused" the other. Being forced to start describing the abuse event at some single point in time increases the difficulty of attempting to view the interaction in a noncausal framework. The attempt will be made, however, to maintain a noncausal orientation in focus in discussing the data.

We will first describe the group of 66 abuser-respondents who were interviewed, present some general overview data regarding the abuse incident, and then attempt to analyze the pattern of interaction in the abuse event from initiation to termination. The data, as noted in chapter 3, derives from structured interviews with the parent who participated in the abuse incident. Interviews generally ran between an hour and a half to two hours in length. Interviews were tape recorded and subsequently transcribed. The interview transcriptions were the principal source of data analysis.

Comparison of Interview Respondents with Nonrespondents

It was noted above that responses were received from 77 parents who had been invited to participate because they met the delimitations of the study. From April 1977 through May 1979 invitational letters had been sent to a total of 215 parents who had been involved in recently reported and substantiated incidents of abuse. The 77 respondents recruited as subjects for the research project and agreeing to be interviewed represented a response rate of 35.8 percent. Interviews with 11 of the 77 respondents were eventually excluded from the study, however, because they were incomplete or had not identified a specific, usable abuse incident.* Actual usable interviews providing the data reported on in this chapter were obtained then from 66 respondents.

There are questions regarding the representativeness of the group of 66 parents providing the data. To what extent does this group differ from the larger group of invitees who chose not to respond and to what extent does the group finally interviewed differ from abusive parents nationally? We will compare the group of respondents with nonrespondents at this point, reserving a discussion of the comparison of the respondent group with abusive parents nationally as this becomes relevant throughout the chapter.

We compared the abuse report forms of 61 of the 66 respondents (5 records were not available) with the report forms of 111 families who were contacted but elected not to respond to our invitation to participate in the study. On almost all available variables, there was no significant difference between the families who participated in the study and those families who were eligible and contacted but rejected participation. There was no difference in the age, sex, race, ordinal position or nature of

---

* This high rate of unusable interviews (14.3 percent) was most often related to the fact that many of our respondents had no telephone. Being unable to confirm in advance by telephone that the respondent admitted to an abusive incident which he or she was willing to discuss resulted in our sometimes arriving to find an uncooperative or resistant subject who was unwilling or unable to present a specific incident, or who denied having been the abuser.

abuse of the two groups of abused children; no differences in the age and race distribution of abusers, their relationship to the child, number of children in the home. There was no difference in the disposition of the cases, the services offered, and the nature of legal action taken, if any. There was a trend, which did not reach a level of statistical significance, for the seriousness of the injury sustained by the nonparticipating group of children to be somewhat greater than that of the children of participating families, and they more frequently required hospital treatment. This was associated with a significant difference in the source of referral for the two groups. Nonrespondent families were statistically more frequently referred by hospital physicians and by social workers. Families in the respondent group were more frequently referred by law enforcement officials, school personnel, and relatives.

One statistically significant difference between the respondent and nonrespondent group is that black male abusers were disproportionately underrepresented in the respondent group. Of 17 black male abusers contacted, only 2 (12 percent) responded to our invitation to participate in the study. This contrasts with the 30 percent response rate received from white male abusers invited to participate.

The respondent group was then, in general, very similar to the total group of abusers who had been invited to participate and is representative of the total group.

Characteristics of the Respondent Group

The following presents some general statistics regarding the abusing parents and abused children who comprised the families interviewed.

Respondent abusers were predominantly female (68 percent), white (64 percent), and young (45 percent being under 30); 77 percent had three or fewer children; 37 percent had less than a high school education, and only 3 percent had graduated from college. Fifty-six percent, almost all female, were single parents—divorced, separated, or never married. Some 40 percent of the group depended on Social Security or AFDC as their primary source of income. For those of the group where such information was available, 36 percent had a family income of less than $6,000 in 1978, but 17 percent had incomes of over $14,000 that year. Respondent abusers, when employed, were concentrated in the clerical, sales, semiskilled job categories.

A disproportionate percentage of abusers are then young, single, female heads of families with limited education and low-level employment skills, caring for three children on a very limited income.

The profile of the group of parent interviews is representative of that of abuse parents nationwide. Nationwide statistics of families reported for abuse in 1978 showed a disproportionate percentage of single parents, although a smaller percentage than the interviewed group (28 percent nationally as against 56 percent of the respondent group). As was true for the interviewed group, only 3.5 percent of abusers nationwide were college-educated. Both groups were economically deprived—median income of abuser families being substantially lower than the national median for all U.S. families, 23 percent of the families in the study having incomes of less than $5,000 in 1978. Nationally, abusers had a slightly smaller number of dependent children to care for than our group (AHA, 1979b).

The group of abused children included somewhat more females (56 percent) than males (44 percent), was 56 percent white and 34 percent nonwhite—of which the very largest majority were black children. The group covered a very wide age range: 10 percent were under 2 years of age; 11 percent, 15 and older; 75 percent of the children were 5 years of age and older. Ordinal positions were skewed toward the older child (43 percent) and only children (24 percent).

The wide age range of abused children in the families interviewed increases the heterogeneity of factors related to the abuse event and increases the difficulty of making valid generalizations. Some 53 percent of the children involved were between the ages of 9 and 18, preadolescent or adolescent.

Gelles and Straus found that violence toward children peaks at two ages, 3 to 4 and 15 to 17, because "these are both ages when parents find verbal control such as reasoning, explaining, ordering, ineffective . . ." (1979:25).

Lourie (1979) points to the fact that some of the principal problems of adolescents—the problems of achieving independence and autonomy—are apt to seriously exacerbate conflict between parents and child. This occurs at a time when parents are experiencing special middle-age stresses. At this point in the family cycle, the potentiality for abuse is heightened.

The age distribution of our sample is generally congruent with national statistics regarding the age of abused children. National reports of abuse in 1977 indicated that 15.7 percent of abused children were under 2, and 34.6 percent were 12 years of age or older. Very clearly, the infants and very young children constituted a relatively small percentage of children abused—66 percent being 6 years of age or older (AHA, February 1979:46, table 14). Nationally, 65.5 percent of abusers were white, 18 percent black, the remainder being Spanish-speaking, American Indian, etc. (AHA, 1979a:115).

General Aspects of the Abuse Events

The action which was defined as abusive involved "beating with hands, slapping" in 40 percent of the cases, or "beating with instruments"—belt, extension cord, wooden spoon, a curtain rod— in 47 percent of the cases. There were two cases of stabbing with a fork or knife, two cases of strangling, two cases of throwing or dropping a child. In 87 percent of the cases, then, the nature of the intervention was such that the consequences for most of the children were bruises or welts which did not require medical attention.

Of the 66 children involved in these abusive incidents, 7—or 11.5 percent—required some kind of hospital care. Most of the children requiring medical attention were younger and highly vulnerable to any kind of corporal discipline. There were no fatalities recorded for this group of abused children.

Similarly, national statistics indicate that preponderance of abuse was in the nature of "cuts, bruises and welts," which constituted 82.3 percent of all substanted physical abuse cases in 1977 (AHA, 1979a: 54, table 2). Only 8.1 percent of the substantiated abuse cases were serious enough to require hospital treatment, less than 1 percent (.7 percent) resulted in fatalities and (.2 percent) in permanent disability (p. 47, table 15).

The abuse incident almost invariably took place in the subject's home—most frequently in the bedroom (42 percent) or living room (34 percent). It usually happened on a weekday (85 percent) in the evening between 6 and 9 P.M. (32 percent) or in the afternoon (26 percent). Typically, at 9 o'clock after a long hard day of caring for six children, the oldest of whom is 12, a mother abused a 6-year-old child who refused to go to sleep and continued to pester her. The mother said, "I felt at that time like I am entitled to a little peace and quiet. I mean, I put up with him all day long from morning to night. I am entitled to a little peace and quiet. By then I don't even want to be a mother."

Interaction Preceding Initiation of Abuse Event

In every instance, the chain of interactions which finally culminated in physical abuse begins with some behavior manifested by the child perceived by the parent as aversive. It is confirmation of Bell's contention that "abuse is most frequently (not 'always'—almost nothing is 'always') a consequence of disciplinary action taken by parents or caretakers in response to a specific act of a child" (1975:417).

In terms explicated by Bell and Harper (1977:65), parents respond negatively to behaviors which exceed upper limits of tolerance and behavior which is below parental standards. Children engage in activities—lying, stealing, disobedience, truancy, fighting, etc.—which parents feel need to be curbed, or fail to engage in behavior—doing chores, schoolwork, responding with respect and affection to parents—which parents feel they should stimulate. This says something about the intensity of behavior which parents think children need to emit. In other instances, parents react negatively to behavior which is initially tolerable but becomes intolerable by virtue of prolongation or repetition—crying or nagging. Parents react negatively to behaviors which are tolerable in some contexts but intolerable in other, situationally inappropriate contexts, or tolerable at one age level but intolerable at another.

The same categorization of behaviors which had been previously employed in reviewing the state report form was employed for categorizing the child's behaviors associated with the particular abuse event which was the focus of the interviews. We were, at this point, concerned primarily with the child's behavior which was identified by the parent as being most proximately related to the interaction sequence, culminating in abuse. It was an attempt to specify the principal behaviors which initiated the abuse event.

The behaviors were categorized in terms of what the child did, the target of the child's behavior, and where the behavior was enacted. A child could fight with a sibling inside the home, or a child could curse at a teacher outside the home at school. Further, the child's behavior eliciting a parental response could be active or passive—doing something that the parent did not want him to do or failing to do something which the parent wanted done.

The group of behaviors most frequently associated with abuse concerned actions in the home which parents perceived as being directed against themselves as the target. In 26 instances, children did something which was in defiance of parental orders or established family rules; in 14 instances children engaged in wasteful, damaging, or destructive behavior in the home; in 10 instances children lied to or stole from the parents; in 10 instances there was verbal or physical aggression against the parents; in 7 instances there was protracted crying, whining, or clinging to the parents; in 7 instances there was persistent overactivity and noisiness. There was a scatter of behaviors concerned with entrance-exit actions such as coming home excessively late or failure to come home; with disapproved habits, such as smoking pot or drinking in the home; and continued association with peers unacceptable to the parents. Siblings were, in five instances, the target of verbal or physical aggression by the abused child in the home, which then involved the parents.

Behaviors outside the home ultimately involved the parents in an interaction which culminated in abuse. There were eight instances of persistent school truancy, tardiness, and other behaviors in the school leading to a threat or imposition of suspension, which were abuse related. There were four cases of shoplifting; and two cases of destructive, aggressive behavior outside the home not involving family members. The child's activities associated with abuse in the sample of families interviewed is very similar to the types of activities exhibited by children included in the statewide sample record review unit of the study.

The frequency of specific behaviors is limited by the relatively small number of interviews, by the variety of possible different kinds of behaviors, different possible targets, and different possible age groups presenting different patterns of problematic behavior.

The total numbers of principal behavior cited by the parents as instigating the abuse interaction chain is greater than the number of children in the abused group. Parents sometimes cited more than one principal behavior associated in their mind with the start of the abuse interaction progression, without being able to make a clear choice of the behavior having the greatest significance. In such cases, we tabulated both child behaviors.

What is more significant than the listing of specific behaviors associated with the abuse event is the fact that, in every instance, the parents could identify some particular behavior on the part of the child which initiated a parental response. The abuse events never, in these instances, started with the child being a passive target of some parent-instigated behavior.

What follows is a series of verbatim excerpts from the interview transcripts detailing the behavior to which the parent was responding in initiating the interaction sequence which eventuated in abuse.

A mother who beat her 14-year-old daughter with a broom said:

> I asked the children [boy 12, girl 14] to do their chores and they have a bad way of talking back to me when I ask them to do something, using bad language and saying they weren't going to do it, and I asked them to do the dishes and clean up the living room, and they were arguing about it, fistfighting, kicking each other, pulling hair, and I—it just upset me real bad. I have a hard time with my nerves, it just made me blow up. It was something that I did on impulse. I couldn't take the pressure and this is what I did.

A 40-year-old woman, separated from her husband and in the process of obtaining a divorce, had the sole responsibility for the care of two sons, 15 and 13. The mother had been seeing a psychiatrist for the last four years because of her own problems. She had been having trouble with the 15-year-old boy, who had been driving her car despite the fact that he didn't have a license, had been missing school, and failing in school. The mother had also been concerned about reports she received that the boy had been using marijuana.

The incident that eventuated in abuse involved the boy's returning home drunk about one o'clock in the morning, having been expected at seven o'clock. The mother, anxious and angered after having called around to many places to locate the boy, whipped the boy with an extension cord, leaving marks on his forehead and legs.

A single mother and her boyfriend had gone out for a New Year's Eve celebration and her daughter, 14, expected them back late. The daughter had told her mother that she had a baby-sitting job that night. On getting home earlier than expected, they found the girl, a 24-year-old man with whom she had developed a relationship, and another young girl, finishing off a quart of whiskey:

I don't know whether it was all worry or all anger when she lied to me. She told me that he just came in off the street, carrying that quart, and I hit her. I had had a high school education, not a college education, but it doesn't take a college education to figure out this man was invited and you're lying to me. And first and foremost, you're 14 and he's 24, and that is absolutely out of the question. And I hit her. Not only hurt her pride, I hurt her in front of her friends. And I did give her a black eye, no doubt about that. And I called the police and pressed charges, that was even worse. Against the man. What really upset me was that she had him in the house after I trusted her. That and the fact that she lied to me about his just walking in off the street. That's when I hit her. I'd been deceived. My pride had been hurt because she insulted my intelligence.

A mother, speaking of the behavior of her 2½-year-old daughter, says:

Coral always seems to be belligerent, as far as I'm concerned. She never listens to me, she never does anything I say. And she just has a real negative attitude about everything. And everything is "no." And I get to the point where I can't stand it anymore when, you know, she says no, and "I don't want to do this," and it's very frustrating for me, so I usually—well, it comes to a head. Like this time when I gave her a spanking. After lunch she wanted to go outside. I am doing the dishes and I wanted to get them done and I wanted her to wait. But she's very impatient and she would not wait for me to put a coat on and it was rather cold and she wanted her coat on. Then she wanted to put her hat on. That's fine. She goes out and I get the bike and put it outside for her and I go back to the dishes. Then two seconds later she wants to come in, and I said no, you play outside for a while. You wanted to go out. But she did not want to do that. But she did stay out for a few minutes. Then she comes—she had taken her shoes and socks off and her coat and hat and thrown them—and her bike is down the street somewhere. And I told her to get those clothes on and get in here, and that she was staying in here and she stands out there and screams at me and cries and says, "No, I'm not going to do that." And she just kept crying and screaming and it was embarrassing that the neighbors could hear that and so I ended up dragging her in here and spanking her and throwing her in the bed.

A mother who suffered from epilepsy said:

When I came into the house my sister's little boy was coming out of the bedroom going to the bathroom, and his private was out and he told me that [her son] Sidney made him do it. And then I told Sidney [11] I was going to whip him because I didn't want them to go into any sex act together. And when I told him that, he got scared and he started crying and running and I chased him with an extension cord. I pulled him out from under the bed and I whipped him.

A mother said:

It was probably during the morning and I asked Harry [3 years old] to put his toys away from out here so that they wouldn't be in my way, and he just kind of turned and says "no," and stomps his feet and runs the other way and cries and runs through the house and twists on doorknobs, and he won't stop and I have to come in and settle him down, 'cause I holler at him and he just don't listen, and so I have to paddle him and put him in his bed. I couldn't get him to mind by trying to settle him down by talking to him, and so I finally had to come and spank him because he didn't mind and he sasses me and he got me overwhelmed and I just couldn't bear it anymore.

A working single mother said:

The kids and I have to get up early so I can catch the bus to work, and they can catch the bus to school. They know if they miss the bus, they can't get to school any other way. So sometimes—this morning we're talking about—the kids sneak in and shut off my alarm. Well, I looked at the clock when I woke up and thought about how late it was and went back there and told them to start getting ready for school. Joyce's school clothes I keep in my room and she's supposed to come back here and get them. But she's sitting back there and I waited. She never did come. I had got fully dressed before I went back there and Joyce is *still* sitting in the same place not getting dressed, not doing nothing— just sitting back there knowing she had to go to school. It made me mad, you know, she knows I am trying to get them off to school. So then I got the belt and went back there and I have to chase Joyce to get her and I must have hit her in the face, the mark was across her face and her eye was black.

A mother, in describing the situation which culminated in abuse, said:

The two boys did the paper route in the morning, and there was constant conflict between those two. And Dean [the older boy, 16] was forever yelling at the younger one. And if the younger boy would say he didn't want to, or this, that, then Dean's voice would raise higher and louder, and it would wake up the whole house. Now with the windows open, it wakes up the whole neighborhood. And I had warned him, I said, "You're going to get slapped in the mouth if you don't tone it down in the morning," 'cause they get up between five and six to do the route, and my husband doesn't have to get up until 6:10, and it wakes him up and he's crabby and I'm crabby—you know, it just sets off a chain reaction, so—This one particular morning I got up and I waited for him. I didn't get up, I was woke up. And I waited for him outside, inside the kitchen door, so when he came up I cracked him across the mouth.

A mother smacked her son, 7, with her hand, making a bruise which led to a report by the school nurse the next day. The incident which initiated the interaction resulting in abuse, as described by the mother, involved her efforts in clearing the house while her son "and 600 other kids around the neighborhood were tearing up the house," running through the house playing:

And I told 'em to knock it off, you know—play outside or whatever. I've got two dogs and they let the dogs loose and everybody was tearing up all over the place and I told him to stop it. He didn't and I smacked him as he ran by. It was just a pile of kids in the house driving me up the wall.

A father said:

It was late in the evening, like 9:30, a quarter to 10, and the two girls [7 and 9] were in their room in the same bed fighting with each other. They were pinching each other and pulling each other's hair. My wife wasn't feeling well. She was lying down and was tired. And I was lying down and trying to get some quiet time, is what I was trying to do. But the children wouldn't settle down. Or else I was going to come in there. And they didn't settle down at all. So I went in there and slapped them both. Sarah, the older girl, has long fingernails and while I was slapping her she was trying to protect herself and she scratched herself with her own fingernails.

The teacher, noting the scratch, reported the child as abused.

A stepfather, describing the circumstances which led to the abuse of his 6-year-old stepson, said:

What led up to it was we had a conference with his teacher at school and he had been getting into fights and totally misbehaving in school, which has never happened before. And they were going to put an M team on him, which is a disciplinary team. This was my first conference with the teacher. My wife has been there a few times before.

He had never pulled any of this shit before 'cause he was in school up north and we had no trouble with him at all and we came down here and he won't eat, won't mind. I mean I pinned him to a wall and he listened for maybe a day or two and then the same—back to the same old stuff. He hadn't been listening to me, hadn't been listening to his mother or anybody else. Generally a pain in the ass.

The teacher showed us—each child had made their own picture on a piece of paper and the teacher blacked it out so that each section was a different child. And he had scribbled all over the whole page all the way down. And I guess I just got royally pissed off. Because he's a very good colorer, 'cause he's got coloring books up to here, 'cause I know he's done better than that.

On picking her child up at a friend's house where he had been visiting, a mother said:

I wanted him [8 years old] to come home with me, and he said, "I don't want to go," and he was pulling back and I said, "Henry, don't jerk on me." He pushed me. I said, "Listen, don't push me." I said, "Henry, you're going to get hurt." I said, "I am going to hurt you," and he pushed on me again. And I said, "Don't push on me like that or I'll hurt you." So then I hit him with my fist and his nose was bleeding. He was pulling back from me and he had pushed on me and he didn't mind—that's the reason I hit him.

A mother reported for abuse lived with her husband and 4-year-old child in a rented, single back bedroom in the apartment of a friend. The landlady complained constantly about the child's behavior, claiming she was destructive.

On the early evening of the abuse event, the mother was cooking supper and the child went to the bathroom to wash up. The mother, a diabetic, was not feeling well ("It's been a long time since I knew what to feel good was"). After washing, the child, as reported by the mother,

poured out the toothpaste and the shampoo and mixed a whole bunch of stuff in the sink, smeared lipstick over the bathroom toilet seat and pulled the curtains down in the bathroom. And the landlady came out screaming, "Look what your daughter did to my things. She done messed up this here, she done messed up that," and I was already tired and just aggravated. I had been telling her all day long constantly, "Julia, don't do," and I had been talking all day and I had just got tired of talking. So we went on and I—I just whupped her. I just got in that room, I picked her up, I'll never forget it—I was so mad at Julia I could have killed her.

A father hit his 11-year-old daughter with a strap in response to her lying. The girl had responsibility for part-time care of two younger sisters, 4 and 5, both parents being employed full-time. The father had stipulated certain rules about the conditions under which the children were to be cared for as a protection to the younger children. The older daughter had ignored the rules while assuring her parents that she had followed their stipulations.

We suspected nothing. She was very neat in her lying and set the younger children to lie to us too. I believed her. Why should I not believe her? I live with you every night. I am your father. It was just a violent streak that you done me wrong. I was most baffled by the degree with which she lied to us all the time when we were supposed to be pals and friends. Being let down by the fact that you'd lie to me and all the time you're grinning, lying here and saying, "Oh, everything's beautiful." You know, all of a sudden to find out what you say isn't true at all. And I believed in you all the time. Jesus, if you can't trust your own kid, who in hell can you trust?

A single parent, very much attached to an only child 4 years of age ("He's the only one I got"), disciplined him when he disobeyed and crossed the street against her instructions.

I was looking out the window and he was starting running across the street and I shouted for him to stay there. "Don't you move. You move and you're going to get it." He moved and it was right across the street and here a car almost hit him. When he came in I asked him what he was doing across the street. He wouldn't say anything. And I kept on asking him, I says, "Leonard, what were you doing across the street?" And he didn't say nothing, so finally, I said "Okay," I says, told him, "One, you don't go across the street on a busy, busy street, and you don't go by yourself." I said, "What if you were to be killed?" I said, "Would you think that would be funny?" I said, "You'd be dead and you'd be six feet under." So, um . . . I gave him one, took the belt and it was where it was folded in half, right? Here I was flopping all over and I got him on his legs and—I think the bruises are still on him. And I grounded him for a whole weekend too. He really scared the living daylights out of me because he was crossing the street and a car just stood on his brakes real fast, and he had to stop. And it's where, almost hit him about this much. I mean, you can't take any chances with that kind of stuff, around here. It was about 4:30. And around here at that time, it's very busy. All the cars coming from all the big factories near here at the end of the work day. I was very angry at him—and I was ready to have the works—I was ready to have a heart failure or faint on the floor. That's how bad it was.

A divorced mother with two young children, who claimed that her child was abused by her boyfriend rather than herself, described the child's behavior which initiated abuse as follows:

When this certain incident happened, we were visiting at Joe's [boyfriend] farm. And well, Ray had wet his pants three times that day and for a four year old that's quite unregular. Well, and when Joe brought him in the house, I said, "Oh, Jesus, he did it the third time," I says, "one and two, it's not bad, but the third time. How come you did it?" "I forgot." I just don't see how he could have forgotten. I really just don't. I guess they're just like everybody else, but—the bathroom is just one thing you shouldn't forget. I just don't understand how he could have forgotten it. "It just slipped my mind." I gave him a swat on the butt and put him out on the porch. Well, then Joe went out and spanked him too. I think he was just aggravated enough that he just hit him too hard. It's just a thing that triggers you off, you know, you get so angry at times and if you got other things you're doing—like we were cleaning out a musty refrigerator that day—it's worse. I just never had that problem with my daughter. I am not saying she's a brain or anything, but once I had her potty trained, she hardly ever had an accident. And I could take one or two accidents, I am not saying I expect him perfect, but these accidents happened three times that day. We could not stay with my boyfriend as long as we wanted because I had no change of clothes for him. I was disappointed, you could say, I was disappointed.

A mother with three young children said:

The kids [twins 3½ and a 1-year-old child] had been particularly trying. Into everything, and my son had been cutting teeth and I'd been up, you know, like three nights in a row, and then one of my girls got the flu and I was under stress with my parents. And Florence (3½) has a habit of asking me for something, and if I tell her no, she'll go to my husband, and nine times out of ten he doesn't know that I've told her no. But this particular time he knew that I had said no and he backed me up on it . . . She kept after me. It was to have a cookie. She wanted to have a cookie. And I was—I had supper in the oven, and I didn't want her to have a cookie. They had had some and I told her no, that was enough. . . . She started to scream and cry, and my husband told her to please go sit down. And she screamed at him no, she wasn't going to, and she knocked over a chair in the kitchen, and he picked the chair up, and she got up on her chair in the kitchen at the table, and sat there crying for a cookie, and she kept repeating over and over that she wanted a cookie. And I was getting very upset, and I—I don't know, my husband says I screamed it at her, I thought I just, you know, told her no, you're not having a cookie. And she says, "I want one," and at that point she picked up—I had this little, just this little thing sitting on the table, and she picked it up and she threw it across the room. And that was when I completely lost control. She got very angry and picked up a knickknack and threw it across the room. And it was just like a breaking point for me. I just—I, you know, I ran in there and I picked her up and I just started spanking her extremely hard.

A single mother of a 7-year-old boy said:

This particular day I got a note from his school saying he did all sorts of things in school and I just got fed up. The note said that he was beginning to be a pig and was biting the child in school and pulling the kid's hair and really being rough and mean to other people, other children in school. Like they were saying that my child was really disrupting the whole class. And I thought that maybe if I beat him, or whipped him, you know, really, I would say whipped, you know, that would straighten him out. But it seemed like when I started hitting him, I was thinking about all the other things that he had done, and I was taking it out on him, you know, instead of realizing that he was a child, you know, there's just so much that he's going to do and so much he's not going to do. But I guess, like I say, a lot of other things flared up in my mind and I just really took it out on him, 'cause I thought that he should know these things, I had told it to him over and over and over again, you know, you don't have to do this, you don't do this and don't do that. And it seemed like as much as I said it, he should have known it. And I just took it out on him. I thought he should know it, and I whipped him.

A single-parent foster mother had been quite ill for two days, and since it was a Saturday, her son Jerry, age 6, was home from school all day. A very active boy, he was eager to go outside and play, but his mother was reluctant to let him go out because she was too sick to watch him. (She tends not to let him play outside unless she can periodically check on him.) Not feeling up to her best, she asked him to stay indoors. Upset because he couldn't go out, Jerry was demanding, mischievous, and aggravating, "doing things like a child would do," until finally his mother, reaching the end of her patience, nervous and upset herself, picked up a belt and whipped him. She admitted being more than normally overprotective because, as a foster parent, she felt accountable to the agency, which periodically reviewed her performance as a parent.

A single mother with two children had served a jail sentence for stealing and reacted strongly to her child's stealing, for which she whipped the child with an extension cord. The child had been born while the mother was in jail and had spent the first two years in a foster home, being returned to the mother on her release. The mother said:

> Selma's [6] been a lot of behavior problems. She would act out a lot of bad feelings she would have inside. A lot of it I think is due to me and our marriage going to hell. And my job did put a lot of mental strain and stress on me. I was worrying a lot about my bills. At that time I had a lot of bad feelings about me, too. My own inadequacy, so I think I was punishing rather extremely. A lot of things she had been doing off and on for quite a while and I hadn't punished her for. And so it just—it like came to a head. And I had had it, fed up. And this time it was a dollar she had stolen from my purse which I found in her sock.

A 21-year-old unmarried mother slapped the face of a 2½-year-old child so that bruises were evident to the day care center staff, who reported the abuse. The mother, describing the initiation of the incident, said:

> I was holding her on my lap and I was trying to get her to go to sleep. She had fallen asleep. I picked her up and put her in her crib and laid her down. Then she woke back up and wanted me to take her up again. And I wouldn't and she started screaming and crying and just jumping up and down in her crib. I picked her up and carried her out of her room and then I slapped her a few times. It was just like on the spur of the moment. It happened so fast I didn't even know I had really hit her until I had stopped.

Among the descriptions of abuse as related by respondents in these interviews, the following instance most nearly approximates the typical picture of the battered child as described in the literature. A 21-year-old single female parent with a 1-month-old child was alone late in the afternoon caring for her own child and a 2-year-old niece. The infant kept crying and none of the mother's initial efforts to quiet her were effective. "Everything was building up inside—everything went—my nerves just left—my nerves are very touchy. They went wild—my nerves did—and I didn't know what I was doing." The mother's repeated slappings severely damaged the infant, who needed to be hospitalized.

The precipitating incident and preceding difficulties may be so closely associated in the mind of the parent that they come together and form a single configuration triggering abuse.

A single-parent mother, caring for two children—11 and 13—whipped her 13-year-old girl with an extension cord. The immediate precipitating incident was that the child attempted to run away after having been sent to her room for punishment. This was, the parent said, "combined" with her "skipping and flunking school," "coming home when she felt like it," "lying" about her activities and "stealing." The girl had been suspended from school and had run away from home previously for varying periods of time. This time the mother caught the girl "climbing out of the bathroom window to run away again" and whipped her.

A father who abused his 12-year-old son detailed a series of recent happenings prior to the precipitating incident. The boy had stolen records, a tape recorder, and other items from a department store, which the father had returned. He had stolen brandy and had gotten drunk and was involved with drugs. The precipitating incident involved the boy's failure to bathe, to change underwear, or his clothes. On going in to wake the boy for school one morning, the stink in the room got to the father and he ordered the boy to bathe. The boy's initial reaction of defiance and resistance intensified the father's anger, and after an exchange of words, he wrestled the boy to the floor and punched him in the face. Here the precipitant of the abuse interaction was the culmination of a series of disappointing, frustrating aversive experiences with the child.

The precipitant, as culmination of a series of related events, is noted in the following account by a mother of her perception of how the reported abuse of her 8-year-old son was initiated:

I'd have to go up to the school, you know, for different conferences to find out what was wrong, and the teacher would tell me a certain thing, and it would upset me, but yet I would talk to him about it, you know. So finally—well this particular day, I had got a note from the teacher and when I got the note, I didn't say anything right then, waited till, you know, wasn't so upset, because it bothered me, upset, and I waited for awhile and then I went to him and I talked to him about it and I told him, I said, I'm going to whup you, I said, because all year, I said, I've been talking to you about how you should carry yourself, you know, at school. I said, the teacher shouldn't have to be screaming and hollering and sending me all kinds of notes about your conduct, or whatever. I said, you shouldn't be fighting, either. And so—I didn't whup him right then, I waited, and then on a Sunday, it was on a Sunday, I be getting ready for church as usual. I told him to do something, and it was like he just ignored me. And so I didn't say anything, I just kept on doing my cleaning. And then I told him, I said, "Bill, didn't I tell you to do—" you know, whatever I had told him to do. And he looked at me and he said, "Yeah." And he just kept on doing what he was doing. And I just walked around for a few minutes to see if he was going to get up and do it. And he didn't. And I told him, I said, "That's been the problem all year." I said, "You've been told to do different things, and you don't do 'em. I told him, I've talked to you, and I've punished you, I've taken things from you to try to get you to just be, you know, more obedient, I said, then I don't have to whup you, I said, but you just don't want to listen. And I looked at him and I got a belt and I whupped him. Usually when I whup him, it's because of things that I have told him not to do, and then he insisted on doing it anyway, and then I whup him, it's like I've reached my limit—okay, this *is* going to stop now. About time.

In another instance, the behaviors which predisposed to abuse were likewise remote from the actual incident which precipitated the abuse but directly related to the abused child's earlier behavior. It represents a classic case of a cry for help by a parent who felt threatened.

The respondent's husband had planned a hunting trip and, as a consequence, his wife was to be left alone in the home with her 16-year-old stepson. The stepson had been telling neighbors fantasized stories of sexual activity with his stepmother. The respondent stepmother described him as

a neat, clean young man, beautiful boy, just absolutely all American blond, blue-eyed, very thin, just absolutely one of the most gorgeous people I've ever laid eyes on. But to me he just had a black heart. He was totally unhappy and he made me unhappy as a result. This kid is the most miserable kid I've ever seen in my life. And telling others that he was imagining having intercourse with me, that did it. That was the end, I couldn't live with that, that was just—that hit too low, and I think I hated him then, really hated him.

Describing the abuse incident, the mother said:

I was cooking. I mean, I didn't go to the drawer and take the knife out, I was cooking. I was using the knife. Preparing food, and this kid probably dropped a glass of milk or—he did something, right? I don't remember what it was, I don't think it was important. My big worry at that point was my husband leaving him here with me while he went out deer hunting and—this was on my mind all the time. I just felt that I could not be with this kid for that weekend. And I couldn't leave him alone. And he did something and I guess I struck him with the knife. In the arm. Twice. I remember the thrust of my hand, you know. It was more of a jab—I don't really believe, neither does the social worker in the case, that I really wanted to hurt Al, because as she said, if you wanted to, you would have. And I would have. I wanted him out. I know I wanted him out. I couldn't take him anymore. And I really think this was my way of getting him out of the house. I know that more clearly than I know what actually happened. I kinda blacked out on what happened when I took the knife to him. I just felt like this is it, either him or me. It was really the survival of the fittest. His brothers, who were there, took care of him, cleaned him up. I went to see what they were doing and that he was getting the care he should have so after I saw he was getting the right care, I came upstairs and went into my room and stayed there.

The following case illustrates a longer chain of interaction in which the mother's anger is gradually intensified to the point where it results in serious abuse to the child.

It started by him aggravating me. All day Louis [9 years old] calls me. I don't mind him calling me every once in a while. It's "Mama, Mama, Mama." I say, "Louis"—nothing. "Mama, Mama, Mama." "What, Louis?" "Nothing," you know. And everybody else is saying "Mama, Mama," you know, but they're wanting something, but—I have to pay attention to him when he don't want anything. He just want to feel that I'm going to come to his beck and call. And after he do that, round the clock, round the clock, it just gets to you, you can't help it. I mean—you know, call me when you want me. Call me when there's a reason, call me when you want something. Don't call me just to call me. And this is what happened that day. That was all day that day.

So it got to be a Wednesday night, at 8:30. I told Louis to go to bed. He had been annoying me all day. And when I told him to go to bed, instead of him going to bed like I had told him, he commenced tearing open my pillows, getting feathers all over the room, jumping up and down in the bed, taking all the clothes out of the closet. Nine o'clock came and he was still showing out. I didn't bother him because I had gotten mad. Ten-thirty Louis commenced to not going to sleep, tearing, banging up the place on the wall by me. I went in there and I said, "Louis, look," I says, "I want you to go to bed, or I'm going to whup you now," I said, "I mean it." But I didn't have any—I mean, I didn't have a switch to whup him. This is the way I usually whup him. By the time I got back in that room, it was about ten after eleven. I said, "Louis, I asked you to mind," I said, "Son, why don't you?" And I reached up against the window and I got a curtain rod, there was a little hook inside. And I took the curtain rod and I went to hit him with it. When I went to hit him with it, he grabbed it, and when he grabbed it, he bent it. He is always fighting me, he always would fight back and that made you even madder. And I commenced to steady whup him with this. When blood went to running all over, and I was steady whupping him. I was—I was angered, you know, I mean I was really angered. And blood was running all over, blood was flying over the wall and over the sheet, and I was still whupping him. And then, when I got through whupping him, I wrapped him up and I took him to the hospital. And they says, "What happened to him?" I said, "I whupped him." They said, "You know you is in trouble for whupping him?" I say, "Yes, I understand," I said, "but at the time, I could not do anything else but whip him." I couldn't. I couldn't help myself, I mean—I was constantly telling this kid to please go to bed. But I—it's just like I have—I mean, I have five other kids other than him. They can mind, he can mind. He don't have to be so aggressive. But he is. God know, I don't know what else to do with that guy, he's running me ragged. But since I've whupped Louis, he ain't gave me no grief. You know, that's strange. But Louis hasn't given me any grief at all. I guess Louis just ran me half near damn crazy for me to put a curtain rod to his back. I couldn't believe that I really did that. But I did it.

Interaction Following Initiation of Abuse Event

In each of the above situations, the child presented the parent with some behavior which was perceived as noxious and aversive. The child's behavior initiated the sequence of interactions which was ultimately defined as the abuse event. The child's initial behavior was the stimulus which was seen as requiring some response.

The parent's initial *feeling response* to the child's behavior in doing something which should not have been done, or failing to do something which should have been done, was one of anger in 85 percent of the cases. Less frequently, the feeling engendered was "sadness, a feeling of depression" (9 percent) or a feeling of being "frustrated or defeated" (6 percent).

The first *action response* to the behavior which initiated the interaction culminating in abuse was most frequently a low-level, noncorporal intervention. In 42 percent of the cases, parents "spoke to the child, admonishing, threatening, warning." In an additional 40 percent of the cases, parents "spoke to the child, reasoning, explaining, instructing." In 4 percent of the cases, parents initially walked away or attempted time out with the child. In 5 percent of the cases, the initial intervention was corporal punishment but of limited intensity, "shook child, light slap or spank." In only some 8 percent of the cases was the parent's first behavioral response more punitive corporal punishment—whipping, beating, slapping, punching.

The response to the aversive stimulus is mediated by the parent's interpretation of the situation, his judgment of the appropriate response, an assessment of the most effective response, an estimate of the likely effects of the intervention on the child. It might even be determined by something as immediate as the availability of the disciplinary artifact. If the belt or extension cord usually used for discipline is at hand, this might determine the action taken. A delay in finding the belt or cord may change the course of the interaction.

The frequency counts indicate that, most frequently, corporal punishment, mild or heavy, was not the first reaction of the parent to the child's behavior which initiates the interactional sequence of the abuse event. The largest majority of parents, even the most unsophisticated, have a hierarchy of procedures, a repertoire of disciplinary responses, which they employ with varying degrees of effectiveness. They talk, they admonish, they shout, they yell, they attempt to ignore the behavior, they withdraw love and withhold privileges, they offer distractions, they distance themselves from the child, or they distance the child from themselves. Parents differ, of course, in the variety and elaborateness of the repertoire they know about and can competently employ. But in most instances, corporal punishment is not their first choice in the hierarchy of procedures available to control the situation.

In responding to a situation requiring disciplinary intervention, the parent is likely to move sequentially through his repertoire from the least punitive and intrusive to the more punitive and intrusive. For most parents, corporal punishment, shading into abuse, is likely to be the result of a series of interactional responses which escalate as parents find themselves having to employ progressively more punitive procedures.

If the varied, less punitive, interventions which most of these parents employed as their first response to the child's behavior, thus initiating the interaction sequence of the abuse event, had been effective, the abuse would have been aborted. The interaction sequence would have terminated with the child's having ceased the behavior which the parents wanted stopped or having started the behavior which the parents wanted the child to perform. The aversively perceived stimulus would then have been dissipated, nullifying the need for any additional intervention.

The child's responses to initial attempts on the part of the parents to deal with a situation perceived as requiring disciplinary intervention either acts to cycle the interaction away from abuse or escalate it in the direction which eventuates in abuse.

At this point in the process, there was the possibility that the interaction in these instances might have gone in a different, more benign direction. Many potentially abusive situations end up as nonabusive events because, at some point in the interaction, a less damaging alternative is available which the parent is capable of implementing and to which the child responds in the manner expected by the parent, aborting a continuation of the interaction in the direction of abuse. The parents interviewed here were, in effect, a residual subgroup of a much larger group of parents who initially responded to some child behavior, perceived as aversive, in a nonpunitive manner. Their fellow members in the larger group do not appear here because earlier nonpunitive interventions of these other parents did have the intended effect of resolving the situation requiring discipline. For the respondent group, this was not the case. They continued to face an aversive situation, which continued to require some response on their part.

If a parent talks, argues, admonishes, discusses, exhorts, yells, nags, and the child persists in his behavior, the parent feels pushed to go beyond this. If the child ignores, or is indifferent to, the parents' first nonpunitive interventions in response to the child's behavior which initiates the interaction, the parents move in a more punitive direction since the initial, less punitive interventions do not achieve the parents' objectives.

A mother who slapped her 7-year-old son for running through the house with friends while she was attempting to complete housecleaning says:

> I asked him, I told him and I yelled at him. Little by little it went up. It didn't do any good to tell him nicely. It didn't do any good to ask him nicely. It didn't do any good to yell. If nothing else, I had to get his attention or something. It was just like he had a wall, he didn't hear anything.

A series of efforts are made to deal with the situation before the abusive action. A young father attempting to deal with his 10-month-old son's crying early in the morning "went over and gave him his pacifier. And that didn't do anything, he just spit it out and the thing goes flying across the room. And I tried picking him up and that didn't do any good, he just stiffened up like a board. And I set him back down and he just stiffened up and almost rolled off the couch and that shook me by a little bit." The father finally spanked the child to stop the crying.

It was noted that, in 8 percent of the cases, the parent's first response short-circuited any efforts at noncorporal, nonpunitive interventions and moved directly to more abusive interventions in response to the child's behavior initiating the interactional sequence. But while not actually attempted, nonpunitive responses were vicariously a part of the parent's calculus of decision making in the choice of the more punitive responses. The effect of nonpunitive disciplinary procedures on other previous occasions with this child was part of the reality of this particular abuse event. The parent's memory of earlier disciplinary interactions determines the parent's decision as to how he might behave now in effectively responding to the child's behavior.

While most of the parents progressively escalated their interventions toward increasingly greater punitiveness as less punitive procedure proved ineffective within the interactional sequence studied, other parents began with the more punitive measures in this sequence because this particular event was seen as the culmination of a series of other, earlier, interactional events in which less punitive measures had proven ineffective. Alternatives to punitive corporal punishment were not initially attempted in this interaction because of the failures in the use of such alternatives in earlier interactions. The previous events merge with this one. The child may act—and the parent may abuse—without any attempts to use alternative options between initiation of the interaction in response to the child's aversive behavior and abuse. But in the parent's mind, the previous attempts at discipline for this kind of behavior are applied as though they were part of the more immediate chain of interactions. The decision as to choice of disciplinary intervention is mediated by such cognitions. Such parents expressed the thought that they had no alternative to corporal punishment in response to the child's behavior which initiated the interaction that was the focus of our interview. They felt forced by the situation which demanded intervention to do what they did, since alternatives had proved ineffective on previous occasions when they attempted to discipline the child.

A mother details the series of steps which led up to the abuse of her 10-year-old daughter. (Margaret, the daughter, had stolen $.75 from a friend's purse and, when confronted with it, confessed.)

> So I sat down with Margaret and had a long talk with her and she told her friend she was sorry, she gave back the money and said she wasn't going to do it again. So I just overlooked it. I thought it was over.

> Then a week later, the police brought her home because she had been caught stealing pop bottles and they told me that a couple of nights before she had been caught shoplifting by the manager of this store, and he told her not to come back in the store. Well, then when the police brought her home, I spanked her because she knew better really, and she was stealing, and she ran out of the house screaming.

A neighbor reported the incident to Protective Services. The mother goes on to say:

> Well, they're (the neighbors) against spanking altogether. They told me I should have talked to her. Well, I had talked to her just the Sunday before for stealing—so I don't know. Talking wasn't going to help her.

A mother who abused her 13-year-old daughter following repeated events of lying and stealing and staying away overnight, without mother's permission, with "friends" unfamiliar to the parents, said:

> It just got to the point that I couldn't discipline her any type of way so I said maybe an old-fashioned spanking would do it. I tried everything. I even called that number, the Parents Help. I've got a counselor talking to her to see what the real problem is, everything. I just did not know what else to do. She got me so aggravated. Took a deep breath and got up and went outside and smoked a cigarette to calm down. So this

time she caught me. She just got me at the wrong time, and I says, "Get up, go upstairs to your room" and I spanked her, 'cause I got tired of her lying to me and stealing and running away for reasons which don't make any sense.

She wanted discipline, but then I tried everything I could think of. "I am trying to help you, but you're not helping yourself. Because I am tired of trying to talk to you and trying to do it your way." I said, "Maybe you need an old-fashioned spanking—maybe that'll help you some, you know."

And I kept saying, "I know that I don't want to hurt her," and I kept saying, "She's *got* to get a spanking."

I was just so upset with my daughter that I, no matter how hard I tried and no matter what I did, it just did not penetrate.

This just kept building up and I says I haven't spanked my daughter in a while and I says maybe she needs a spanking. So she repeated the incident and I just got so upset that I spanked—overspanked her.

I didn't do it because I was vindictive and wanted to hurt her. I did it 'cause it just came to the point that I didn't know what else to do.

A mother said:

I tried like closing him up in his room to punish him and not saying anything to him, you know. And I thought not speaking to him would hurt him more than anything else. Well, sometimes it does and other times he doesn't care. I tried to make him stand up in the corner and he gets in the corner and counts his fingers like it was no big thing about being on punishment. And I think that's what really would get to me sometimes, 'cause I couldn't get to him but he was getting to me, you know, so I said, well, I see punishing him is not going to do any good. I am really going to have to tear his behind up. Nothing bothers him. See, he's a tank. He's undestructible.

A father said:

I didn't think about any other action to take because I had taken different routes with him before this incident had happened, so I didn't think of any other way of trying to discipline him.

Another father said:

Well, I've tried other things like not letting her go anyplace and things like that, but it never does any good either. I need to do the beatings since nothing does any good. . . . Ground her, take away her privileges, maybe don't let her go to the show or something she wanted to go to. Nothing does any good.

The alternative efforts are detailed by a father who finally "punched out" his 12-year-old son. Two grades behind in school, the boy was described by his father as having a "controllability problem." The child had been stealing for some time from local stores—records, tools, flashlights, bicycle accessories.

> I tried to cope with this by talking to him, advising him, hollering at him, belittling him, telling him such as "Boy, you're going to end up a bum less you change your attitude, appearance and general outlook on life." I reprimanded him and I grounded him.

In trying to explain the abuse event to herself as well as to the interviewer as an unhappy alternative, one mother says:

> I did it for all the things I let go and tried to talk to her about, for all the times I tried to explain things to her and she never listened or never understood, for using and abusing me. I had a lot of deep remorse because I thought adults should handle it better. But I felt trapped and pushed against the wall.

Another mother said:

> Before, I wouldn't whup her. I'd just sit down and talk to her and try to get her to understand why and I try to understand her as much as I can. I try to get her to understand me. But *that* I tried to do and it never worked. That's why I led up to the whipping, you know.

The parent's more intimate knowledge of the child's habitual pattern of response dictates choice of initial disciplinary procedures and the age of the child dictates choice. It is difficult to reason with a 1-year-old child, and some children are more persistent, or more obstinate, or more independent than others. Bell and Harper note, "Learning to be a parent consists very largely of expanding and sequentially organizing one's responses within repertoires to make possible appropriate responses to a variety of child behaviors and to give primacy to those responses in the hierarchy that produce the desired results, or other feedback, with acceptable levels of effort" (1979:69).

Sometimes nonpunitive alternatives are not considered because of situational constraints, and the first response evoked by the child's behavior is a punitive one. The parent may have neither the time nor the energy available to engage in less punitive control procedures. The parent has a schedule which needs to be maintained, and a one-room apartment may not permit the effective use of "time out" procedures. For example:

A single parent caring for a 3-year-old boy generally made him sit in the bedroom in his "little chair" as a disciplinary procedure. "He doesn't like that but he does it automatically now. When he's crying, he knows he has to go in his bedroom and sit on that chair."

The mother worked in a CETA training program, and the child was in day care during her work time. Consequently, when he cried in the morning about not wanting to go to day care, there was no time to employ the usual procedure of making him sit it out. "Mornings are real hectic times—pushing for time."

So one morning I says to Ben, "You're going to have to stop crying every single morning," and then the next day I told him, "I'm going to spank you," and so I spanked him with a spoon. But the spoon had holes in it and that's what—and they made little marks on his butt.

And I think the reason I spanked him is because I had to go to work and he had to get to school and we couldn't spend the whole morning with this.

In another instance, a mother had a dental appointment and her ride was waiting for her. Her 4-year-old boy, whom she had to take with her because there was no one available to care for him,

just wouldn't get dressed—he just wouldn't go, he was screaming and kicking—he just kept screaming and kicking and he wouldn't go and I was really, really upset because, you know, it was getting to be the last minute, I couldn't cancel, I knew we were going to be late and they would be mad. And I just started hitting him and screaming.

The stress was aggravated by the fact that her estranged husband had taken time off to give her the ride to the dentist and the mother was nervous with him around generally, but particularly under these circumstances.

It was noted above that the initial intervention of 92 percent of the parents in response to the child's behavior which started the abuse interactional sequence was a nonabusive disciplinary procedure. What followed from this depended on the child's response to the parent's response. As indicated above, if the child's response to the parent's intervention was a change of behavior in conformity with the parent's expectation, abuse was not likely to have taken place and the family would never have been part of our study sample. The fact that the family was reported signifies that the first intervention was ineffectual and the situation required continued involvement in the situation on the part of the parent.

But now the fact that the child has not responded positively to the parent's initial intervention is, in and of itself, an additional consideration intensifying the parent's anger and escalating the violence of the subsequent parental response in the interaction.

The failure of initial efforts of the parents in response to a child's behavior which they seek to control, or change, itself contributes toward the direction of interaction which eventuates in abuse. Not only are the parents upset, annoyed, aggravated, irritated by the behavior itself, but now this feeling is intensified by the fact that the child has frustrated the hoped-for, anticipated, and desired response to the parents' initial interventive efforts. If the child's behavior, which precipitated the initiation of the interaction chain, suggested the parent's general overall inadequacy in teaching the child to act in a desired manner, the failure of the first interventive efforts is further confirmation of parental failure. The anger aroused earlier by the child's behavior is incrementally intensified by the anger in response to the feelings of frustration and failure evoked by the child's rejection of first disciplinary efforts.

If the parent picks up the child in an attempt to stop his crying and the child struggles to free himself from the arms of the parent, this action by the child is frustrating. Now the parent is responding not only to the crying, which is a source of irritation and discomfort, but, in addition, is reacting to the child's rejection of his efforts to comfort him, and to the frustration of the failure of his intervention.

Furthermore, if during the earlier interaction in the sequence the parent threatens or "promises" more punitive measures and the child continues to engage in aversive behaviors, the parent feels committed to implementing the threat and the promise. Failing to do this, it is feared, would lead to a loss of credibility in the parent on the part of the child, and to a parental confession of weakness and ineffectuality which might be exploited by the child. This then acts as an additional pressure moving the interaction in the direction of increasing parental punitiveness and abuse.

In addition to the children's failure to change their behavior in response to the parent's initial interactions, parents report that children engage in both passive and active behaviors which further intensify the anger of parents and escalate the interaction from the first nonpunitive response to mild corporal punishment, and finally to the abuse which led to the report of the family. It is behavior emitted during the interactional sequence which arouses incremental anger. What starts as an intentional disciplinary procedure within the acceptable definition of that term may escalate into abuse because of the child's response to the parent's intervention.

In passive response, children can be indifferent to what they have done or they can be indifferent to, or ignore, the parent's response. The child's response frustrates the parent and stimulates feelings of being rejected and disrespected. Indifference communicates to the parent that he is ineffectual and can be ignored. It reduces any parental hope that he can change the situation, since the child is unreachable and is, consequently, frustrating. As one parent said, "It is difficult to discipline a child who refuses to acknowledge that what you're doing is punishment. That she is being punished." Nonresponsiveness to parents' initial interventions is as frustrating and ego-threatening as is a negative response.

A mother responded to a perception of the child's defiance in her refusal to answer her. Her description of the abuse event follows:

I was having trouble with Annie [15] because she was running with a girl who I didn't entirely approve of—because this girl can just about do anything she wishes. All I can recall is that she got up for school that morning, and I asked her a question and she wouldn't answer me. I walked into the bathroom where she was combing her hair and I said, "Annie, answer me." And she wouldn't, like she didn't care. If I want to answer you, I will; if I don't want to, I won't. She didn't respond, that's what got me so angry. I grabbed her by the shoulders and I says, "Answer me." And she wouldn't, and that's when I swung on her and I hit her. I must have hit her in the nose with the rings I wear because her nose started bleeding. Sure, maybe I didn't have to slap her in the face for not answering me. I could have let it ride. But it was like, Annie was almost like—not pushing it onto me, but—more or less like just trying to get the best of my goat. I didn't want Annie to think that she could run me. In other words, "Mother, I am going to tell *you* what to do, you're not going to tell me."

Parents indicated that they are made to feel unimportant, inconsequential, rejected when children fail to listen, when children tune them out and ignore their requests or commands. While not labeling it as such, these reactions from children make the parent feel emotionally abused. "I thought she was hurting me by not listening."

In addition to the frustrations felt as a result of not getting done what needed to be done, or the frustrations resulting from the failure to change behaviors which were annoying, irritating or anxiety provoking, the parent faces the additional penalty of feeling denigrated as a consequence of being ignored.

In the following instance, the child's behavior that occasioned discipline does not in itself lead to abuse. It is the child's failure to respond to the mother's invitation to discuss this that escalated an initially nonpunitive disciplinary interaction toward abuse.

A mother was very much concerned about her 13-year-old daughter who had stayed out overnight away from home on a number of occasions. On the particular occasion which resulted in the abuse report, the child had stayed out overnight and the mother, who was employed, cruised through the area on her lunch hour in search of the child. Seeing her daughter in the company of a young man, the mother tried to pick her up but the girl refused and ran away. On the child's return home the mother talked to the child, asked "why she did it."

> She wouldn't give me no explanation. She wouldn't say anything. So I whipped her for it. . . . She refused to say why she had run away or why she hadn't went to school that day. She wouldn't give me no reason for it. . . . I kept asking her why and she just looked at me and she wouldn't give me no reason why. . . . I was disgusted with the whole idea, the way she was carrying on. I asked her to go to her room, that I was going to give her a whipping for it. And I whipped her with a belt.

Another mother said that her son (7) had been playing away from the area where he was supposed to have been playing. The mother could not find him and was very worried as to what might have happened. Finding the child, the mother admonished him for having wandered away. The child appeared indifferent to the mother's anxiety.

> He didn't seem to be concerned that I had been looking for him and that he was not supposed to have gone. So I spanked him. He didn't seem to be concerned that I spanked him so I spanked him *again*. He seemed to have a real flippant attitude toward the whole thing. We're having a real struggle as to who is in control between us.

In describing her intensification of corporal punishment, a mother said:

> Then I started spanking her and she wouldn't cry—stubborn, she's just like I am, she just wouldn't cry—like it was having no effect, like she was defying me. So I spanked her all the harder.

One abuse event was precipitated when the parents came home from a visit to a friend to find that their 15-year-old daughter had just accidentally broken a 10-gallon aquarium, the water flooding the floor and an expensive stereo set. The father said that, "What bugged me the most was that her attitude was real nonchalant, like it was no big thing, you know." Steaming mad, the father "took to her room and used the belt on her." The incident was the culmination of a series of anxiety-provoking happenings—money missing around the house and a strong suspicion that his daughter was stealing, conferences requested by the school because of the girl's truancy and failure in schoolwork. The abuse was precipitated not by the breakage behavior per se but, within the incident, by the child's indifference to the breakage.

In another interview, a single mother reported that she came home early in the evening and found the whole house was torn up—"I mean the drapes were hanging, it was a complete shambles, like somebody went through here and just tore everything up." Her 7-year-old daughter and three boys from the neighborhood, 8, 10, 14, had been having a party in the mother's absence. They were in the bedroom when the mother returned, playing a game called "do it up" which, as the girl described it to the mother, involved kissing. In response to the mother's questions, the girl said it also involved, "well, you know." The girl had been raped when she was 6, had contracted syphilis, and had been through a series of counseling sessions at a rape clinic.

The mother's reaction which resulted in abuse was only partially a response to the damage to the house and the sexual activity. The triggering element was the daughter's casual attitude toward what had happened:

> She didn't care if she talked about it, because she thought it was cute. And she's laughing when she's telling me, "Well, you know, Mom." I really lost my temper at her. Because it wasn't cute. To have a 7-year-old give sex here like she's a grown woman and you know, make a joke of it. And if she didn't know the difference between right and wong it would be one thing, but we've gone through it many times. The point where I lost my temper was when my daughter thought it was cute. I just told her to get her clothes off, for I was going to whip her ass and show her how funny it was.

Parents feel that proscribed behavior should be regarded seriously. Anger may result not only in response to the nature of the behavior manifested by the child but further by the fact that the child refuses to take such behavior seriously. Unless the offense is regarded with seriousness, the parents recognize that they are likely to be frustrated in motivating toward a change in the behavior. Consequently the disciplinary action is in response to anger at the child's indifference to the behavior and the intent is to communicate their own perception of the seriousness of the behavior.

More active responses within the interactional sequence, intensifying parental anger and spiraling the interaction toward abuse, involve verbal and physical aggression toward the parents and attempts to evade or thwart punitive interventions by the parents. The child fights with the parent, sasses, "bad mouths" or curses the parent or attempts to ward off blows or run away from the parent. In response to parental efforts to apply corporal punishment, 15 percent of the children "attempted to run away" and 9 percent of the children attempted to "fight back, kicking, punching, scratching."

A father of a 9-year-old boy, recalling the abuse incident, said:

> Well, he's been misbehaving quite a bit at home. A few days before this incident happened, he was throwing eggs at the kids, squirting a water hose in the house, stuff like that. And I punished him for it. I even took his bicycle away from him, 'cause to him that's his life, and I took that away, and it hurt him. So—came home one afternoon in

July, and before I knew what happened, I saw him chasing kids with a butcher knife. And I went after him and brought him in the house. I said, "Son, I went my limit with you." I said, "I'm going to have to spank you now." Took him to his room and I spanked him. I bent him over my lap, pulled his pants down and spanked him on his bare butt. And before I knew it he fought me off, and as he was fighting me, I hit him with the open hand in the face.

A mother said:

It all started when Camille [age 14] slammed the door on her little sister's leg. Camille was in the bathroom and realized there was no toilet tissue. She asked her little sister, the 9-year-old, to get some tissue, which she did do, and apparently her sister wasn't rushing out of the bathroom fast enough and Camille kind of pushed the door, and in the process, she caught her sister's leg in the door, and with the child screaming as she did from the pain, it got me very angered . . . it was so sudden and the scream itself aggravated me so much, it's that—I didn't have time to really think about it. I just acted impulsively, I believe, and I didn't think about it at all. It's like when I heard the noise, I just jumped you know, right out of the chair. . . . And I think at that moment I lost control completely, and I went over and I swatted Camille with me—you know, my hand, and Camille turned around and she swung back to strike me, which she did do and that got me even more aggravated. And before I knew what really was going on, I had pounded Camille several times. She had run a tub of bath water to take a bath, and suddenly I realized I had knocked Camille into the bathtub. And apparently I had struck her in the face, which by no means was intentional. But she had a swollen eye, and she didn't say anything to me that night.

A parent interviewed was concerned about the use of alcohol and drugs by his 13-year-old daughter, who was flunking out of school, and who was dating a 19-year-old boy, from whom she had received "speed." On the night of the incident, the girl came home drunk about midnight and her father

asked her who she was out with, and how much she had to drink, etc., etc. . . . anyway, to make a long story short, I told her I didn't want her to see this fellow anymore, I wanted her to stop the drinking, and she started swearing at me. I think one of the issues, a big issue with her, is the fact that we've chased a lot of her friends out of the house because she's gotten in so much trouble with them. I wanted her to clean up her act, kind of. And she started swearing at me and this time that provoked me so much that I hit her, and as I was leaving the room, she threw a stool at me, she—continued to swear at me and she had one of these little footstools so she threw that at me and it caught me in the elbow and that really made me mad and I threw it back at her and she put up her hand to ward off the stool and broke her hand.

Another mother detailed both verbal and physical aggression directed at her by her daughter:

It all started when Laura [16] came home way after the city curfew for teen-agers—but we have been having trouble for some time because of her fights in school and truanting and forging some of my checks and use of drugs, etc. When I admonished her for coming in late, she began to swear at me. She was in a general freaked-out condition. I told her to shut up but she just kept on swearing at me. And I swung at her and slapped her and then I said I was leaving and I think she knew I was thinking of calling the police because they had picked her up before when she was on drugs. She picked up a pair of scissors and said, "If you try to leave I am going to stab you." I can't remember how I or maybe her brother got the scissors away from her and I left and found a squad car and they took her to a detention home.

In another instance, a mother told her 14-year-old daughter to do something, exactly what the mother didn't remember. The daughter refused.

She was very hostile about it. If she would have said, "I don't feel like it," or something like that, I think I just would have overlooked it and said, "Well, when you get ready or whenever." But she was very nasty about it. It made me very angry. I just questioned her and asked her why she felt the way she did, why she was being so nasty and taking it out on me. But she kept getting more bitter, "I hate this house, I hate you, you're a bitch and you don't have to tell me what to do." Well, I just didn't like her attitude. It made me very hurt that she was saying things about me, and—but I couldn't key into why she was so down. But when she would call me bitch and things like that, I just forgot about the others, you know, I just became very angry.

A father described building an extension on the house in his spare time after work and on weekends. He was doing some electrical wiring and asked his 13-year-old son John to "go in the house and get me something" he needed to do the job.

And I am waiting and waiting and no John. And I'm wandering around looking for him, looking for him, looking for him. Come in the house and he ain't there.

The boy had gone over to his grandmother's house next door and was watching TV. When the father found him, he told him to go home.

So he's giving me lip service, you know, so I take a swap at him with the electrical cord I had coiled up in my hand, and I was mad at the time, I took a whop right at his butt and he got it. I started to give him hell for being over at Grandma's house and he started to give me more lip and more lip. I don't remember what he said, but finally he said something that was just way out and I grabbed onto him, trying to turn him around and crack him again. He's flailing with his arms and I took maybe two or three swats at him with that thing and he got it in the hand and in the lip.

Another father said:

She's not going to get her way like talking back, sassing. She does have a smart mouth. If I could just get her to understand that she's not going to talk back to me to get her own way. And I think that's what she was trying to do. And if she wouldn't have talked back to me, none of this would have happened.

Defiant ignoring of the parent's first nonpunitive disciplinary interventions evokes more punitive responses. A father describes an interaction sequence of this kind, which eventuated in abuse:

She came in. She says, "The dog got out." I asked her, "How did the dog get out?" She said, "Well, I opened the door and out he come." I says, "Did you close the gate doors?" You know, the gate's in the yard. She said no. And he got out of the yard. "Now you go to your room." She went to her room and I says, "You go to bed too, now. I don't want you up." About fifteen minutes after that, I got up to go to the bathroom and I heard noise in the bedroom. The door was closed. Opened up the door—my nephew and her were in the bedroom playing. Told him to get out, and I asked her what did I tell her to do. And she looked up at me and she wouldn't answer me. So I slapped her in the face. I said, "What did I tell you to do?" She still wouldn't answer me. She still wouldn't answer me, she just kept on looking at me. And—the more she looked at me, I think the more violent I got. I felt myself getting angrier because I wasn't being answered. And I took my strap off and I spanked her and put her to bed. And my wife called my parents then. They arrived and my Dad looked at the side of her face. He says, "You got to be nuts," and they put the kids in the car and took 'em over to his house.

The description illustrates the fact that abuse was not the first reaction but that another form of punishment was attempted—sending the girl to bed. It further illustrates the fact that the child's behavior in the interaction—her failure to respond to the father—was an additional source of frustration and an instigation to abuse.

Lying to the parent, when confronted with the parent's efforts to discuss an aversive act, is perceived by the parent as an act of defiance which in itself provokes harsher discipline.

A mother first sat and talked with her 10-year-old daughter brought home by the police for shoplifting.

And she kept lying to me. She made up all kinds of excuses and none of it was making any sense. I sat there for about an hour trying to talk to her and she just kept coming up with different stories, you know, instead of telling me the truth. So that's what made me mad, that she had sat there and told me a lie and that's when I spanked her.

A father said:

It wasn't anything I observed. It was something that my wife told me Bill [4] had done that she sent him to his room for before I got home. So I knew from her what the full story was. But I wanted to get it from him. And I went in when I came home and asked him what happened, and I was just not getting what Ann [wife] had told me. I was getting anything but. And this went on for maybe ten or fifteen minutes, you know, getting the same—if you'll excuse the expression—cock and bull story all the time. It was just too much for my patience—just the lying aspects of it, that more than anything else, getting me very steamed up. I just was getting—he wasn't telling me the truth, it's as simple as that.

I just continued asking him questions. By this time here, I had lost all control. I wanted—the big thing I had in mind right then and there was, I wanted the straight answer to the question I was asking. It had gotten to that point. I was that aggravated. Like I said, lost control.

Parents' initial intervention escalates to abuse if, when confronted with the behavior instigating discipline, the child lies in refusing to accept responsibility:

What made me mad is when he says it's all somebody else's fault, I didn't do anything. I stood there and watched him do it and it's *all* somebody else's fault. He never takes the blame for anything. No matter what you say to him, you can't get him to take the blame for anything.

In self defense children attempt to ward off or run from the first parental attempts at inflicting corporal punishment. This intensifies parental anger and frustration escalating the level of punitiveness of the parents' subsequent interventions.

A single parent caring for four young children had been home from the hospital two days after a Caesarean section. While she was resting after a heavy shopping trip, the stitches suddenly opened and she started to bleed. Getting up to attend to this, she noticed, and was upset by, her 6-year-old son, who was throwing Kleenex tissues onto the gas-stove burners, watching them catch fire.

As she was preparing to whip the child with an extension cord for playing with fire, the boy kept pleading for another chance. This angered the mother still further. She detailed for the interviewer her attempts at "other chances" for earlier disobedience on the part of the child. When she finally did attempt to whip him, the boy started running around the table, intensifying the mother's anger. She lashed out and, swinging wildly, caught the child in the face with the extension cord. The mother said, "His running around the table made me much angrier—it was like very, very bad anger."

A mother talks of what happened when she got ready to whip her 8-year-old son with a belt:

He started to run and I had to chase him. A lot of time when they're running, I'll be standing there hollering, "Get back now," and "you better stand right here" and they'll still be running. When I have to run after them, that makes me more upset. And that's with anybody. If you're whipping a child and you have to run after him, that itself is going to make you more upset.

The parent's intensification of discipline from corporal punishment to abuse in response to the child's reaction to corporal punishment is described by a mother:

He's really afraid of a licking. If he would think you're going to hit him, he's screaming then, you know. He always has been like that, and I told him to turn over, and he was looking at me instead of trying to turn over like I asked him to, and I said, "Well," I said, "I'll just give you a few licks if you'll turn over," and he looked the other way. "And just let me give you a few licks," I said, "because I got to punish you some kind of way," you know. But he wouldn't turn over, and then after he wouldn't turn over, when I pushed him down to turn him over and I hit him, and that's when the anger just really blew up and I just constantly hit him, then, instead of stopping.

As this suggests, frustration in attempting to implement discipline may further intensify the degree of anger felt. A father says:

I was watching TV with the kids playing upstairs. And all of a sudden I could smell something like—to me, I knew what it was, it was pickles. And I went upstairs, pickles were scattered all over the house. They said they were playing house. . . . And all of a sudden I said, "Who did this?" And they all said Libby [8 years old] did it. And they were all running all over the house to hide, like they generally do—underneath the beds, or in the closets, and I got to look all over for 'em. Well, anyway, Libby got underneath the bed, and the bed is very narrow and it's a steel bed. And I was sliding it around the floor to get her out to give her a licking for it. And I couldn't get her out. And I kept getting more mad, and more mad, my temper was getting up there. And my kids had found these weight-lifting blocks in the toy box downstairs here, and they had 'em upstairs. And they were using 'em for exercise. I seen 'em laying on the floor, and I picked it up, and I slid it underneath the bed. I don't know how fast it was, I don't know how slow it was or anything, all I know is that I hit her in the head, and when she come out from underneath that bed I was very upset, my temper had gone down, and I quick rushed her to the hospital.

A mother who had found that her 6-year-old daughter had been stealing money from her purse deliberately decided to delay a planned whipping as discipline until another day when she felt more in control of herself. Having waited a day, she told the child she was going to get a whipping. The child's response to the discipline intensified the mother's initial anger at the child because of the stealing. The mother said,

I waited a day because I was determined to prove to Selma that I was the parent and she was the child, and to find out that I can whip her and be calm. I wasn't really upset during the whipping, except that she made me madder and madder because she's one of those kids that she's not going to stand still for nothing, especially a whipping, so that overweight as I am, I had to chase this little kid that's super hyperactive. At first I told her she was going to get a whipping and to take her clothes off. And she wanted to discuss it. And I said there's going to be no discussion. You're going to get a whipping. So she finally sat and took off her clothes. After the first couple of licks, she started running through the house. I sat down and watched TV while she was zipping, and running and going under the bed and under the couch and stuff. So I would rest awhile until she decided to come out wherever she was hiding in. Then we would discuss it and it would start up again. When I finally got done—after about four hours of whipping and running and waiting and discussing—she understood that I was the parent.

There is some available research which confirms the likelihood of these responses to the child's response to parental disciplinary interventions. The research notes that if the child submits at the first blow and immediately stops doing whatever it was that had provoked the parent, there's a good chance his punishment will cease right away (Patterson, Littman, and Bricker 1967). On the other hand, the child might retaliate in one way or another, striking back at his punisher physically, verbally, or with some defiant gesture. Detailed observations of family interactions have shown that this retaliation frequently leads to much stronger counteraggression so that the hitting accelerates (Patterson and Cobb 1973). Parke, Sawin, and Kreling (1974) have demonstrated that adults tend to display an intensification of aggression when children defy their attempts to discipline them.

Going beyond their original intent in being carried away and acting impulsively is in itself a further frustration which accentuates hostility toward the child. If some component in initiating the disciplinary interaction was for the purpose of reestablishing control, the fact that the parent acted in a way that had not been anticipated and which may be regretted is antithetical to that purpose. Rather than establishing that they are in control, the parent's behavior is indicative to themselves and to the child that they have, in fact, lost control. Recognizing this, however dimly, leads to further aggression toward the child, but for whose presence and behavior, as the parent perceives it, none of this would have happened.

The child's response of indifference to the parent's interventions or to the parent's concerns and/or their more active oppositional response to the parent in verbal and physical aggression and defiance, challenge parental authority, power, and prerogatives. Such a challenge and a threat is very likely to provoke additional feelings of anger which accelerate the propulsion of the interaction ultimately in the direction of abuse.

Having asked a child repeatedly to do something and having been ignored, a father said, "I felt right there that my authority was gone, my words meant nothing anymore. I had said it in a firm enough voice so that he knew I meant it. That was the final rejection of my authority as a father. That's when my temper failed."

While the challenge to parental authority is sometimes explicitly perceived, the parent often recognizes that abuse, in and of itself, is implicit confirmation of the failure of parental power and authority. If the parent had been in adequate control of the situation, the need to abuse the child should never have arisen. Parental intervention at lower levels of punitiveness should have sufficed to change the child's behavior in the direction desired by the parent.

In some instances, what apparently started as run-of-the-mill corporal punishment ended up as child abuse because of inadvertent, accidental circumstances. Unanticipated happenings within the abuse interaction sequence converted what was intended to be corporal punishment of limited intensity to accidental, more serious injury to the child as a consequence of some action by the child as the event unfolded. Kotelchuck notes, "Many accidents have parental concomitants and many child abuse cases have strong accidental characteristics. Thus while the diagnosis of accidental abuse seems distinct, the underlying reality is much less clear" (quoted in Shapiro 1979:118). What started as the use of reasonable force accidentally had results identified with unreasonable violence.

A mother living alone with her 10-year-old daughter in a rundown lower-class neighborhood was enrolled in night school. She had admonished her daughter to stay home after nightfall but the daughter kept staying out beyond the agreed-upon time. The night of the incident, the girl had stayed out again and the mother was worried and upset in trying to locate her. While she was trying to discipline the child on her return home by whipping her with a belt, the daughter ran under the bed. In moving the bed to dislodge the girl, the girl was bruised in being pinned between the bed and the wall. The school reported the bruises as abuse. The mother's intention had been to discipline rather than to hurt. The fact that the child was more seriously injured than had been intended in the difficult-to-control context of the disciplinary interaction was more or less accidental.

Another incident which ended up in accidental injury was initiated as a result of a 13-year-old girl's failure to do some chores expected of her and then persistently lying about the fact that she hadn't done them. Just prior to the abuse incident itself, the girl had been suspended from school for smoking pot, truancy, and lateness. The father, after a discussion with the girl about the chores and assuring himself that they had not been done, was preparing to whip the girl with his belt. "Since I had already promised her two or more times, I was going to do it." The girl, running to get away and chased by her father, ran into a glass door in the hallway and was injured.

A child ducks and a slap intended for the buttocks catches the child in the eye; a child falls in running away from a parent intent on discipline; a hot-water bottle is overturned on the child in a struggle between parent and child.

The thin line between nonabusive discipline and accidental abuse as the interaction unfolds is illustrated in one of the pretest interviews conducted with a volunteer Parents Anonymous respondent. A single parent, mother of three children, said:

> I guess I just had a bad day from the older kids. I was feeling kind of bad and it seemed like Dick [9] had just constantly done things to irritate me, one after the other. And it got to be about 8:30 and I was reading a book that I was really interested in. And it seemed like every time I would sit down to read my book, then it would be something else I would have to get up and take care of. Dick and his sister [8] were supposed to be getting ready for bed, but he was hitting her and she was just screaming at the top of her lungs. And I felt very mad at what was going on. I was feeling like it's not fair that I should always have to be the one to break up their fights. It's not fair that I should have to be the one to do everything. And my kids are always talking about being fair and they aren't fair to me. For a long time I just kept going in and breaking up their fights and leaving it at that, but then finally I just got so mad I went in there. It was almost like I was in a rage and I couldn't really think straight. I didn't know what to do. I just wanted to hurt him, I think. I picked him up by his feet and swung him onto his bed and as I swung him his head just missed the metal

part of the bed. But it really scared him. He just turned white and it just really shook him up. And he said things like, "You could have killed me." And after I'd thought about it, it really shook me up, 'cause I could have. He would have hit the metal part.

Parents' Interpretation of the Child's Behavior

Whatever the objective reality of the child's behavior, the parent's response to the stimulus presented by the child is mediated by the parent's memories, feelings, and expectations derived from his prior actual experience with the child. It is also mediated and determined by his image of how children of that age should behave, his perception of what might be appropriately expected from such children, and his general knowledge of child development. Further, the parent's response to the stimulus presented by the child's behavior is mediated by the effort to understand the child's behavior, to explain it, to interpret it. Some potentially abusive interactions are aborted at this point if the parent makes an interpretation which excuses the child, exculpates the child.

Parents were requested to reconstruct their understanding of the child's behavior which initiated the abuse interaction. This may have been an ex post facto interpretation, but may also have been a factor in the parent's thinking in determining his choice response to the child's behavior.

Attempting to interpret the reasons for the child's behavior, parents infrequently felt that the child's behavior was motivated by a desire to arouse the parents or a manifestation of hostility toward the parents. In only 8 percent of the cases did the parents present this as the principal explanation for the child's behavior, saying, "He does it to annoy me"; "He knows it bothers me when he does that"; "I mean, it's wrong to feel that way, but she does things to get back at me to make me mad, you know"; "I think she [2-year-old child] is trying to get back at me—she makes a dirty face at me and she'll say something in baby talk like in a real snotty voice, like she's really trying to cuss you out or something."

More frequently, however, other factors were cited by parents as the principal reasons explaining the child's behavior. In 25 percent of the cases, the parent, in retrospect, felt that the child was upset about something and that the behavior was in response to the child's needs. In 21 percent of the cases behavior was attributed to "peer pressure." In 7 percent of the cases, the child's emotional or physical illness was cited as the cause, and in an additional 7 percent of the cases, the desire for "attention" was cited as the reason for the behavior. In many instances (32 percent) the parent felt unable to present an explanation for the child's behavior. Parents seek an explanation that makes sense ("If I knew, it would be half the battle"), but very often find the child's behavior incomprehensible.

Failure to understand why the child should engage in behavior which presented such obvious difficulties for parent and child was, in itself, a source of frustration for the parent, stimulating anger and consequent aggressive, abusive behaviors. As was noted in several statements in the previous section, parents did attempt to elicit from the child the "reasons" which would make his behavior explicable and understandable. The supposition is that the child "knew" why he was doing it. The failure of the child to "share" his reasons, to explain his behavior, was perceived by the parents as an act of defiance and a rejection of them. It was this deliberate withholding by the child of what he was thought to be able to share, rather than the initial aversive behavior itself, which intensified anger and prompted abuse.

Some parents explained the child's behavior in cost-benefit terms involving a contest of wills. The child wanted to do what the child wanted to because it was satisfying and pleasurable. They were ready to risk possible punitive parental reaction as against immediate gratification. They were ready to test the limits of how much they could get away with. Wanting to do something pleasurable which is against the parent's dictates, family rules, and/or community requirements, the child weighs the certainty of pleasure against the uncertainty of punishment. He knows he's not supposed to do it but there is the certainty of pleasure in doing it. The certainty of pleasurable benefit is weakly opposed by the uncertainty of costs. The parent may not learn about it; if he learns about it, the parent may not punish; if the parent learns about it and punishes, it may not be so hard to take. In seeking to discourage the behavior, the parent decides that the certainty of punishment that does hurt may be an effective cost deterrent. This calculation, communicating the certainty of punishment that hurts, mirrors the suggestions of reputable social scientists in dealing with crime.

As noted above, the largest percentages of explanations offered by parents for the child's behavior involves some appreciation of the child's needs. There appeared to be some not inconsiderable capacity for empathy on the part of these parents.

A mother who severely beat her 4-year-old daughter with a belt for destructive behavior said:

> Children do things but there's a reason why they do them. They don't do things just to be doing them. I think she did it because before that, me and my friend had got into an argument, then me and my friend's husband, they, me and my husband, and then I hollered at her and she went into the bathroom and I guess she said well, you know, everybody else is doing it, why not me? If I am going to get a whipping, I might as well get a whipping over something.

A father who beat his 6-year-old stepson for repeated disobedience in school said he realized the child had problems because of his recent move from one school district in the state, where he had been comfortable, to another strange, unfamiliar school. A mother who used a belt on her 10-year-old daughter who stayed out beyond agreed-upon time limits said her daughter said she did it because she was lonesome. "Okay, I'm not going to say she wasn't lonesome. You can't tell another person's feelings."

A 21-year-old mother who slapped her 2½-year-old daughter because she refused to go to sleep in the crib said the child had previously slept with her. She was trying to help to wean her to her own crib but she knew the child "didn't like the idea of being in the crib because it was new to her."

A mother who severely spanked her 7-year-old boy for disobedience says:

> I think he was just playing with his friend and he probably wasn't thinking about what he was doing. Possibly, it wasn't as clear-cut to him as it was to me that he wasn't supposed to go to this particular place without telling me where he was going, and so, when things aren't real clearcut to him, he sort of gives himself the benefit of the doubt, and goes ahead and does what he wants to do.

A mother who slapped her 2½-year-old daughter for negatavism said:

> She did it to get all my attention. This all started since the baby was born. She's very jealous. She had all my time before and now she doesn't.

Another mother who spanked her 6-year-old daughter for failure to pick up her clothes dropped around the house said:

I don't really think she was trying to irritate me. It was just that it was something interesting to her on TV and she didn't want to stop watching. Maybe it's her time for being alone, you know, when she's watching TV.

Parents recognize the pressure of peer-group patterns of behavior with which they might not agree. A mother discussing her problems with a 16-year-old daughter says the daughter behaves like that because she likes to be like the others. "They're free to go out and their parents never even say nothing."

Trying to explain her 13-year-old daughter's defiance of her mother's request which eventuated in abuse, the mother says:

I think she was just feeling a little independent because she was starting junior high and she just—she just had to spread her wings.

A mother felt that the child's sex play behavior, for which she was whipped, was the result of "the wrong environment, where you look out the window and 90 percent of the time somebody who walks by is a prostitute, pimp, or wino." She made a successful effort to move the family to another neighborhood after the incident which precipitated the abuse.

A mother, recognizing a child's disability in attempting to explain his behavior, said:

I think he does it because he's mentally slow. It's terrible for a mother to say, but—I don't know. I just think so. Just sometimes—like my boyfriend says, too, you can sit down and you can talk to him and he looks at you like he doesn't even understand what you're saying. And you're talking English. You're talking a language he knows. And like [my boyfriend] says, too, he just seems like he's a little bit slow. You know, not completely retarded, just slow.

A mother who whipped her 6-year-old son because he disrupted classes in school said:

I can just see how he felt, well, he never got a chance to do anything at home, so when he got away from home, things that he desired to do he did it, you know. Things that he should have been doing at home, like running me crazy, he was running the teacher crazy instead of me, 'cause I had him up so like he was a little soldier here, and that's just the honest to God truth, he was like a little soldier. When he came home from school, it was change your clothes, have a seat, don't make a move, don't be noisy, you know. And when he got out this is all he did, go to school, make noise, he wanted to be seen. He does all those bad things in school because he doesn't get his way at home, he can't get his way. He tries to get his way at school because he doesn't get it at home, you know.

While anxious to "understand" the child's behavior, parents indicate that "understanding," however adequate and satisfying the "explanations," is not sufficient in dealing with the situation. They indicate that understanding why the child is behaving in the way that upsets them carries them only so far. The child's behavior, aversive to the parent, perceived as having potential negative or harmful consequences for the child, behavior which disorganizes family life, etc., still needs to be dealt with, responded to, changed, even when understood. The parent needs to respond to such behavior, do something about it.

An understanding of why the child did what the child did was not decisive in determining the parent's response in these cases. Where understanding of behavior did lead to a mitigation of the parent's reaction, as it did in some interactions which might have eventuated in abuse, the incident was not reported.

It might be said, parenthetically, that one can see mirrored in the abusive parents' responses some of the protective service worker's reactions to child abuse. While we may seek to understand the nature of such behavior, the bottom line is that, whatever the reasons, such behavior cannot be tolerated and needs to be changed. The parent cites similar reactions to the child's behavior associated with the abuse event. However understandable the child's behavior, whatever the nature of the justifications presented, the behavior, it was felt, was not to be tolerated and needed to be changed.

Some of the parents' "understanding" as expressed in the interview might have been the result of discussions with the protective service worker subsequent to the incident. Furthermore, the degree of rationality implied in the verbalization of understandings in the interview may not have been operative in the emotional upheaval of the abuse event as it was actually acted out.

Parent's Intentions in the Abuse Event

Parents, in response to our probing, were capable of advancing reasons which explained their own behavior in the abuse incident—the intentions which prompted their actions. It was difficult to separate a statement of intent regarding the particular segment of the abuse event concerned with the actual infliction of physical abuse from the more extended event itself, of which physically abusive behavior was only one subunit. Parents saw the whole event as a unit and found it difficult to separate their thinking at one point in the process from their thinking at other points in the process.

Violence, including abuse, can be employed for the purpose of inducing a change in the child's behavior, in which case it has an instrumental objective. The intent is to induce the child to carry out some act or to refrain from acting in a certain way.

Where abuse is employed with pain or injury as an end in itself, without any further deliberate intent, or where the intent is to meet the emotional needs of the abuser for relief of tension or pleasure in inflicting pain or satisfaction in revenge against the abusee, the intent is categorized as expressive.

Parents initiated the disciplinary interaction most frequently with the intent of changing the child's behavior—reducing or eliminating the aversive stimulus. This was true in 32 percent of the cases. Somewhat similarly, in 30 percent of the cases, their intent was to "teach the child a lesson" so that ultimately behavior would be changed. In 14 percent of the cases, the intent was to reassert parental control which they perceived as having been threatened or eroded. These are all in the nature of instrumental intentions. Expressive intentions were less frequently expressed. In 6 percent of the cases, parents said their intention was to "hurt the child" and in 5 percent of the cases the intent was to relieve "anxiety" and "frustration." Some 12 percent of the parents could not define an intent, indicating that the act was primarily impulsive behavior. As one mother said in response to the question of what she had intended to accomplish through her behavior, "I really didn't think about it. It was an impulse reaction for me to do it." A father said, "I didn't have any intention of doing what I did. It all just happened."

Such parents talk of the interaction as feeding on itself once it got started. As a consequence, beyond a certain point, the interaction develops an autonomy of its own like an activated machine out of control.

Parents describe this tumescent tension-building that leads to impulsive, abusive action.

> . . . It all developed, I won't say fast, but it was to the point where I didn't have time to think or to back off or any—because I had committed myself. And I was just—kind of running away with—And I didn't

actually realize where it was going to, because I think if I had more or less in the beginning, it would have been enough time then that I could have put the brakes on me. Backed off a bit, but just—it just built and that was it.

The parent does not define his action as abuse at the time he is engaged in it. For almost all of the parents, their actions are defined by them as disciplinary procedures required in response to the child's behavior which is the focus of conflict. This is evident in the parents' explication of their intentions in initiating the interaction which eventuated in abuse—in defining what they hoped to accomplish by their actions.

As noted, most frequently the parent initiates action in an effort to change behavior and/or teach a lesson.

A mother who used a belt in disciplining her 16-year-old son who was failing in school said:

I hoped that by disciplining him this way it would shake something up in him to say, well, hey, I got to do better or do something—to make him angry or to make him think. That's why I did it. . . . I don't feel that in any way I have did what do you call it, brutality. No way. If I used what they say is brutality with my children, it was because I was overly protective or trying so hard that they didn't slip into the same thing that happened with their father [an adult offender who had spent considerable time in jail]. . . . I've told him if I do discipline you, it's because I love you. If I didn't care, I could have given it up just like your Dad. But instead I buckle down harder.

A girl 7, involved in heavy sex play with three boys, infuriated the mother because her daughter thought the whole thing was "cute." When the mother told the girl she was going to whip her to show her that it was serious,

she thought it was a joke. See, I've never—seldom hit my kids, and she thought, you know, I wasn't going to do it. Then when she saw the belt she got a little worried. She started crying and I *did* whip her. And it *did* hurt her. I meant for it to hurt. . . . I wanted to make her change her mind and to realize that what she did was not cute and not a game. It wasn't so much to make her hurt, it was to stop her from doing what she was doing, to let her know it wasn't funny. And when you've tried everything else, you know, what else are you going to do?

Parents said:

By my spanking, she knows that she shouldn't be doing what she's doing.

I did it for them not to do it again. I think that was the thing. Maybe if I discipline this one time, they won't do it again.

In explaining abuse of a daughter [age 14] who slammed a door on a younger sister, "I hoped to have her understand that she does not wilfully, purposely hurt another person."

I want him to learn to take orders and to listen. I want him to listen when people tell him to do things and I want him to do them especially at home. I don't want him to talk back and call a dirty name or curse out or totally ignore when people ask them. I want them to respect people and charity begins at home. If they respect me and people that come into the house, then they'll learn to respect other people. This is a thing I try to instill in them, and I don't like to do the whipping, but if it becomes necessary, that's what I'll do.

For one thing, hopefully, that he would start listening to us when we say something, we mean it, and that he wasn't going to keep getting away with it, you know. Like I say, this behavior went on for some time before I hit him. I figure he's old enough now where hitting should not really enter into it. Talking should be able to get through to them, but it doesn't.

I even found myself telling him that I was sorry, that I wasn't trying to hurt him, I just wanted him to be good, that's all, and obedient. I guess my whole thing was trying to make him obedient, whereas that, you know, if something was ever happening to me, just learn how to be good without me, you know. You know he need me standing over you in order to be good. If you gotta be good, you're gonna have to be good whether I'm there or not, you know.

As I told her, you have got to learn that you can't have everything you want. I am not going to do everything when you want to do it. You're going to have to be a little more patient. And that's what I hoped to teach her by doing it.

I just wanted him to stop peeing in his pants. I mean, I worked on it for so long that—I think it was starting to be a habit, and I just wanted him to stop this habit, you know, I wanted him to quit it. And I don't think sometimes he even had his ears open when I even talk to him. He doesn't seem to even want to hear it. You know, just by the way he'd look at me—like, "What'd you say?" you know. So I knew there had to be a different way, I had to get to him besides just talking to him, because lots of times he doesn't even seem to hear me.

I hoped that by doing it he would learn to listen and pay attention and want to mind and pick up his toys and stop running through the house and behave himself better. I didn't want to have to paddle him again. I wanted him to be happy and to learn to mind and behave himself and do what he was told to do when he's asked to do something.

A 36-year-old mother, who worked as a teenage counselor, used a belt in whipping her 16-year-old son. The mother had become progressively more concerned with the child's failing work in school and a growing irresponsibility in his behavior. The immediate precipitant was the son's loan of the house key to his girlfriend. The family rented in a duplex with an older couple who were very concerned about people breaking into the house and were very strict about the use of the keys. The mother said she had tried talking about his schoolwork and irresponsible behavior.

So I talked to him. I started talking to him like an adult, a grown person, letting him see and letting him know what his future's going to be like if he doesn't study.

The situation just kept getting worse and the mother made a deliberate decision to use corporal punishment. She said:

If you feel the irresponsibleness and how much it bothers me from the things you have been taught—if this whipping will remind you of that, I am going to give it to you.

A mother made clear her intent in slapping her 16-year-old daughter. The girl had been suspended from school for truancy and misbehavior and was taking drugs. The mother said:

Well, I hated her incredibly much because she has ruined the last nine months of my life. Certainly she made it incredibly difficult to work and just function as a human being, and I really hated myself for letting her do this to me, and I was determined that she really wasn't going to continue to behave the way she had been behaving.

A father who had used a belt in disciplining his 15-year-old daughter for damaging an expensive stereo set that she was not supposed to touch said that his intent was to remind her that you got to respect somebody else's property whether it's your family or your sister. She definitely wants everybody to leave her things alone and respect her property. But in turn, she doesn't follow that same principle with everybody else's property. I don't know, the only thing was the discipline at the time. To me it's something that she wouldn't forget. Hopefully, won't do it again. There's no guarantee that she won't.

The interaction is sometimes initiated in response to parents' intent to implement their definition of their role responsibilities. In confronting a 13-year-old girl with her behavior—a confrontation which ended in abuse—the abusive father said:

Well, I felt like it was my responsibility to—well, protect isn't the word, but to—number one, state my position you know, I mean, to kind of reaffirm my position as to what the rules were. You know, the rules are that she can't go out and drink, I don't want her riding around in cars with older men—at the time she was only 13 years old. She wanted to ride around in cars, and I just wanted to kind of lay down the law, so to speak. And I guess, probably, in a sense, to punish her for her bad behavior.

Intent to change behavior through corporal punishment is concerned with the consequence for the future if present patterns of behavior persist. It is felt that if disobedience is not dealt with when children are malleable and still subject to the control of the parents, there is less possibility that the necessary lessons will be taught effectively in the future.

Talking of her 8-year-old son's failure to listen to her and mind her, a mother says:

'Cause he'd get that mind and then would keep that mind. And then when he gets 11 or 12 years old, I won't be able to do anything with him.

Another mother said:

She got it mostly because she wasn't obeying me and I feel it's really important that she learn to obey now or she's never going to obey anybody.

A mother who whipped her 11-year-old son for engaging in a homosexual sex act with a younger boy says she whipped him because "I didn't want him to grow into it."

Another mother said, "I didn't want to spank him but I didn't want him to grow up to be a brat either, you know."

Corporal punishment is nonverbal confirmation of the seriousness of the situation and the seriousness of parents' concern. It underlines and emphasizes the verbal communication. It may not be facetious to suggest that the parents hoped to make a stronger impression on the child through the use of corporal punishment. Parents talk of slapping, spanking, beating, and whipping as nonverbal communication designed to emphasize, underscore, and reinforce a verbal message. "Violence can serve as a means of communication and as a catalyst bringing about needed changes when all else fails" (Straus and Steinmetz 1974:323).

The intent in the use of corporal punishment is to focus the child's attention so that he listens and to emphasize the fact that parents are serious about their expectations.

One father who used a belt in disciplining his 13-year-old daughter said:

> What I was hoping to accomplish was getting her to understand things that when I tell her something, I really mean it. 'Cause I don't think she really believes that you really mean what you say. I don't think she does. And I was trying to get her to understand me that I did believe that, I *did* mean what I tell her to do. I meant it so that she should take it seriously. Otherwise, anything I say, it don't even register. She blanks herself off from what you're saying. It makes me feel bad to have to spank my kid. I don't feel good doing that. When I do whup 'em, I go to 'em and tell 'em that I am sorry, you know, the thing happened like that, but that's the only way I can get them to understand what I mean—you know, sometimes you just have to throw away your feelings and just whup them.

The mother of a 16-year-old girl who has been rebellious, running away for periods of time, involved in an affair with an older married man, suspected of drug abuse, says:

> She wants to do everything she *likes*, you know. I don't like the way she behaves, that's why she is with me all the time like this (gestures to indicate conflict). She no listen no more. She no listen no more. She don't care about my ideas, only her own. She says all the time that she don't want to change. I want her to listen, you know. I said listen, attend me. I am her mother. See, I don't have no choice. She don't care. She don't care for nothing, just herself, all the time. We thought

the police could help—they came here (after she had run away and returned) and they talked to her. But she laughed at them, right in their face.

The father supports this, saying:

We want to show that we won't allow what she want to do in this house. Come anytime she feel like it, six o'clock in the morning. We just couldn't go to sleep waiting for her, you know, waiting for maybe a call from the police, maybe a call from somebody that something happened. It was really a bad time. She make everybody, you know, sad, nervous.

Some parents see what they regard as discipline, defined differently by the community as abuse, as a communication of their concern. One mother who beat her 13-year-old daughter with an extension cord, said:

Well, for one thing, I wanted her to know that I *did* care and I was worried. To let her know that I care. I do think that right now she doesn't realize, and maybe when she's older, she'll probably know, understand that I didn't do it because I was vindictive and wanted to hurt her. I did it 'cause I just came to the point where I didn't know what else to do.

For some parents the intent in initiating the interaction was to call the child's attention more explicitly to parents' reaction to the child's behavior, to communicate more forcefully the effects of the child's behavior on the parent.

A single-parent mother who disciplined her 9-year-old son for fighting with siblings said:

I think I just had it in my mind that—they take up all of my time. I'm with them all the time. If I go anyplace, they go anyplace. I just wanted him to realize that I'm a person too, that I have things I like to do—that they have free time and I don't impose on their free time, why are they always imposing on the little time I take for myself? I just wanted him to see that I'm—just as important as he is. That it's no fun for me having to break up fights, it's not fun for me having to play policeman all the time.

Another mother said:

I don't know that I thought it out that well, but I guess I wanted him to have more thought for the effects of what he does or doesn't do and more concern about how I feel and what I have to do as a result.

More expressively oriented intentions were articulated by a more limited number of parents who indicated that they had initiated the disciplinary incident with an intent to hurt the child or relieve frustration. The principal component here was satisfaction derived from some expression of strong feeling.

Parents said, in discussing this kind of intent:

> I was just hurt and angry and disgusted at her [daughter, 13] behavior and I—it's possible maybe I just wanted to hurt her like I felt she hurt me, even though this may not have been her intention, maybe it was revenge, my way of revenge, I don't know.

> I know it'll happen again and I feel like—the only way *I* can get any satisfaction *is* to hit her. I feel some satisfaction from doing that, to release my anger on her, and I feel better.

> Probably at the time I was just thinking of, you know, hurting her. Maybe I thought she was hurting me by not listening.

> It's like I said to him, I am so tired of you and your negative behavior. I know this whipping is not going to do you any good. But if it doesn't do you any good, it's going to do me some good.

A mother who slapped her daughter for throwing and breaking a statuette during an argument said:

> It was just—she hurt me. It was something I had cared about, and she hurt me, and all I could see is, I wanted to hurt back. And—I couldn't think. It was like—I really couldn't even see. It was just like kind of— maybe it's what they call a blind rage, I don't know, it was just kind of—everything was just—out of focus—I felt anger. Very very deep anger. And a little bit of hurt, that she would do it. Afterwards I felt very frustrated.

And once a beating starts, the expressed satisfaction in the release of anger is a stimulus to the continuation of abuse. A mother said:

> And I grabbed her and I looked at her. She wouldn't even look at me. You know, she did look at me. She looked at me like I was poison. And I whupped Julia and I whupped her and I whupped her and it looked like the more I whupped her, the more I wanted to whup her. I couldn't whup her enough.

A mother of a 14-year-old girl expressed her intent as a response to frustration:

I did it for all the things I let go and tried to talk to her about, for all the time I tried to explain things to her and she never listened or never understood, for probably using and abusing me.

Expressive and instrumental intentions—changing behavior, teaching a lesson, and satisfaction of parents' own feelings—are sometimes mentioned together. This is noted in what a father said about his intentions in beating his teenage son:

My anxiety and my anger was to teach him a lesson. And now it was venting out all that had transpired inside of me and the hurt that I was seeing my son go down the drain. This had turned around inside of me, that now I—it was my last resort, you might say. And the anger grabbed me and I took him—I held him down and I hit him in the face with my fist.

Child behavior which suggests doubt about who is in charge, where power and authority lie, generates a response with the intention of clearly establishing or reestablishing parental authority. Control in their own home, a sense of authority in their own home, may have greater than average salience for the high percentage of abusive parents who are low-income. Not having control over much of their lives, expecting to have control over the limited but significant segment of their lives concerned with parent-child relationships, they feel more than ordinarily frustrated and depressed when they sense a loss of control even here.

The intent of one parent in initiating discipline which eventuated in abuse was clear when she said, "I was determined to prove to Harriette that I was the parent and she was the child."

The intent in disciplining is to win the struggle for control, but a control which parents feel they have not only the right but also the responsibility for asserting and maintaining.

In response to one child's overt resistance to a parental request, a father said, "I thought, my God, I've got no authority at all when he tried to get by me and refused my order to take a bath which to me was a very legitimate order and that's what I hoped to accomplish, to just show him that he just could not disregard everything I say and start running his own life at 12 years old."

Parents recognize the conflict in the struggle between themselves and particularly the older child for control, autonomy, independence, and the dangers premature autonomy might pose. A father who disciplined his 15-year-old daughter with a belt said:

I just wanted to show her, I suppose, you know, her attitude is not going to defeat me. As far as her independence that she wants and feels she should have, I jokingly say she's 15 and thinks she's going on 25. But the maturity is not there.

Using corporal punishment with the intent of communicating a message regarding the locus of control in the relationship was expressed by a mother who spanked her 7-year-old son after he had wandered off and she had been anxiously looking for him for a long period of time. She said:

Ideally, I should talk to him—in this case, telling him how worried and inconvenienced I had been about not being able to find him—and maybe grounding him for a couple of days. But I am beginning to think that kids have to know you're in control and that if you have to, some physical way of doing that, preferably not spanking, but maybe physically—I don't know, it seems like kids have to know you're in control, so I am really ambivalent.

More idiosyncratically and atypically, the intent of the parent in abusing the child may be to justify taking a step, such as placing the child, that might otherwise be unacceptable to them. Here too, however, there is some behavior on the part of the child which triggers the abuse incident:

I woke up from a nap in time to find that my son [Larry, 4] had taken and lit a cigarette and I abused him pretty badly. His face was all black and blue when I got done with him. Immediately I could see what I had done and thought God, what did I do to this kid, he didn't deserve that kind of punishment. He hadn't done anything that serious to just brutally beat him the way I did. See, there were a lot of things in my life that I didn't like at the time—nothing to actually do with Larry— and I didn't like it so I was bad to the kids. I didn't feel too good about myself either. I was under a great deal of pressure at the time. I was down on myself and down on things that were happening in my life. I took it out on Larry. And the next day after this happened, I took him to a social worker to have him placed in a foster home and he stayed there for about a year.

Whatever the intent in the parent's response to the child's behavior, once the abuse action itself was initiated (the point at which the parent started to slap the child, beat the child with a belt or extension cord, etc.), the parent's reaction was most frequently that of feeling "overwhelmed—out of control" (44 percent). In 39 percent of the cases, the dominant alternative feeling expressed during this subunit of the abuse event was one of "hate, anger." There was a scatter of other feelings identified as "feeling righteously indignant" (6 percent) or feeling "anxious" (2 percent).

A mother who whipped her 13-year-old daughter with an extension cord " 'Cause I got tired of her lying to me and stealing and running away," said, "I guess I really didn't realize that I was spanking her. I think maybe I did realize—I don't know, but I was just so upset I overspanked her that time."

The parents sometimes make explicit an awareness that their reaction to the child's behavior appears unusual, unreal to them. There is a tendency to dissociate themselves from the abusive behavior. This is not merely a convenient excuse. The feeling communicated in the interview by the parent is that he actually did feel his "true" self was not involved: "During the time that I was beating on her I guess I was just falling apart. I didn't—I didn't feel like I was myself."

Another parent expressed this sense of dissociation when she said, "A lot of things I do through my anger, you know. If it was ordinary me, it wouldn't happen, you know."

Termination

Termination of the abuse event is in response to a variety of considerations. There is some break in the continuity of the incident, some interruption, some change. The abuser may become aware of the extent of injury being inflicted by the child's pained response. The abuser may stop as a result of seeing blood drawn. The abuser may feel pain or exhaustion. It might terminate as the abuser feels growing anxiety, sense of shame, or lowered self-esteem as he becomes more explicitly aware of what is being done.

Sometimes it is terminated by the intervention of others—the other parent, older siblings, friends—who might be witness to what is going on. There is a danger when abuse takes place in the absence of others who might be prompted to intervene and stop it, and there is danger in abuse which is potentially damaging but where evidence of damage is not immediately observable. Very young infants, who cannot communicate the extent of hurt they are feeling, are, by virtue of this, vulnerable to abuse which might be excessive.

Sometimes the child takes the initiative in terminating the abuse by successfully fighting back, warding it off, or running away from the abuser. Once again the younger child is in greater danger because of the inability to take such initiatives.

In only a limited number of the abuse incidents studied here was anyone else present and in a position to intervene between abuser and abused child. In 27 percent of the cases, a spouse was present; in a more limited number of cases siblings old enough to possibly intervene were present; and in 12 percent of the cases a boy- or girlfriend of the abuser was present. Where others were present with some potentiality for intervention, they were most frequently, however, passive witnesses to what was going on. In 10 instances, they attempted to stop the abuse by verbal interventions; or in 8 instances, by physical intervention. In the few instances in which physical intervention to stop the abuse was attempted, the attempt was generally made by the spouse of the abuser who was also parent of the child. In 3 instances, others present verbally encouraged or supported the abuse.

The following citations illustrate different ways in which the abuse event terminated. Respondents said:

> I stopped when I saw that she was bleeding, just to look at her, what I saw coming out her mouth, it made me kind of catch hold of myself.

> What stopped me was my oldest little girl. She was crying and she said, "Please, Mama, Jimmy's bleeding all over, please, Mama, please leave Jimmy alone."

> I spanked her hard enough that I broke a blood vessel in my finger. And that stopped me, that amount of pain to myself stopped me and I realized, hey, you know, look what I'm doing.

> I finally—I think what really made me stop was, I did see—I think it was blood on his behind where the buckle of the belt—you know, I hit him with the buckle of the belt on the behind, and that—I guess the little point that sticks inside the hole must have punctured his skin. That's really what made me stop, when I seen his blood, I got scared. So I stopped.

Experiments in aggression have found that a recognition by the aggressor of the victim's pain and injury tends to exert an inhibitory effect.

A father who slapped his 13-year-old daughter in the face said the incident ended when she ran out of the house. She had her shoes off already, I guess, and she ran out of the house without a coat, without her shoes on, barefooted or stocking feet, and a bloody nose—which I didn't know at the time, but she ran out the front door and ran up to MacDonald's and called the police department.

If the child's reaction is one which suggests that he is contrite or apologetic, this tends to inhibit the parent from continuing abusive action and abuse terminates.

A single parent notes the response which stopped her from slapping and screaming at her 8-year-old daughter.

And then she started feeling really bad, I mean, she was feeling bad when, you know, she was—she started crying and hanging her head. And I thought, "Oh, poor thing, it's not her fault." And so I just sat down on the couch for a little while.

Parent's behavior was varied, immediately following the termination of physical abuse. In 20 percent of the cases, the parent walked away from the event at termination thinking their behavior was "justified." In some 27 percent of the cases, parents attempted to apologize to the child for their behavior, tried to explain their behavior to the child, or to make a gesture of reconciliation or restitution. In 16 percent of the cases, the parent cried at termination; and in 8 percent of the cases, isolated themselves. In an additional 8 percent of the cases, parents' initial behavior following termination involved treatment of the injury inflicted.

If damage to the child was evident, if there was a cut, bleeding, a scratch after termination, parents made some efforts to deal with the damage. And this sometimes has positive effects for the parent-child relationship.

I tried to help her with the mark on her face [as a result of the use of a belt]. I tended to her cut and she seemed to like it. I was paying whole lot of attention to her and she was really happy.

The dominant thought of most parents (42 percent) following abuse was one of regret. "I should not have done it." An additional 10 percent of the parents were puzzled as to "how they could do a thing like that." Eighteen percent thought to themselves that it "was all the kid's fault—he deserved it."

The initial thought of a more limited number of parents (3 percent) was that they were behaving just like their own abusive parents, and an additional 3 percent of the parents thought their behavior inexplicable.

The dominant parental feeling at termination was one of guilt (34 percent) or depression (23 percent). Other negative feelings included feeling "anxious" or "scared" as a result of what was done (9 percent) or feeling "inadequate" or "inferior" (5 percent). Positive or neutral feelings were less frequently felt at termination—6 percent of the parents feeling "satisfied," 3 percent feeling "indifferent", 2 percent feeling "relieved."

The percentage recapitulations above regarding parents' behavior, thinking, and feelings following termination fall short of 100. Frequently parents couldn't provide the requested information; sometimes answers were so idiosyncratically unique that they were categorized as a singular "other."

Parental reaction to the event is often different immediately following the event, at a time when parents are still emotionally involved, and after a short period of time when tension has subsided and reflection is possible. Feelings of guilt, anxiety, depression are gradually activated. These feelings are intensified as the physical results of beatings, whippings, slappings, punching develop. Discoloration, welts, black and blue marks take time to surface.

The largest percentage of respondents, in reporting their thinking, feeling, and behavior following the abuse incident, indicated a negative reaction to what they had done.

Parents said:

I wished somebody had been around and kicked me on my butt. I felt about two feet tall.

I just sat down and started crying.

I am not proud of what I did. I felt very bad. I was sick, I was crying. I really felt bad.

I felt like—I just felt like nobody. I felt—I felt I don't think nobody in the world could feel as bad as I did. I just—oh!

I kind of have mixed feelings about what happened. I certainly didn't feel good about it. I am sorry that it all happened. I sure didn't like my reaction at the time. It's—I don't know, it bothered me.

Well, I regretted what I did, you know. I regretted it, but I didn't feel really bad about it until the next day. You know, until—you think about things. I was just still angry with him, that he was doing the things he was doing, you know.

I regretted what I had done. I felt kind of remorseful. I felt kind of sorry for him. But I felt I had to do it, and I didn't want to let it go for the simple reason that if I let it go, he would've done it again.

Then afterwards I couldn't believe myself for doing it, you know, I just felt like, you big—because she's so young, so innocent, you know. It just made me feel like a complete, total asshole. I looked like a great big old bully, you know, picking on a little kid. Probably, maybe I was.

I was not pleased with what happened. I was not denying it, but it was a thing that just momentarily happened and I really hoped that it hadn't happened. I kinda wished that, you know, I hadn't done it.

I broke down and cried. I told my wife I really didn't want to spank him, 'cause I feel like I am hurting myself as well as him, but I didn't know what else to do. I didn't really know what to think.

I felt frustrated, I guess. Why does she have to lie to me like this? She makes me do it. I am just such a failure. I am doing something wrong, I am not bringing them up right. I just *hate* it when I get this way.

I know I was angry with myself for getting that way, for flying off the handle. I just felt that there must have been some other way I could have handled it. But how? I just didn't know. Just completely, totally helpless. And I felt bad for her and I tried to control myself by saying, "Well, she deserved it."

I had a lot of deep remorse about it 'cause I thought adults should handle it better. But I felt trapped and pushed against the wall. It probably let the hostility out of me.

And then after I took the broom [with which she hit daughter, 14] away, I was really shocked because I didn't think I'd do anything like that. I was crying really bad. The shock was that I would really beat her with something. I've slapped 'em across the face or something when they get mouthy—or I slapped them on the butt or something like that, but this was the first time I actually beat them—and it shocked me. I felt really bad 'cause I don't want to hurt my children anyway. I don't want to beat 'em or, you know, do things like that. It's just something that happened. And I felt really bad and I was really sorry for what I did.

Later, when I looked at him, I'd just cry and I cried. I said, "did I really do that? I didn't even realize how much damage I had done to this poor child, and I thought, "Well, that's part of me, I actually birthed this child, you know," and I thought, "How could I hurt him like that?" Then I'll also pray very hard that it never happen again. I felt like a big bully, you know, and then I tried to make up by giving him different things and I think he sort of knew, you know—I told him that I was sorry and that I was wrong. Mom can be wrong sometimes too, nobody's perfect. But I did, I felt so bad, I couldn't even look at him. Every time I would look at him I would go into tears. It seems like this one whipping just really brought us much closer together, and it made me more watchful of my own behavior so that I don't do it again.

I was shaking, I was trembling, in a high state of emotional despair. Because I thought, my God, you know, has it come to this between boy and father. I really—I felt bad, I felt bad, but I just somehow I felt justified and I was, in the back of my head I thought, maybe this will do it, maybe what I have tried before has failed but maybe this will do it. Later I knew I overreacted on him and I felt bad about it. I felt that I was too harsh in my actions. I treated him like a man when he is just a boy. But I felt deep down I had justification. Maybe not justification, but I just felt that I was at where I didn't know what to do anymore. It's like a guy provoking you in a bar. You take it and you take it until the anger builds up and finally it's a fight and this is what happened here. It was that kind of situation.

I cried about it 'cause I didn't mean to hurt him. And I saw that I had. I cried about it. I tried to pamper him and wash him up. Really—it really didn't take the pain away. I mean after, once you've done something like that—you can't take that pain back. But it hurt, and I just sat there and cried about it. That's what I was feeling. I wasn't angry anymore, I was just hurt, more hurt. I did—kind of like cried because I was trying to figure out why wouldn't he just obey me? You know. And then when I saw the bruises, I just—that's all the feelings I thought about. And I was very upset. Not with him anymore, with my own self. Feeling that I could have controlled myself better. I could have handled the situation in some different way than what I did.

The act derogates the parent to himself because he is unflatteringly confronted with his own loss of control, his own reversion to more infantile behavior; and there is anxiety about the need to recognize the susceptibility to unacceptable behavior:

I felt sorry for him and I felt sorry for myself because I showed myself that my temper can get out of control and that's something I feel everybody should be able to control.

I was very angry. At the same time, I didn't want to do what I found myself doing. I was afraid of myself.

I felt terrible that I had beat the little guy like that and I still don't understand how I could have let myself get so angered. It terrified me.

In response to their negative feelings about their abusive behavior, in dealing with their upset feelings of anxiety and guilt, and in trying to resolve feelings of conflict between themselves and the child, parents attempt to talk to the child about what had happened.

A mother who beat her 13-year-old girl with an extension cord said:

I told her to wipe her face off, clean her room up, and lay down . . . so we sat there and I talked and I says, and she cried and I says, "Look, babe, you asked for it. You're doing all these things that's really hurting me and you" . . . I talked while she was crying and I was trying to make her understand. I just kept saying why. I know she wants my attention but she's going about it the wrong way.

Another mother said:

I sat down and I started to think, oh, no, how am I going to undo this? How can I—I couldn't understand what I had done. And I sat down and I started saying to Debbie, "Oh, God, Debbie, it's not your fault." And I think I told her I was feeling bad. And I said it's not your fault, it's my fault. But even, you know, I thought, well, you know, it wasn't all my fault, either, well, it ain't all my fault. I asked her if she'd forgive me and she said "yeah" and I told her to come over and sit beside me, and I gave her a hug and I just sort of tried to just tell her a little bit that, you know, I was sorry. But it still didn't—still didn't make up for what happened. And I kept thinking afterwards that, you know, I had given her another negative image of myself as a mother in telling her it was all my fault. See, lots of times I see her as being really critical of me and this just increases it. And she's free, she's clear, but look at *me*, you know, I'm just a rotten person.

The parent's behavior is shaped in part not only by what the child does before the abuse interaction actually begins, by what the child does during the interaction, but also by what the child does after the termination of the interaction. The incident continues beyond the termination of the abuse interaction.

If the child responds by a positive gesture to parental overtures at making restitution, to tentative parental efforts at reconciliation, the negative cycle of parent-child interaction may be ameliorated or reversed. If conversely, the child carries a "grudge," if the child does not assist but actively resists the parent's attempts at apology and reconciliation, the negative cycle is intensified, increasing the risk of subsequent abuse.

Sometimes the child's behavior after the abuse results in reconciliation. A mother who beat her 13-year-old daughter with a belt for persistent lying describes the interaction shortly after the beating:

I put my arms around her and I told her I was sorry, and—if she just wouldn't lie so much, we'd get along so much better. And I started crying, and she started crying, and that's the first time I've ever seen tears flow out of her eyes. I remember that so well. It's the only time I've ever seen her cry tears. I'll never forget that. Of course, I apologized. I told her, "If you just wouldn't lie all the time."

In other instances, the child's behavior in response to the parent's initiative intensifies hostilities between parent and child. A father who used a belt on a 13-year-old girl said at the end:

I just called her into the room where I was and sat down and asked her things. I told her I was sorry for whipping her, you know. But she didn't say nothing; she just stand up and pick her nails like this when you're talking to her. It's as though her mind were blank. She blank herself off from what you're saying, it seems.

A mother said:

I got very distressed about it because it really upset me that, you know, I would lose control like that, and it really bothered my husband too, he didn't think I would have been able to have lost control like that. The kids and I just kind of spent the rest of the day crying. I want to make it up to them—you know, I wanted to hold them but they didn't want me to, and that really upset me, because, you know, I wanted to make it better but they didn't want me to.

A mother who sought to discuss the abuse event with her abused daughter said:

I say to her, "Do you think you'd feel better if we wouldn't care where you went, let you go when and where you want, come back when you please. If we didn't love you, we wouldn't even be trying, you know." And she doesn't give me any feedback, I don't know.

The child may refuse the parent's effort at reconciliation. This response stimulates a feeling of frustration and a sense of rejection in the parent. The anger that is felt as a consequence evokes additional abusive behavior. The nature of the way one episode of abuse terminates may precipitate the initiation of another episode, as in the following instance.

I was involved in something personal, either trying to sew or rest—I don't remember—and I wanted him [6] to rest in bed and he wouldn't stay in bed, he kept coming out, and I would either send him back or take him back in but he kept getting out of his bed coming out, and I guess I needed some time alone and that he should give me some time alone. And he would be safe in his bed and that would be a place where I wouldn't have to check him or worry about him for awhile. And if he would sleep, that would give me some time alone, and so when he wouldn't stay there, it finally got to a point I vented it, taking him physically and throwing him on the floor and hitting him.

At first when I hit him and threw him on the floor, he laid in a little heap and he cried. Then I regretted what I had done. I felt kind of remorseful. So I picked him up in my arms to comfort him, but he didn't want to have anything to do with me, he wouldn't be comforted. He tried to push himself out of my arms. So I felt well, if you don't want me to love you, so I'll punish you again. And at that time I felt most frustrated. So actually what I did was to throw him on the floor again, and he kept on crying and I went out of the room. And I felt a little bit justified after the second time when I threw him, because I felt well, maybe he deserved part of it, of what I did to him, because he won't let me love him.

A small group of parents felt comfortable with what they had done and felt justified in their behavior. One mother said:

I felt foolish after the thing happened. I said, 'My gosh, what am I doing?' I felt I was ready for basket weaving in a rest home. I felt like they were trying to run me and it was way over bounds, the pendulum was too far to the left and I didn't like it. Well, I was tired and frustrated and I was blowing off steam. But they had it coming, they had every bit of it coming, and I don't feel bad for blowing off steam. They had it coming royally.

Another mother said:

She had it coming and I did not feel guilty. And I did not want to hear about her scars; that's her problem. If she had been still instead of running around and had apologized for stealing a dollar, she wouldn't have had all those scars. At the end I was thinking that I had a very stubborn child.

Outcomes of Abuse Events

The abuse event having been terminated, we were interested in the respondent's evaluation of the incident—what they thought was accomplished, what they perceived to be the outcomes of the experience.

Given the fact that the principal conscious intention of the parent in initiating the interaction which eventuated in abuse was to change behavior and/or teach a lesson, we were interested in learning to what extent these objectives were achieved.

In 47 percent of the cases the parents recognized that they did not accomplish the intent of the intervention which culminated in abuse, that the procedure was ineffective in achieving their purpose. However, in 44 percent of the cases the parent did feel that, as a result of the intervention, the child's behavior changed in the direction intended by the parent. Changes related to behaviors which were the focus of the abuse event and related, temporally, to the period immediately following the abuse event. A few parents said that they felt less frustrated as a result of what they did, and a few others indicated that what they did relieved tension in the relationship.

The principal arguments against corporal punishment are not only that it is morally wrong, but further that it is ineffective. This is designed to influence parents to abandon such procedures for other more ethically acceptable procedures, which would—at the same time—be more effective in achieving their own purposes. Many parents, however, apply their own pragmatic and empirical yardsticks to such communications. It should be recognized that some of the parents in the group felt that corporal punishment is an effective procedure because it has worked for them, reinforcing their tendency to employ such procedures in the future.

The immediate proximate objective is often achieved as a result of the abuse. Whatever the long-range consequences—which, because they are divorced in time from the event, are not perceived as consequences of the abuse—there is pragmatic satisfaction that the child's behavior is changed, however temporarily, in the direction desired by the parents. In responding to our question about what they thought they had accomplished parents said:

> I got these kids out of here; he settled down. I got the toys back in the house.

> It seems to me like every—the only time I use force, then there is a lull in her rebellious behavior for a while, for a period of time. Even though it is hatred or whatever, she feels she will cut down and she tries. But then it seems as soon as I give her more privileges again, then she's right back to rebelliousness.

A father who had punched his 12-year-old son in the face after a series of difficult experiences said:

> I don't regret what I did. The reason for that being that a day or two after the beating I sat down with Hank and I said Hank, what I did hurt you and it hurt me. And I explained to him why I did it. He had pushed me to my limit and any love I had shown him he had rejected, so whether it was the beating or my conscience, I'd started treating him real gentle. And now he listens to me more and does what I ask him to do.

A slightly larger percentage of parents (47 percent), however, felt that abuse was ineffectual in changing behavior as intended. In addition, the abuse event, in and of itself, created additional difficulties in the relationship with the abused child. Parents said:

> Nothing was accomplished. I hurt him and upset myself. I don't like to hit [child] but I feel terrible afterwards.

> It was just one of those spur-of-the-moment things. Something comes up sparks and you have that short circuit—and you have accomplished nothing. The only thing it accomplished was giving a red welt on the side of her face and me with a guilt complex.

> What it accomplished is that I hurt her and I probably hurt myself, too, because that's not the kind of person I want to be.

> I'll probably punish her some other way next time. What good is beating her going to do? It's only hurting both of us. It maybe makes her more defiant.

> I think I just made myself feel guilty and made him feel angry. I think people can accomplish something by spanking, but not if they feel as ambivalent about it as I do. I didn't want him to be anymore but it made him just that much more fearful of me.

The sense of failure, but also a sense of frustration, is expressed by the mother who said:

> What did I accomplish from the spanking? Nothing. Nothing. Leaving bruises. That's all I accomplished, I know how to leave bruises very good now. No, I didn't accomplish anything. It's not going to be anything compared to what, probably, talking to him would accomplish more. But I had talked to him before that, before I gave him his spanking. That just got me nowhere either. So—you know, like, I don't think it comes to anything either.

The outcome is often perceived by the parents as damaging to whatever positive relationship they have had with the child. A mother said that at the end of the incident:

> Probably Sue didn't really like me too well. I wouldn't. If I had to put myself in her place in her age, I'd be totally afraid of me. Probably even hate me. I mean a total hatred feeling for a while. Because what happened is I broke a certain relationship between us. I feel we do have between us and our children a good relationship. A certain part of your relationship just sort of took a deep blow. What I did would had to have hurt the children. It broke a part of the relationship.

The alienation between parent and child that often results from the abuse incident is poignantly described by a mother of a 13-year-old girl whom she beat with her hands as a consequence of the child's persistent stealing, school truancy, pot smoking.

> The next day I went to school and I was in the principal's office and they brought her in the office too, and her and I were just sitting there alone together and we sat there a long time without saying a single word. It was very strange.

Where the parent-child relationship had been problematic, the abuse incident further intensified the difficulty. A father who abused his 13-year-old daughter by beating and choking her and who had described his general relationship with her as having been very conflicted, said that as a consequence of the abuse incident his daughter

> doesn't have that good a relationship with me. She said, "I am not going to like you anyway. I don't care what you do to me." She thinks I am just an old meanie, that no other parents beat up their kids like I beat her up. She says, "Why are you like that? What's your problem? None of the other parents do that to their kids. You can't stop me from going out. I am going out twice as much now, you know, all my friends can stay out late. You haven't accomplished anything."

Noting adverse changes in the relationship as a consequence of abuse, other parents said:

> She was scared. I had really scared her bad. I can see she's scared of me. You know, when I raise my voice and come toward her, she'll start to cringe. And I don't like to see that in my kids.

> For the next couple of days, she just kind of sidestepped me. She didn't trust me, I guess. The whole weekend the kids were giving me sidelong glances and going to my husband instead of me.

She didn't want to have anything to do with me for a week. She probably hated me for what I did.

A father said that, after the incident, his daughter:

didn't say anything to me for a long time. She stayed out of my way. And even now when I try to talk to her she ducks, she automatically ducks. She flinches and she started that then.

The fact that abuse had negative consequences for the parent-child relationship is confirmed in response to another question we asked regarding the parent's perception of the child's feelings and behavior at the end of the abuse incident. Here the parent, once again, is speaking for the child, making inferences about the child's feelings and interpreting the observed behavior. There was a loss of data here because some of the parents felt that they were not able to discern what the child felt; others had not carefully observed, and could not describe, the child's behavior following the incident. Nevertheless, when parents shared this information, the parent's answers indicated that they most often perceived the child's feeling response to abuse as being negatively directed against the parent.

The child's reaction immediately following termination of the physical abuse was most frequently perceived by parents as being "bitter" or "resentful" (52 percent). In 12 percent of the cases, the child was perceived as feeling "frightened" or "anxious" and in 10 percent of the cases the child was perceived as feeling "rejected." In only some 10 percent of the cases was the child's feeling perceived as internally directed. In 5 percent of the cases, the parent perceived the child as feeling "guilty" and in 5 percent of the cases the child reflected a feeling of being "contrite" or "apologetic."

The most frequent behavioral response of the child following termination of physical abuse was to "withdraw from the parent," to "avoid the parent" (28 percent). Less frequently active counter steps were taken to "remonstrate with parent" or "curse or threaten parent" (13 percent).

Parents, when asked what they imagine the child was feeling and thinking at the end of the incident, perceive the child as responding negatively to them. Parents said:

She wanted me dead.

He probably didn't like me.

She carried on for an hour afterward, crying and saying that she doesn't like me and I hurt her.

She thinks I am bigger than she is and I am mean and I always hurt her.

Probably that she didn't like me too well. I wouldn't, if I had to put myself in her place, in her age, I'd probably be totally afraid of me.

She probably hated me.

Total defeat and probably being unwanted and unloved, that she was unjustly pushed around, probably. She has even mentioned not being loved.

She was feeling that maybe I don't love her because if I did, how could I treat her this way?

I don't think you can really push anybody, force anybody. Me, if somebody hit me, I'd get even more belligerent. "That's your best shot, what's your next one? It's going to have to be better." So I figured— that's how she must have felt.

He was probably thinking I was a terrible mother.

That I hated her; that there was no love here. That she didn't want to stay here.

I think his feelings were very hurt and he probably felt confused because of what I did, he probably felt I didn't like him and then when I tried to love him up because I felt badly—that would be confusing, he didn't think love goes along with punishment.

A father, talking about his 12-year-old daughter's reaction to corporal punishment, said: "I think she probably had a lot of hatred towards me, which is probably the reason why I think the thing came to light at the clinic. It was probably a way for her to get back." The girl, in going for a TB test the day after the abuse incident, had shown the nurse the marks of a beating.

A mother described her 7-year-old daughter's reaction after a whipping with a belt:

She was thinking probably how much she was hating me at the time. And she didn't say or do anything. For a long time she just sat there. She didn't say anything for a long time. It was just her and me sitting there.

As noted, much less frequently did the parent perceive the child's reaction to the incident as inner-directed. One mother said:

I think maybe she felt guilty, causing this reaction in her parent. You know, what have I done to make Mother that mad at me? What have I done that makes Mother hate me?

A father said: "I think he was sorry he did it. I think he was feeling ashamed of himself."

In three instances, some 4 percent of the cases, parents said that as a consequence of strong feelings generated by the incident, there was a positive effect of bringing parent and child closer together. The emotionally charged situation permitted the release of feelings which tended to erode barriers to communication between parents and child. Children were prompted to share more openly, and parents, perhaps in making restitution for their behavior, made efforts to be more empathic and understanding.

Another outcome cited was the fact that as a result of the incident, which is given sharper visibility and explicitness by the agency's intervention, parents often reflect more consciously than ever before on their disciplinary procedures.

An awareness of the ineffectuality of this kind of disciplinary procedure resulted in a change of attitude on the part of some parents toward corporal punishment. The abuse incident is for some parents a highly charged learning experience.

A father, who abused his 8-month-old son, discussing what, if anything, he might do differently in response to a situation similar to the one which eventuated in abuse, said:

I sure wouldn't have spanked him. Because I realize now that was the worst thing I could have done, was to spank him. This baby didn't know what was going on. And I thought he did. And I just proved myself wrong. When I found out that the spanking didn't do no good, it just made the situation worse, I couldn't cope with it. I thought I was right in my mind, by disciplining him but I found out that it was just total chaos 'cause he didn't understand what I was doing.

The incident accomplishes a reassessment by the parent conscious of the hurt he has inflicted, of his disciplinary procedures. A father said that, after the incident,

I went to talking with her and asked her why does she do these things, why don't she try to do things like I tell her to do, why is she so hard-headed, how come she stay in trouble at school and different stuff like that, you know. I said, "Well, just go upstairs to your room and stay there." And I stopped putting so much pressure on her. I just lighten up.

The abuse incident itself, particularly when its seriousness in the perception of the community is made explicit by protective-service intervention, generates reactions that make for changes. The parents see themselves acting in a way which they had not previously conceived as possible for them. They see themselves as capable of behavior which reduces their self-esteem and tarnishes their self-image. They make an effort or a resolve not to repeat the behavior which defines them as an abusing parent. As one parent said to the child, "I am never going to let you make me so angry that I am going to hit you. There's got to be a better way to do this."

Some of the effect of agency intervention on the outcome of abusive incidents is noted in the response parents give to the questions as to how they might handle the situation now if they were faced with a repetition of the child's behavior which initiated the abuse interaction. The mother of a girl of 10, bruised in running away from her mother attempting to whip her with a belt, said:

Through the incident, I did go through a lot which will make me stop and think, just by having to see so many different people. That upset me. I just made up my mind from then on that I would just think things out, slow down and if I am too angry, don't hit her, 'cause I mean, I might hurt her.

The incident and the consequent intervention of the agency has taught constraint and compliance. One parent said that next time

I think I'd just get up and walk out of the house and go out and go for a walk or something. Because I found that you can't punish your own child without being taken to court or something.

Just as an abuse incident is potentially a learning situation for the parent, it is likewise a potential learning situation for the child. This is illustrated in one mother's account of the child's behavior following abuse for which the mother apologized:

I think I got across to her that sometimes Mommy loses her temper and doesn't mean to hit her. Well, I know there's times now where she'll come to me, after, you know, I usually cuss a lot, and there's a lot of times where I get mad and tell her I'm going to have her put away or something like this, and—she'll come to me later when she sees where my anger is kind of toned off, and she'll say, "You didn't really mean what you said, did you? You were just mad at everybody, weren't you?" And I says, "Yeah, I'm just in a bad mood today." She said, "I kind of figured that, that's why I stay out of your way." And it's really been helping, you know, with her coming to me and saying that she understands how I felt, because she even, you know, when I get into some of those moods once in a while now, she even says—to her little sister, "Debbie, get out of Mom's way, she's in a bad mood," you know, so she's starting to really catch on to what's going on with me.

But, for some parents, realizing the ineffectuality of corporal punishment and the failure to accomplish the purpose for which it was intended does not necessarily result in the parent's rejection of the procedure. Even while there is a recognition that corporal punishment is not a particularly effective disciplinary procedure for achieving the parent's objectives, there is an awareness that there is difficulty in exercising self-control in the volatile parent-child interaction which risks abuse.

Discussing his use of corporal punishment, one father said:

It wasn't a good armament in the first place, because it never did the job anyhow, hitting 'em, you know. . . . Like I say, you blow your cork and hit 'em with what you got handy, now you shouldn't do that. But you take it and you take it and you take it because it don't pay to hit 'em anyhow. And then, you lose your temper. Now you take a look at the situation I got around here. Hey, this isn't no picnic, you know. And I got a lot of stress at work, and I got a lot of stress here, and these kids are hard to raise.

In a further effort to determine the possible learning outcomes for the respondent, we asked if, in retrospect, the respondent would have done things differently if they had the opportunity of reliving the incident: 15 percent of the respondents said they would have repeated their behavior without modification; 29 percent of the respondents replied that they would repeat their behavior but they would try to keep under better control; 25 percent indicated that they would have persisted in some alternative noncorporal method of discipline; some 12 percent would, in retrospect, feel more inclined now to ignore the situation; 11 percent would have appealed to a spouse, friend, or professional for help in dealing with the situation. It might be noted, for emphasis, that about 44 percent of the respondents would have opted to repeat what was done or repeat it with a greater measure of control—this despite the fact that all of these parents had been reported for confirmed abuse, and all had had some contact with a protective-service worker between the abuse event and the time of our interview. These parents say that they would continue to employ corporal punishment as a disciplinary procedure but perhaps be more careful, less impulsive, more restrained, more deliberate.

Some would use corporal punishment again but attempt greater control by allowing a cooling-off period for the anger before starting to discipline, and some would do it over again, but controlling by using a less lethal method.

A mother who whipped her 13-year-old daughter with an extension cord said:

> I would find the belt, period. I wouldn't use the extension cord, I would find the belt. I think the extension cord may be, you know, too hard on a child's rear end. A belt's not too hard. And I think I would have waited another 15 minutes sitting down because it would keep me calmed down and don't let my hostility, you know, whatever it is that got me so upset, come out on her. But she would still get the spanking.

Some would do the same thing, but would be more careful. A mother who whipped her 8-year-old son caught him on the neck with a belt as he was running away from her. The teacher, seeing the welt on the child's neck, reported it.

> I would whip him just like I did before; I would whip him. I would've whipped him but I would have just hoped that I wouldn't hit him, you know, on the neck. That would probably be the only difference. I would've whipped him and it probably been just as hard.

Similarly, another mother said:

> If I was going to whip her, I would make sure I had hold of her, have her in a certain position—you know how you put a baby over your lap or something. That I would make sure that I am not whipping anything but her butt—that way, I know there's no bruises. . . . It's not hurting her body really, it's just giving her the understanding that I mean what I say and giving her something to think about.

A mother who beat her 10-year-old daughter with a wide belt, resulting in lacerations to her back, said

I wouldn't beat her so severely. She would have got it. She definitely would have got a whipping. But not as bad as that.

Another mother said:

If I had to do it over again, I would do it over again. 'Cause I'll tell you something, I'll tell you why. A belt or an old-fashioned spanking wouldn't hurt no kid. And I told the same thing to my mother. And my mother said he deserved it. And also because it's happened quite a few—about three or four times already, before this, but I handled it by talking to him and telling him and asking him not to do it, and he promised me he wouldn't do it again. But he did it again, just recently. So I thought with the spanking, I could accomplish that he wouldn't go across a dangerous street by himself where he might get hurt or killed.

A father said:

I would use my hand next time instead of a wooden spoon, which I did use. Using your bare hand, you can tell better how much you are hurting them.

A father who had punched his 12-year-old son in the face said that if he had to do it over again, "A belt, a good ass-tanning, might have accomplished the same. I felt I was too harsh in my actions. I treated him like a man and he's just a boy."

One parent said, "Not only would I have done it again, I would have done it sooner."

And a mother, who had slapped her 7-year-old son in the face for having persistently refused to do what she had asked of him, said that the protective service worker came and gave her this "psychological mishmash" and I said, "You're crazy if you think I am not going to ever slap him, or any of 'em.' If I had to do it over, I wouldn't have done anything different."

Those parents who said, in retrospect, that they would now handle the same situation differently, opt for talking to the child, explaining more, giving the child more attention, trying to use noncorporal disciplinary procedures more persistently.

A mother said:

I would do it altogether different. I would listen more to his side of things and there really is no harm in things that he's done because that's the way he thinks. He's a child and I wanted him to think on my level. I really didn't get what I wanted just by beating him, you know. Just by letting him be a child, I found out he's much happier. It made me much happier too.

Another said:

I would have sat down with the county [social worker] and ask if there was any way that they could help a mother who was being abused by her children [laughs hysterically]. That's a good point. A new agency must be started. Parent protection.

Recapitulation via Illustrations

We have discussed the child behaviors which initiated the abuse event interaction, the course of the interaction during the event as determined by the parent's intent and the child's reaction during the event, the termination of the event, the parent's and child's reaction to what happened, the parent's evaluation of what was accomplished and the effect on the parents and child of the abuse experience.

Extracting statements from the interviewees for the purpose of confirming and illustrating the analysis does violence to the unitary nature of the incident as described by the parents. The following incidents, presented from initiation to termination, help to restore some sense of the living reality of the incident and the continuity of the interaction. For clarity of focus, it should be noted, once again, that the abuse event interaction per se starts in each case with a behavior stimulus emitted by the child and the child's behavior during the interaction is a significant determinant of the parent's behavior. Incremental to the child's immediate behavior as precipitant is a situational context which predisposes to an aggressive response conditioned negatively, in some instances, by the more general relationship to the child. The choice of a specific behavioral response evoked by anger, in these cases abuse, is determined by an attitude toward corporal punishment brought to the situation as a consequence of previous learning. The complexity of these interacting factors is illustrated in the following account of an abuse incident by the father of an 8-month-old boy, and by the detailed additional incidents which follow:

I got up real early that morning and I got off from work about 1:30 in the afternoon. I worked construction, which is pretty hard work in 105 degree weather and it didn't take anything to get mad out there. Especially out in the hot sun. But I guess I did come home and I was very aggressive, because my kid was screaming and my wife had to go to the store and I just couldn't take having him screaming and having my nerves shot all at the same time, so—I might have took it out on him. You know, spank him, and he just kept crying. He wouldn't stop till my wife came back and picked him up. And I couldn't handle it; I went crazy. 'Cause I was in a little argument with my partner too at the same time that worked with me.

When I came home my wife had to go to the store and I was left with the baby and he was screaming and wetting and everything else and I wanted to take a shower and get cleaned up. First off I tried picking him up, to try to shut him up. He didn't shut up. I don't know what was wrong with him. I couldn't figure out what was wrong with him. And that's when I gave a spanking at that time, when I just didn't realize what was wrong. And I figured that would shut him up. It didn't, that just made it worse. I tried everything, and he just got worse and worse on me. He didn't recognize me, I don't think, so—covered with dirt when I went in the house, I don't think he recognized me, really. I think he was scared of me. But it made me so mad I didn't understand why it didn't work for me to get the baby calmed down, no matter what I tried. That's another factor, in the first three months when he was born, he wouldn't come near me. The baby wanted to be by mother all the time, and I sort of didn't like that very much. 'Cause he wouldn't—I couldn't hold him or anything, he just cried.

Every time I hold him, he wanted Ma. And that's what the problem was at that time. No matter what I did, I couldn't keep him quiet. Had to have his mother. I couldn't take it, him not wanting me. First three months were the hardest. The baby would not accept me at all. I didn't understand why the baby wouldn't accept me and would accept his mother instead. It kind of hurt, you know. He wouldn't want to be left alone with me and I wouldn't want to be left alone with the baby either—like it happened this time.

Anyhow, when my wife got back, she started yelling at me, "You don't hit little kids like that. They're too young to be disciplined at that age," and I argued with her 'cause I thought you could discipline. I told her straight out I thought he needed it and she told me you can't do that 'cause he didn't know what he was doing and I thought he did know what he was doing. I raised kids from a year, a year-and-a-half to about nine years old—and I've always disciplined children, 'cause that's the way I was raised and I thought I was right in my mind by disciplining him.

A female single parent with three children 3, 4, and 6, had a nervous breakdown during which time her parents cared for the children. On release from the mental hospital, she received responsibility for the children although she was somewhat hesitant about caring for the subsequently abused child, a girl of six:

> There was this frustration between us and there was always like anger, I always stayed mad, you know, and I never reacted like this toward my sons. And when we did move here together, she got to the point where she was telling me I couldn't tell her what to do, she didn't want to stay with me and the pressure was just building up.

On the day of the incident which precipitated the abuse, the mother got up feeling ill and upset. The girl went out to play, and after a time, the mother went looking for her but couldn't find her. She finally found her in back of the house, lying on the ground crying, having been raped by an 11-year-old neighbor boy. The mother took the child to the hospital for an examination which confirmed intercourse but no further damage.

On returning home the mother was "wound-up," "tight," upset. She went in to talk to her daughter:

> Well, when I went into the room she was just standing there, and I said, "Well, Ruth, you know," and she didn't answer me. I said, "Ruth I'm talking to you." She still didn't say anything. And I said, "Well, when I told you to go outside, what was you doing in the back garage?" And she just looked at me, she wouldn't answer me, she never said nothing. So then I hit her when she didn't answer . . . I wanted to knock her down. I wanted to stomp her. So—then, like, she just, after I hit her, I said, "I'm gong to ask you one more time, and if I don't get an answer, then—I don't know, you know, what's going to happen, so—" she stood there and she still didn't say nothing. The next thing I know I just kept on hitting her. She wouldn't answer me, so I kept on and I kept on and finally, she just like turned away from me and the next thing I know I just grabbed her and pushed her head into the wall. The next thing I know she—like turned back to me her mouth, up here she was bleeding and everything, so—you know, I kind of hesitated a little while and—I guess I just—and I said, "What am I doing?" And she looked at me. She looked at me kind of like— like the way of her eyes were telling me, you know, get away from me. You know, she was scared. She was very frightened of me, she was afraid of me. And all she could do was just kind of—just stand there and look at me. But her eyes were kind of doing the talking, and she

was just looking me up and down, and I was just looking at her, I wanted to just reach out for her, she just seemed like—she was trembling, she'd jump. So I didn't, you know—pulled my hands away. I just put 'em down. I just stopped and said, "My God, what am I doing, you know, what's wrong with me, why am I doing this to her, you know." So then I just—I started crying, you know, she was bleeding, and everything, and I said, well, we'll have to take her to the hospital. So I took her to the hospital, and I told them that I did hit her, had pushed her head into the wall and I caused her mouth to bleed, but I hadn't harmed her, you know, to where I had swelled up her body, but she was swoll.

Another parent, in detailing the abuse event, demonstrates the complexity of factors contributing to the interactional sequence initiated by the child's behavior and culminating in abuse.

The father, 19, who abused his 8-months-old stepdaughter, works in a fast-food restaurant.

I went to work like at six o'clock and get off at two in the morning. That was a hell of a hectic day, to put it bluntly. It was a hard day at work. It was too busy all day along. I just came home and I was grouchy. I was tired, I wanted to go to bed, you know, and the baby wouldn't keep quiet, you know, so anybody could sleep. Like she was you know, just a problem that I could live without for a while. It seemed like that, she was becoming a problem. The way she kept crying all the time. All the time she wanted, you know, wanted to cry. And it just drove me nuts. Working such a long time at work, you know, a really busy day, coming home at two in the morning and, you know, getting stuck halfway on the way. That night, it dropped about six inches of snow, all night long and I think the snow was this deep, and I didn't have snow tires or nothing, I got stuck about five different times. Had a hard time getting home, and it took me till about a quarter after two to get home, and the place I work is only a hop, skip, and a jump away from here. Just up the road there. Boy, it was a hectic night. Man, I pushed the car twice to get out of the ditch. I just wanted to go to bed. I was tired. When I got home, it was late at night and she was fussing. I mean, she was *really* fussing. I held her, wife held her, I held her, wife held her. We just kept passing her back and forth, and she wouldn't keep quiet. We laid her on the floor, and she didn't like that, you know; put her in the crib and gave her a bottle. She didn't like that. Hold her and she didn't like that, then put her in a walker, and she didn't like that.

You know, I got really pissed off and I started hollering and screaming and yelling at her and telling her—shut her you—know—what

mouth, you know, and she just kept crying and crying, you know—
bam! Cracked her across the ass a couple of times. Shut up, kid! Put
her in bed right away and put a bottle in her mouth and covered her
up and said, to hell with you, if you want to scream, go ahead and
scream. I don't have to listen to that. I guess she went to sleep. She
was sick, too. No excuse for that. Then again, maybe there is. I feel—I
feel small because I hit her. Then I went to bed and boy, it felt good to
sleep. I didn't feel too good because I hit her, but it felt pretty good
that she was sleeping so I could get some sleep.

A 29-year-old mother with five children ranging from 5 to 12 years of
age, separated from her husband and living with a boyfriend, describes
the abuse of her 10-year-old daughter—the context, the instigation, the
abuse action, the termination, and the aftermath.

I had just come off two 8½ hour shifts, a night shift and a day shift—
worked straight through with a 45 minute break on one and a half-
hour break on the other, no break in between. I can remember those
shifts very well.
    It was part of my daily routine, per se, as a nurse's aide, but I had to
dress and we call it, at the nursing home we call it, lace up three ca-
davers. By myself, because those other girls out there are scared to
death. And like I've got to plug the nose, the rectum, the ears, to keep
any discharge for the autopsy. And I had three of those. One of them
happened to be one of my favorite patients. There were three, plus I
had 19 or 20 incontinent patients. And this was the time that they were
given the second round of swine flu shots. Everybody and their
grandma had diarrhea. I had—all of them are heavy, they cannot
move themselves, the majority of them had to be turned every two
hours. All of them had intake output, whereas you have to give them
so many cc's of fluid. They dispense so much in a catheter bag. I had
to change all the catheter bags. And by the time I got home, I was the
perfect bitch. I was bitchy, my old man passed me by going out the
door. He was there for a little while, and I started bitching at him
because the house wasn't this and the house wasn't that, and he just let
it go, he said, "Damn, a man can't even go to work happy." And I was
bitching also because I had been on my period about a week before
that and had just come off. He told me he was going to take off from
work, and he didn't take off from work. And so we were working different shifts. And I'd come in and we'd say "hi" and "bye," you know.
I am high strung and very sensitive. I am a woman that at times I have
to have a man for sexual reasons, for emotional reasons and this was
getting on me too, because I couldn't be with him, it was "hi" and
"bye" and that's not anything. And I was bitchy because I couldn't get
my sexual thing off. And when I can't get myself together like that, I

don't get along with nobody. Nobody can get along with me. And I was feeling, nobody cares anything about me, I got the whole load on myself—you know, feeling sorry for myself.

Anyhow, I had come in from working this double shift and I had finally gotten a chance to settle down and get some rest. I had been trying to sleep but the kids were playing and fussing and arguing and I had been yelling at them to do their work, to finish washing the dishes and finish what they were supposed to do but they weren't—they weren't moving fast enough.

I'd taken the ground beef out of the refrigerator to defrost for supper and she must of thought it was spoiled because after it gets out of the freezer, it turns kind of brown. She had taken it and thrown it out. And when I got ready to make supper and asked for it, she went out to the garbage can and brought it back to me in her hand. And that did it. I blew up. It turned my stomach. It made me mad to think that she was that stupid, to bring it to me in her hand, you know, and expected me to fix it for dinner. And she handed it to me and I believe I slapped her, I backhanded her, and I told her to get upstairs. She started crying and I told her to stop that yelling and she went upstairs and I told her to get out of her clothes and lay down on the floor in front of me and I got a wide belt, a wide leather belt about that size and I began to beat her and beat her and the more I beat her, the more I couldn't stop. At first you know, she cried a little and then she took it, but when I really started giving it to her, she had the worst look on her face, as if she was begging me to stop. "I am not going to do it no more, I'm sorry"—you know. She had a really horrified look on her face. And I was thinking and feeling, "I don't care, I don't give a damn. You don't do nothing I say do. I am working hard. I can't get any rest. I'm tired and you don't listen to me and I'm just going to make you mind. I have to repeat over and over again what I'm telling you to do and you don't listen to me."

I believe, I really believe what really made me stop was I got tired. I got tired, and then I went through a—my doctor said I went through an anxiety attack. I lost all control of my bowels and my bladder, I was crying and I just—my whole body started shaking and I couldn't stop. And I managed to call my doctor and he came out to the house and gave me Thorazine. I don't want to go through that again. It was something bad.

And after I got calmed down I called Reba into the room and I tried to explain why she got a whipping. And even now when I try to talk to her or reach for her, she ducks. She automatically ducks. She flinched and she started to run. She flinched and I told her to get the hell out of my face because you see you're not even paying attention to what I'm saying now, you know. And after it was over, I felt bad, I really did, I really felt bad. I was thinking I was losing my mind. I was living a situation that was hopeless. Messed up my relationship with my daughter and possibly, you know, with my family taken away from me completely.

And then she went to school the next day and said that one of the girls in her class in playing pulled up her sweater and saw the bruises on her back and called the teacher. I did not know how extensive her bruises were. I had beaten the girl so bad she had open lacerations on her back. When a policeman showed me photographs I felt really bad because I didn't know that I had beaten her that bad. And I was really scared about how I had lost control. It was a long time before I even yelled at her. A real long time before I even yelled at her.

REFERENCES

AHA (American Humane Association). 1979a. *Annual Statistical Report: National Analysis of Official Neglect and Abuse Reporting, 1977.* Englewood, Colo. American Humane Association, February.

—— 1979b. *Annual Statistical Report - National Analysis of Official Neglect and Abuse Reporting, 1978.* Englewood, Colo.: American Humane Association, October.

Bell, Richard Q. and Larence V. Harper. 1977. *Child Effects on Adults.* New York: Wiley.

Bell, Richard Q. 1975. "Reduction of Stress in Child Rearing." In L. Levi, Ed., *Society, Stress and Disease, Volume 2: Childhood and Adolescence,* pp. 416–21. New York: Oxford University Press.

Gelles, Richard J. and Murray A. Straus. 1979. "Violence in the American Family." *Journal of Social Issues,* 35(2):15–40.

Lourie, Ira. 1979. "Family Dynamics and the Abuse of Adolescents: A Case for a Developmental Phase Specific Model of Child Abuse." *Child Abuse and Neglect: The International Journal,* 3:967–74.

Parke, R. D., D. B. Sawin, and G. Kreling. 1974. "The Effect of Child Feedback on Adult Disciplinary Choices." Manuscript.

Patterson, G. R. and J. A. Cobb. 1973. "Stimulus Control for Classes of Noxious Behaviors." In J. F. Knutson, ed., *The Control of Aggression: Implications from Basic Research,* pp. 145–99. Chicago: Aldine-Atherton.

Patterson, G. R., R. A. Littman, and W. Bricker. 1967. "Assertive Behavior in Children: A Step toward A Theory of Aggression." *Monographs of Society for Research in Child Development,* 32:1–43.

Shapiro, Deborah. 1979. *Parents and Protectors: A Study of Child Abuse and Neglect.* New York: Child Welfare League of America.

Straus, Murray A. and Susan K. Steinmetz. 1974. "Violence Research, Violence Control and the Good Society." In S. K. Steinmetz and M. A. Straus, eds., *Violence and the Family,* pp. 321–24. New York: Harper and Row.

CHAPTER 6

FACTORS ASSOCIATED WITH THE ABUSE EVENT

Contributing Factors

THROUGHOUT, we have been emphasizing directly and indirectly that the onset of the abuse event interaction was precipitated by some behavior, on the part of the child, which was perceived by the parent as noxious or aversive. Some child behavior was identified by every parent interviewed as the starting point of the abuse interactional sequence.

The interviews provided additional data, however, confirming the generalizations in the child abuse literature that other factors were operating which contributed to making any aversive behavior of the child high risk for abuse. Such factors intruded to provide an explosive milieu which increased the probability that some behavior on the part of the child would ignite the start of an abuse interaction episode. Further, these factors were operative in increasing the intensity of parental responses once the interaction commenced. A stressful socioeconomic situation, residuals of previous difficulties in the relationship between the parent and the child, the parent's own childhood abuse experience, children's handicaps and noxious personality characteristics, negative identification associated with the child, are factors recurrently cited as being etiologically significant in explaining abuse.

Each of these factors was alluded to by some percentage of the respondents in elaborating on their description of the abuse incident. It should be noted that while some aversive child behavior was cited by all respondents as associated with the initiation of the abuse incident, there was a very uneven distribution of these secondary factors. Not one of these additional, incremental considerations was cited by more than 70 percent of the group; most were cited much less frequently.

The uneven distribution of secondary factors is similar to the distribution of such factors in the families whose records were reviewed as part of the first unit of the study.

SITUATIONAL STRESS

The general situation at the time of the incident—that day and the preceding day—was characterized by 68 percent of the respondents as "worse than usual." A variety of different problems were being felt more intensively at this time. Intensified parent-child relationship was cited by 34 percent of the respondents as being associated with the abuse incident. Intensified marital or boyfriend/girlfriend stress was cited by 29 percent of the respondents, job related or unemployment problems by 29 percent, stress as a result of physical illness by 24 percent, financial problems by 21 percent, housing problems by 8 percent. Relatively few respondents cited substance abuse or alcoholism as problems associated with the abuse event: 12 percent of the respondents admitted drinking on the day of the incident; 5 percent admitted drinking more than usual.

On the day of the incident, 9 percent of the respondents described themselves as feeling sick, 20 percent felt depressed, 33 percent felt tired or irritable; 35 percent said they felt the same as usual.

In describing the general situation at the time of the abuse, a 22-year-old stepfather who had beaten a 6-year-old stepson said:

I had just lost my job and I was trying to figure out where in the hell my rent was going to come from and I was depressed to begin with on that day. I was mentally down in the pits. I was very tired. When I get depressed, I get very, very exhausted. I had been smoking pot and was high.

In another instance, a father who abused his pre-teen daughter had been on strike for two months, was trying to maintain a family of six on $50-a-week strike funds, with the aid of public assistance. He had recently lost his driver's license and the insurance on his car and his mother had died shortly before the incident. "Things were pretty rough— maybe it was me. I don't know, maybe I was a little too harsh on them. I don't know."

A mother, having asked her 9-year-old daughter, Lori, "two or three times" to do something for her, was refused. After the girl talked back to the mother, the mother slapped her in the face and left a mark. The woman had just had an argument with her husband about his working arrangements and said, "Things were going fine between Lori and me until Frank and I had that argument and she just smarted off and she just caught me at a bad time. Any other time it wouldn't have bothered me." The father was on long-distance truck hauls for extended periods and the mother was often both father and mother to the children for 24 hours a day, 7 days a week.

A mother who slapped her 15-year-old daughter in the face said, in describing the context in which the incident took place:

I had a lot of pressures. My mother was ill, I think that was part of my—how do you say, the state I was in at the time. 'Cause my mother was—had just gotten out of the hospital—she had a heart attack. I had that on my mind. My husband was in the process of going to the hospital for surgery. I had that on my mind. I was under a lot of pressures when all this occurred.

A father who whipped his 9-year-old daughter with a belt describes the confluence of stressful events that presented a fertile situational context for abuse:

There was an awful lot of things that had built up. I was laid off work for seven weeks, and right after I got called back to work we went on plant shutdown for two more weeks. And then I had a pending court trial coming up for a speeding violation, the dog had got out the week before, and we had just gotten the dog back from the Humane Society. And my wife was baby-sitting at the time, and she had my sister, her sister's children here, and I get very nervous, uptight when they're around, because they don't listen, and they tear things apart. I had three double martinis that day in the house. And she just caught the wrath of building up of my sister-in-law's children being here, and the dog being, you know, being escaping the last time and then again this trip. So, I went overboard a little bit.

A 34-year-old father who used to do outdoor work as a construction worker had been out of work for four months and confined to the house because of bad weather. After abusing his 10-month-old son he said, "It just got on my nerves 'cause I haven't been working and have been sitting at home listening to him scream and throw his fits all day long, you know, it was trying to me."

A mother said:

When it happened I was married and I wasn't getting along with my husband. He was never home, going out on me all the time. If there was a problem at home with the kids, "Well, that's women's work," and I didn't get along with my family. I was isolated, not having any money, and not having a car and two little kids and Carl had diarrhea all the time. I couldn't stand him. He had diarrhea about seven times a day, almost every day. And it would be in his hair and his bed and when he'd come down the stairs he'd crawl in bed with me and I couldn't stand him. And I just really was angry with him because I couldn't figure out what I was doing wrong. And one thing that used to make me really mad was if I was talking to another person—and it may have been that—that he would demand my attention and be taking away from me having a conversation with somebody. It was like the kid was always getting what he wanted, you could never put him off, it was whatever he wanted, and he was real demanding of me.

Rather trivial behavior on the part of the child can, given a stressful context, instigate an abusive action. A single mother caring for four children, ages 12, 11, 10 and 4, said:

It was on a Sunday night. I felt very down. I laid in bed that morning because my kids refused to clear the table for me. They refused to help me. And I felt very down. I was very tired and very upset. I've wanted to get a break from my children, to send them to this camp, and they won't go. I felt really down and really rather overwhelmed—I felt it was really like I had given so much and received nothing in return. And life at work has not been too rewarding. And I was having difficulty putting up the aluminum siding on my house, which I am trying to finish and didn't and what I put up was wrong. I really felt I was really down. I was at a low, low ebb. We were eating and he said he had a bone in his mouth and he spit it out. It was the way he spit it out. He didn't take it out of his mouth, he goes [blows] and I said, "You don't do that." And I put the knife to him. Well, I pressed it in him. I was so damn mad.

A single mother of an 8-year-old girl describes her introspective ruminations, presenting her assessment of her general situation, which predisposed her to abuse:

I had just gotten up and I was feeling miserable when I woke up. Debbie was downstairs watching TV and I was upstairs, and I know exactly what I was thinking about. It was the day before her birthday and I was going downtown to pick up some film projector and some film for her birthday party, and I was just feeling kind of miserable because I was doing a lot for her, and it didn't seem like nobody was ever doing anything for me, including me, and I was upstairs getting ready to go downtown. And I was looking in the mirror and I was thinking how ugly I looked. I thought I'd started to look bad and there was nothing I could do with my hair, short from cutting it off. And I was thinking that maybe I would meet, maybe I would run into somebody downtown who might think I'm attractive. But then, the thoughts that I was having were just bad thoughts. Downtown there are just a lot of people who when I looked at 'em they always looked so happy and they had places to go and people to meet and things to do. And I always feel real vulnerable when I'm downtown.

I thought—I didn't want to run into anybody, I just wanted to sneak downtown without anybody seeing me and sneak back again. And Debbie was downstairs watching cartoons on television, and she started hollering about the TV not working and so it just enraged me, I also felt like she was complaining at *me*, you know, which I knew later she wasn't, she wasn't hollering at me or making me feel bad, I just, you know, I just——

I felt like she was down here complaining and because she was upset, I felt like it was my fault. So I just came downstairs and I just grabbed her, you know, I was just so mad that I grabbed her and I shoved her over here by the window. And then I went and I just grabbed her by the throat, you know, I just—I really wanted to hurt her. That you know, was where it was at, I wanted to hurt her. I wanted her to know, she thinks, you know, that her rotten TV is bad, you know, let me just show her what real pain is, you know, something like that. And I slapped her, and I screamed at her, you know, I just was screaming things at her like she's bad and stupid and—and I wished she wasn't here and I wished there was something I could do with her, you know, stuff like that.

For one mother, a stressful housing situation contributed to increasing the risk of abuse. A single mother caring for two children, Ruth (3) and Celia (1½), said:

About a year and a half ago I moved here with my girlfriend. And that's mostly when it started, when she wanted the kids not to be in the way. She didn't want nothing to be messed up. She was a very clean woman. And she got mad when the kids went into her kid's room and played with his toys. And most of the time I just left them in my room.

Because, since she wanted it to be like that, just me and the kids were in the room all the time. We didn't go hardly no place. And that's mostly what it was about. And then if Alice [girlfriend] started some stuff, if I got angry at her, I took it out on Ruth. And this one time me and Alice got into an argument. And I was kind of—I was kind of not up to anything that day. And I was angry at—I don't know who I was angry at. And I came downstairs and I told Ruth to eat, and she wouldn't eat anything. I guess that's what I got mad at her from. And I picked her up and threw her on the floor. And she went—she passed out for a little while. And she woke up and she couldn't—she couldn't stand or walk or anything like that. And then Alice called my social worker and we took Ruth to the hospital and then they put the kids in a foster home.

The foster care placement decision was based, in part, on the fact that there were previous incidents of abuse involving the same child which the mother discussed in the interview.

Since the largest group of respondents were single parents caring for children on the limited incomes provided by public assistance or social insurance programs, it can be contended that social stress was chronic and severe, making for a situation which was persistently predisposed to abuse. If 32 percent of the respondents, in answering our specific questions, said that the situation at the time the abuse event occurred was "about the same as usual," the definition of "usual," it might be said, was stressful enough. However, the steady-state situation does not help to understand a specific, clearly defined event which is differentiated from the repetitive, nonabusive interaction with the child that was manifested in the chronically stressful context.

PARENTS' CHILDHOOD EXPERIENCES WITH DISCIPLINE

We asked respondents about their own childhood relationship with their parents and, in particular, the nature of the discipline they experienced as children. The relevance of these questions relates to the supposition in the literature that "abuse begets abuse" and that parents who experienced abuse would be predisposed to act abusively.

Because of death, divorce, parental illness, parental maltreatment, etc., 37 percent of the respondents had been separated from one or both parents during childhood.

Overall, however, a sizable number (43 percent) of respondents characterized their relationships with their parents as primarily positive; an additional 27 percent characterized the relationship as mixed; 30 percent characterized their relationship with their parents as primarily negative.

Almost all of the respondents had experienced corporal punishment during childhood, and in 44 percent of the cases the disciplinary experiences, as described, were clearly within the spectrum of child abuse.

Respondents said:

I had a very terrible relationship with my family. My father was an alcoholic, my mother was an alcoholic. My father used to beat on me just for practice, and I have memories of five years old, maybe even a little earlier than that, that I'll never forget, of being strangled and beaten and I was covered with bruises before they took me away from my father.

We grew up in an awful atmosphere. Mother and father fighting all the time. We been beat with fishing rods. We had to pick splinters out of our backs. My mother even burnt 50 cent pieces in our hand. I used to suck my thumb. She beat my nail. She beat my thumbs so bad one time the nail came off.

I never really had a mother love, hugging, and kissing and all like that. My mother didn't raise me, but when I did stay with her she used to beat the hell out of me on general principles. Maybe this [the child abuse] is a throwback from that, I don't know.

Dad had a razorstrap, and he used to whip us with the razorstrap. And Mom lost control several times at us kids, whipping us with switches. One time she whipped me really bad, she whipped me—I had welts all over everywhere—at that time, police couldn't be called in for child abuse and stuff, it was allowed to—you were allowed to make your kids mind, and Mom whipped me with the switch and left welts all over me. I guess I really hated her at that time 'cause she whipped me like that.

Less frequently, these respondents presented descriptions of childhood experiences which might be characterized as psychological abuse:

My Mom would holler at me and slap me. How bad I was, she would tell me how bad I was. I just recently got over the feeling that I was the worst person in our family. It seemed like I always felt like I was being looked down upon and I was the black sheep of the family. And I knew when she was after me, too—how bad I was. I felt like I had to live up to it. You know, I'm this way, and that's what they think, so that's the way I'll be. I hope I'm not putting that impression on my kids.

Mom used to give us the silent treatment. She'd say, "All right, if that's the way you want to be, forget it. Just forget it." And shut up, and she wouldn't say another word. And that made you feel so guilty that you ended up doing it anyways.

Some parents explicitly confirm the classic supposition that abusers learn to abuse as a consequence of their own childhood experiences as abused children, modeling their own behavior in terms of those experiences.

A father said:

It's just that when they get me mad, I try to do the things my Dad did to me, which I think now is wrong, but I was born and raised that way. I don't know what to do anymore. I am lost. I guess the kids are just going to have to grow up being just like we were when we were kids. We were never raised to be able to know how to raise our kids, I guess.

One abusive mother said,

If I hadn't been brought up the way that I was brought up, I don't even believe it would have happened like that, because it had a lot to do with the way you raise your own kids. [The mother had experienced considerable physical abuse as a child.] You know, when you're raised in an atmosphere like that, it's hard to pull yourself out of it. . . . I don't *want* to do this to my kid. I don't want to raise him like that because I know what it have done to me.

What was communicated was not only that corporal punishment was an accepted and common method of discipline, but that children should expect to be punished this way if they did something wrong:

A father says:

Discipline for us was pretty common physical discipline, which is probably why it carried on to me. But even though I got hit, I knew I had it coming and I don't know, I never reacted that way. When I got hit, I felt I had it coming. We respected it.

Having experienced corporal punishment in childhood, the parent has learned this method of disciplining children. By virtue of having been used by their own parents, they see this as a sanctioned, acceptable method of discipline.

But the experience as an abused child impacts differently on different children and affects parental behavior in a variety of ways for a variety of reasons.

As implied in one of the quotes above, despite the fact that the mother felt she was influenced to use such punitive procedures in disciplining in response to her own experiences, she also was more keenly aware of its negative consequences for parent-child relationships, and, as a result, was motivated to change her behavior. The lessons learned in childhood of how to deal with problems of child discipline are potently influential in determining behavior as a parent. Yet the lessons are resisted and the childhood experience prompts a desire to find a better way to deal with problems of child rearing.

A father said:

My Dad kept beating me all the time. Broken back I had, you know, broken legs. My nose was broke up here. Scars here and scars on my back and scars down here, and when I'd started really getting mean and ornery toward Lori [his child], the more I thought the less I could, you know. The less I picked on Lori. I ain't going to be all that strict with her, but she'll know the difference between right and wrong. And I ain't going to beat her like my Dad used to beat me. There's no way, 'cause I don't want to—I wouldn't put my kid through that.

Another parent said, "You know, I hate my Dad because he hit us. And I don't want Sidney to hate me—and I am afraid he will."

A stepfather (22), describing his feelings after beating his 6-year-old stepson with a strap, an interaction initiated by the child's repeated misbehavior in school, says:

I was very angry, very upset. I don't know, I guess I was pissed off at myself for doing it. The way I felt myself about myself—'cause I can remember the way my stepfather was. And he was a natural-born prick. He believed in corporal punishment and that's the way he felt. I felt like him. And it upset me very much to feel like him. I was totally upset.

Some element of the acceptance of corporal punishment as a disciplinary procedure on the part of parents who were themselves disciplined in this way as children is based on the experience that, for them, corporal punishment worked. In retrospect, they see themselves as having been induced to change dysfunctional behavior as a result of their parents' punishment. It was for them, as they perceive it, a positive learning experience which they are then motivated to repeat, for this reason, in their own child-rearing practices. Having experienced corporal punishment, they have not only learned to employ it as a disciplinary procedure, they are convinced of its value in child rearing.

One mother, recalling her own childhood experience, says:

When my mother whipped you, you were well whipped. We got whippings with an extension cord. I got marks on me now that I got from whippings when I was very little. I got to a point I almost hated my mother. But you know now, I think the Lord for every whipping she gave me then. I didn't see it then, but now, every whipping she gave me I needed. If I had to go through it again, I wouldn't change it a bit. If I could change, I wouldn't change, 'cause I needed every one I got.

A mother who whipped her 7-year-old daughter for stealing said:

When I was a teenager I started picking up stuff that wasn't mine and my mother whipped my ass. At that time, I hated her for it, but it broke me of it. It stopped me from doing what I was doing because I wasn't going through another whipping.

Having experienced corporal discipline as a child, one parent says:

It's been a long time but I am sure I wasn't too happy about what she [mother] was doing, that's for sure. It didn't make me happy, but you know, since I grew up, I think I am kind of happy that she did some of the things she did, you know. Because you know right from wrong, you know what to do and what not to do, you know.

A father said in discussing his daughter's problematic behavior:

I figured maybe she needs an old-fashioned spanking. I mean, you know, it helped me a lot. I got spanked when I was a kid and, knock on wood, I am very proud that it helped me.

A mother's intention in whipping her daughter with a belt was to stop the child's persistent disobedient behavior. She said, "Maybe she won't do it. I remember what whippings I got. I wouldn't do those things again."

Other parents said:

Well, I didn't know what to do 'cause I don't discipline him very much and I talk to him a lot, you know. So I thought well, I'll just give him a spanking. I thought, well, it's about time we do it, you know. My Ma used to spank me and well, I'd shape right up.

I was always getting into things and running my mouth and doing things I wasn't supposed to and my mother, she never physically hurt me, you know. She'd pop me in my mouth or, you know, whip me with the ironing cord and I think it did me some good because, like I shouldn't have been running my mouth.

And sometimes the childhood experience with minimal discipline prompts exactly the opposite behavior as a parent. A 27-year-old mother who abused her 7-year-old son said she never "got punished" by her mother. She could always manipulate her mother so that her mother never stuck to any discipline. She feels her mother was "definitely wrong—I wouldn't have done half the things I did in my life if she would have just, for once, stuck to something she said." The mother nows feels that stricter, more definite discipline, is desirable.

HISTORY OF ABUSED CHILD/ABUSIVE PARENT RELATIONSHIP

The developmental history of the abused child/abusing parent pair and the nature of the relationship pattern established as a consequence of such experiences contributed in some cases to increasing the probability that aversive behavior would incite the inception of a child-abuse interaction sequence.

One might hypothecate residuals of hostility directed toward the child, deriving from earlier traumatic pregnancy and birth experiences, as contributing to onset of the abuse event. A disproportionate percentage of the children were admittedly unplanned (64.3 percent) and a disproportionately large percentage (46 percent) were born out of wedlock. Some 57 percent of the mothers were 21 years or younger when the abused child was born, 15 percent being only 18 or younger. In 35 percent of the cases, the pregnancy was perceived as difficult because of physical, social, or emotional complications; and in 43 percent of the cases, the delivery itself was perceived as difficult. In 32 percent of the cases, the child was born at a "bad" time for the parent, there being more than usual stress in her life at the time. All of these considerations would suggest that the mother might, logically, be expected to harbor some resentment and hostility toward the child, predisposing her toward abuse.

A mother articulates the connection between the birth situation and her subsequent relationship to the abused child. She was 17 at the time she gave birth to the child conceived out of wedlock but born after marriage.

> I don't know, for some reason, I've always had a thing against her. I've always, you know, been cussing at her and telling her that, you know, she's dumb or things like that. Maybe it's just the fact that I was pregnant with her before I got married. This is one of the reasons why I might be picking on her more.

However, less than 5 percent of the mothers had considered either abortion or adoption as a means of "unburdening" themselves of the child, and the reaction to the presentation of the child at birth was positive for the largest percentage of these abusive parents (73 percent). They were "happy, excited, pleased" when presented with the child after birth.

The complexity and discontinuity in the planning, pregnancy, and delivery process itself is summarized by one respondent when she says,

> I got married because I was pregnant and my ex-husband probably wouldn't have married me if I hadn't been pregnant. But all the same, I didn't have an abortion. I didn't even take birth control. I wanted to have a baby so I don't know if you could call that planning or not. And the pregnancy was with much pleasure. I was exulted. I just felt terrific all the time. But the delivery was extremely horrid.

An additional source of possible resentment against the child lay in the fact that, in 31 percent of the cases, the birth of the child had negative effects on the mother's relationship with a spouse or lover. The pregnancy and birth of the child intensified difficulties in the relationship resulting in abandonment, divorce or separation. In the largest percentage of cases, however (64 percent), there was no change or a positive change in such relationships as a consequence of the pregnancy and birth of this child. In most instances, also, the first year's experience with the child—the year that might be thought of as determining the direction of the relationship—was generally regarded as positive.

In 85 percent of the cases, the child's health was either good or characterized by "minor problems or problems of brief duration." In only 9 percent of the cases did the parent see the child as difficult to live with during the first year. Most parents rated the child as fairly easy to live with during the first year, requiring only "average amount of care." These assessments were being made retrospectively in response to our specific probes, which makes the general positive picture presented even more surprising. We were focusing on the abused child with whom the parents had had some recent difficulty. It might have been anticipated that having had an aversive experience associated with the child would have intensified a tendency, in recalling the past, to give emphasis to past negative perceptions and to intensify the memory of past difficulties.

Discontinuity in the relationship is occasioned by changes in the child's pattern of behavior with maturation. While rejecting the dependent infant and the associated feeding, crying, diapering, etc., the parent grows gradually more accepting of the child as he becomes progressively more independent, more capable of interacting with the parent as a companion. Or the reverse might be true.

One mother described the comfortable relationship between herself and her child as a young infant, which changed subsequently. Perceived primarily as a love object, the child in the total dependency of infancy could adequately play this role:

> Then suddenly Valerie turned a year old and boom, there it was. Maybe I expected Valerie to be a baby always, you know, somebody that all I have to do is bathe, dry, and feed her and she was fine, you know. When Valerie started growing up, that was it.

The demands a child makes by virtue of being dependent, the sacrifices that are inevitable in becoming a parent, occasion resentments that predispose to abuse. A mother said:

> Then I thought, too, I guess when I went to whipping him, like when I—like I was telling him that it had been many a winter I wouldn't buy nothing, have any boots, but I made sure you have some. Then I thought, you know, if it hadn't of been for him, I probably would have been a nurse by now, you know, and I—all kind of things was just like running through my mind, and it all boiled down to this one little child stopped me from doing all of this, you know.

The child might have been born at a particularly inconvenient time in a parent's life. A father expressed resentment against a child he abused because, as a consequence of her birth, he felt trapped. His first child, Ruth, abused at 13, was unplanned:

One of my underlying desires was to get a divorce from my wife, and since Ruth came, I felt that—kind of obligated, because—I guess my reasoning over the years has been that I never had a father, I was going to make damn sure—well, after I decided that I would—irregardless of the marital problems, I would stick it out and be a father to my children. And I guess, in a way, I guess—in a sense, you could say I held it against the kids. 'Cause if it weren't for them, there's no way I would stay with my wife. The birth of the child changed my relationship with my wife in that it made me more compliant with her wishes, you know, about what job to take and, you know, more compliant. My job situation was bad. I was fairly reasonably young then. I hadn't made up my mind what I wanted to do in life. Some of the things that I really wanted to do would now be impossible. I wish in reality they would have been, but I knew they wouldn't.

The abused child may have been born too soon after a previous birth. The short interval in spacing imposes a difficult burden, creating a negative reaction. One subsequently abused child was born one year after the birth of a previous child. The mother said, "It would have been nicer if it would have been a couple of years." After the birth of this child, her third, the mother had a serious postpartum depression, which lasted close to a year, during which time she required psychiatric help.

Being the first-born made two of the children in the study group high risk for abuse. The first-born child moves a person from nonparent to parent status. As a consequence of the birth of the first child one has to assume the burdens, penalties, restrictions, limitations associated with parent status. Subsequent births compound these effects, but the birth of the first child is decisive in initiating the change.

A mother, in talking about her year-old daughter, whom she abused, said she had rejected the pregnancy and had considered an abortion.

Here I was going to school and I wasn't going to let the child tie me down, but she was going to take away kind of my privileges of doing a lot of things that I wanted to do when I was not pregnant. I could just go where I wanted to go, do what I wanted to do. There's the frustration between us and there's always like anger. I always stayed mad and I never reacted that way toward my other children. Rose is my first child. I had given birth to her and everything, but at that time I just wasn't ready for a baby, and I didn't know what to do.

The mother was 18 years old when she became a parent for the first time. Subsequent to the conception, pregnancy, and delivery experience, some parents and children experienced events that were damaging to their relationship.

The abused child (Ann, 5) was in a foster home for the first two years of her life, during which time the mother was serving a jail sentence on a charge of forgery. The putative father never knew of the birth of the child and had no contact with the mother subsequent to her arrest. Regaining custody after her release, the mother found it difficult to establish a positive relationship with the child and the difficulty persisted:

> I took over from there [foster home] and it's hard for her and me to communicate. I don't know, me and Ann has it out lots of times. I used to say [to Ann], I wish I wouldn't have never went and got her, and you know, that's a bad thing to say to a child.
>
> I don't think [Ann] likes me at all. I just think that she hates me, you know. I don't know what she would be thinking, but I feel that she hates me, really, you know.
>
> This woman [foster mother], she had better things than I did, you know, more money and everything—Ann had a whole bunch when she was with her—way more than she's got now. So she was quite scared of me. We had to trick her in order to get her to come with me to come home.

There was specific notation in 25 percent of the cases that the child manifested some mental, emotional, behavioral, or physical problem. The most frequently cited disability was a mental disability such as retardation, palsy, or an abnormal EEG (8 cases). In 4 cases, some serious behavioral problem was noted, such as hyperactivity or extreme shyness and withdrawal. The largest percentage of children (75 percent) were perceived by their parents as essentially normal.

Disability might increase the risk of abuse, since a disabled child presents the parent with a greater than normal burden of care. However, this did not seem to be a dominant factor associated with abuse in this group of children.

Low birth weight and prematurity as risk factors in abuse, because of the disruptive effects of these factors on the mother-child bonding process, seems, once again, to have been characteristic of only a limited number of these children. Some 7 percent of the children were low birth weight babies and 4.5 percent were premature.

Forty-six percent of the respondents indicated that they had similar kinds of disciplinary problems with siblings of the abused child as they had with the abused child; 6 percent of the respondents admitted abusing a sibling as well. More frequently, however, similar kinds of problems manifested by siblings of the abused child were handled with less punitive disciplinary procedures.

In a few instances, parents frankly explained the difference in approach on the basis of the fact that they liked the nonabused child better. Sometimes the difference was a matter of age; the sibling being young, less was expected of him, so that more aversive behavior was tolerated.

Dereliction of duty, failure to do chores, is less excusable in an older child. "They should know better. They should have learned by now and, if they haven't learned by now, what's going to happen to them when they go out into the world and have to do what they have to do." Here anger is mixed with anxiety for the future, mixed with a sense of inadequacy as a parent for having failed to teach the child to behave in the way intended.

The older child is higher risk for abuse because he or she is regarded by the parents as modeling behavior for the younger children to follow. As the oldest, he is expected to set a good example. If he fails to set a good example, he can be accused of misleading the others. One parent said if there was disobedience on the part of the children, the oldest was the target for discipline, "Because Rich [the youngest child] is at the point where he follows and copies Bob [the older, abused child]. If there is trouble, it is usually instigated by Bob."

A father said he whipped his daughter for disobedience:

'Cause I don't want her ruining the other kids that's here, you know what I mean. 'Cause now my next oldest girl just started yapping off at the mouth. She got this from Lily. If Lily stays on here, she'll have all of 'em repeating after her and I don't want that, you know. By you being the oldest child, you're supposed to set an example for the rest of the kids. I don't want them going out doing what you do, 'cause you're going to lead them off in the wrong direction. You be spoiling the other kids.

More frequently, however, the abused child here was perceived as being different from his more easily disciplined siblings in terms of some dispositional, temperamental characteristics. In explaining the difference in approach to the same behavior on the part of abused and nonabused siblings, parents indicated that the nonabused child did not engage in the aversive behavior as frequently, or as persistently, and that the nonabused child responded better than the abused child to initial nonpunitive disciplinary approaches.

Comparing the abused child, Vicky, with her twin sister, their mother described the sister as less obstinate. "She doesn't get as angry as Vicky does. She just cries. She just doesn't get as violent as what Vicky does."

In distinguishing between her two children, Lawrence and Helen, a mother says she has no trouble with Lawrence:

Lawrence is more easy to live with because I would say—I can trust him more than I can Helen. He's—you know, he's more trustable than Helen is. If I tell him "stay, I'll be back," he stay. If I tell him to come down to the job to pick up something and pay a bill for me, he'll do it. Helen, she'll forget it. Or she'll lose the money.

Describing her two daughters, a mother said:

The difference between the younger and the older child [the abused child] is that the younger one is a very passive little girl who will go play someplace by herself. If she gets time, she'll, without saying anything, disappear and you'll find her in bed sound asleep. The older one is not like that. She's there all the time and she lets you know she's there. She's not about to be ignored. She's noisy and boisterous. She's got a temper and she'll spend an hour throwing a temper tantrum, and at times she gets on my nerves.

Delineating on the differences between her two sons and showing a clear preference for the nonabused child, a mother said:

And my oldest child [Steve] is the extreme opposite of Carl (the abused child)—very timid and quiet and you could set him aside and he never broke toys and I like his sensitivity. I liked him better from day one. Yeah . . . I see Steve in me even now . . . I really empathize with him—that kid brings up so many feelings in me, and I get really angry with him sometimes, but I'm more apt to understand him and try to be nicer to him. And Carl, I just don't understand him at all. It's like he's not like me at all. He rarely shows feelings, he is bullheaded, strong, real aggressive. And when I first came home from the hospital with Carl, all I could think of was protecting Steve from this intruder. I felt that the baby [Carl] was an intruder between him and me. So I guess I'm very partial to the older boy.

A mother talking about her two daughters, one 16, the other 14, distinguishes between the two in a way which suggests the younger as being higher risk for abuse.

> The oldest one was, I guess, very much like me, and she was just always a very mature kind of person, whereas the second one has always been immature, playful, and even yet she is. In fact, I would call her the class clown or the family clown, however you'd like to say it. She never takes much of anything serious. And she has caused me a lot of problems . . . I remember years ago when my husband and I were together, Yvette was about five years old, and he said at that point, Yvette was a manipulator. I couldn't believe it, I really couldn't accept that. And finally when I saw too many undesirable things coming from Yvette, I did take her to a child psychologist, and he indicated to me that Yvette could be very manipulative, and if not corrected, she could cause—not herself, but other people around her, a lot of pain and heartache.

Parents are perceptive in individualizing their children, in identifying differences, and in noting differences in their own responses to the children. The mother of two children, a boy of 5 (Dick) and a boy of 3 (John), found herself reacting more negatively to the 5-year-old who was abused. She described him as hyperactive, always seeking attention, a constant nuisance, unable to play by himself. The younger child was described as "just the opposite, easygoing, able to play by himself for long periods of time without bothering others. They are two completely different personalities. I wouldn't usually clash with John. He does not provoke me as much as Dick does." The abused child had viral encephalitis as an infant and showed abnormal EEG responses.

In another instance, a father showed more patience in dealing with a disciplinary problem of another child than he had demonstrated with the abused child. In explaining the differences in response, the father said of the nonabused child that

> he's provoked me less often. In a sense, he's been a good kid. I suppose I can't deny some probability of some favoritism, you know. But he's like always been first string on the sports, he's a good athlete and most valuable player in football and he's like—he's a pretty good clean kid.

In talking of another child who was not abused, a mother is aware of the child's behavior which acts to inhibit abuse:

I can't whip her because she's got those big eyes and she comes to you, "Well, I didn't mean to do that," and she cares more for me than the other children.

Sometimes it's a question of dispositional dissonance between the parent and the abused child. The abused child, unlike his siblings, acts in a way that just rubs the parent the wrong way.

A very noisy child and a mother somewhat allergic to noise present an example of dissonance—a lack of fit between mother and child which predisposes to abuse with the particular child as the preselected target. In illustration of this, one mother said:

> The other children do things too to misbehave, but they don't act like Reuben. They'd stop if you tell them to, not just keep right on like he does. Real persistent and just keeps on doing it, kind of like he's waiting for you to get up and spank him or see what'll do just to push you so far. And he's very noisy, more than the others, runs through the house and bangs on doors and I think I'm kind of a high-tension person. I can't put up with too much noise, it gets on my nerves and it gets on my mind just too much and I just can't take all the noise he gives me.

In 62 percent of the cases where a choice could appropriately be made, the parent interviewed selected the abused child as "the child in the family hardest to live with." A sibling of the abused child was selected as "easiest to live with" in 93 percent of the cases where parents made a choice. Parents were clearly differentiating between the abused child and a sibling, giving clear preference to the sibling in selecting the child easiest to live with.

But while the abused child may be the less preferred child, this is not the same as implying that the child necessarily is a rejected child. It would be easy if there was undeviating consistency between the abusive behavior toward the child and a persistent feeling of rejection of the child. Apparently things are not that simple. There was considerable ambivalence in the attitude of the parents toward the abused children, components of rejection laced with affection, pleasant experiences as well as difficult experiences.

Results on this are based on two sources of data. One of the questions, asked toward the end of the interview, requested the parent's description of the child—the kinds of things the parent liked about the child, the kinds of things the parent disliked about the child; the nature of the satisfactions the parent obtained in relationship with the child and the sources of dissatisfaction. In addition, the parents were asked to complete a checklist form after the interview was completed. The checklist included words and phrases that might describe a child and his behavior in both positive and negative directions, i.e., "is selfish," "is impatient," "is self-sufficient," "cries easily," "is warm," "is competitive," "has sleeping problem," etc. Parents were requested to complete the form describing the child in terms of a 5-point scale from "not at all like my child" to "very much like my child."

The verbal descriptions at the end of the interview and the responses on the form were generally congruent with each other. The means of the ranking of the form items tended to suggest that parents described these children in both negative and positive terms.

On the scale, a mean score of 3 in response to a word or phrase represents a perception of the child as being like this "about half the time;" an average score of 4 indicates that the child is "usually like this but not always;" a score closer to one indicates the child is "not at all" like this. Scores between 3 and 4 then describe the child as he usually is.

Responding to the checklist, children were pictured by the abusing parent as being "friendly" (mean score 4.2) "healthy" (mean score 4.1), "affectionate with me" (3.7), "sympathetic" (3.6) with no serious sleeping, eating, toileting problems and few disabling nervous habits. On the other hand, the children were described as having "strong personalities" (mean score 4), "stubborn" (3.9), "impatient" (3.6), "noisy" (3.6), "aggressive" (3.5), "competitive" (3.5), "dominant" (3.5), emotionally labile, i.e. he "gets angry easily" (3.5) and "gets hurt easily" (3.4) and is "constantly seeking attention" (3.4).

Descriptions of the children in the interview indicated a similar ambivalent characterization. Criticism and dislike are cited alongside of affectionate concern, strong feelings of compassionate, positive regard for the child.

A mother said of her 16-year-old daughter, who was the object of abuse:

> She's an attractive girl and she makes friendships easily, although they're all on the surface. I see her as very selfish and also very lazy. It bothers me that she lies all the time and that she's really destroying herself. She sees herself as not mattering and she has very low self-esteem and that bothers me. Then there are times she surprises you, she

can be very compassionate, she's very good with little children, she's a good baby-sitter and she's done volunteer hospital work where she was very patient and helpful.

A mother, describing her 3½-year-old daughter reported abused, said:

She's a very easygoing, self-sufficient type of little girl, very eager to learn about everything and very helpful to her younger sister who's a little bit slower in learning physical things. But I enjoy her when we're doing things together, like this morning I baked cookies. We read to them a lot—and I enjoy doing that with her and being able to watch her when she's playing really good together with other kids. But she's very obstinate and very persistent and can be constantly going on about the same thing for all day and whining and crying. And that gets to me. I can't take the whining and crying and I can't take the persistence.

A mother, talking of her school-age daughter, said:

She's a 7-year-old who thinks she's 17, very mature in some things. She's a leader, not a follower, she's interested in everything. She's still sweet but at times she can be downright mean because she is spoiled rotten. She's pretty, a very pretty girl. At times she's very hard to get along with, 'cause she's stubborn. Most of the time you can reason with her, most of the time, but she knows what she wants and she'll go pretty far to get it. And she can maneuver people very well. But to me, she's wonderful 'cause she's mine, you know. But a lot of bad habits are rubbing off on her.

Other parents describing their abused children said:

I enjoy the way she looks when I've combed her hair and dressed her for school, and the way she does when she brings me her report card and she's a very good student, very good. And she's got a certain way of saying, "Mama" that just knocks you down. She's a quiet child, very impressionable and she takes up habits that are . . . nauseating. She's sneaky, very sneaky.

He's a very imaginative 6-year-old, very talkative, curious, very curious, "nosey" keeps coming to my mind, very smart, very alert. I have pleasure having him around. But he likes to be a big attraction in a crowd of kids, daredevil, and I don't like his attitude toward school, his attitude that he wouldn't mind, his constant trying to fight, doing things behind my back, and lying to me about them.

NEGATIVE IDENTIFICATIONS

The child might generally evoke negative feelings in the abusing parent because of the nature of the identification with which the child is associated. At the time of the interview, the child was identified in the abuser's mind with some familiar person in 65 percent of the cases. The child most frequently reminded the abusing parent of the child's father (28 percent of the cases) or was identified with the abuser him/herself. The direction of these perceptions was positive or ambivalent in most cases (52 percent), but was clearly negative in 48 percent of the cases. In some of the cases, the name the child carried, and the recollection he evoked in the abuser's mind as a result of the identifications imposed on the child, presented a heightened risk for abuse.

Where the child is identified in the abuser's mind with a significant other who caused pain and trouble, and where the child's behavior mirrors that of the rejected person, the child is reacted to with more than expected vehemence.

Speaking of the husband who walked out on her, the mother of the abused child said:

> I didn't want him to be nothing like his father. I tried to prevent him from being like his father and when I saw him acting like his father, it upset me very much. So I guess that might have a lot to do with it too.

A mother made the connection between the identification of one child and her father, which made the child high risk for abuse:

> You know, I beat her—I didn't touch the other children, just her. She looks like her father. She reminds me of him in her mannerisms—sneaky, very sneaky—and I can blow up. She is the image of her father, and sometimes I can sit there and listen to her talk, or watch her do something, and I get so mad, because she's just that much like him and his people. I'm thinking about what's happening to me, why I am in this lousy situation—with five children, separated, on welfare—which I cannot stand, being a totally independent person—and if it wasn't for her and her Daddy, I wouldn't be where I am now—all of this falls on her.

And further illustrating the awesome complexity of identification patterns that relate to abuse, the same child reminded the mother most explicitly of herself:

She's hard to live with because she's so much like me. She's got her own mind, she knows what she wants to do and where she's going. She's determined that whatever she's going to do, she's going to do it, she don't give a damn whether she's going to get a beating or what. She's going to do it regardless. And that's the kind of thing, in me, that got me into a lot of trouble.

A parent identified the abused child with himself in another interview. As a consequence, an intensified awareness of the problematic aspects of certain patterns of behavior resulted in reacting strongly to what the child did:

Well, like he's always been a very hyperactive child, which—he takes after me, temperament, attitude, the whole bit. When I see him, I see a carbon copy of myself. And—just knowing the hell that I caught from my parents kind of makes me more aggressive to him, so to speak, because I can see him going the same way I did. And I don't want to have myself and him going through the same experiences that I went through with my father when I was growing up. Which I think has a lot to do with the way I handle him sometimes. 'Cause there are times when I am, shall we say oppressive, more so than I should be.

The incisive memory of their own mistakes makes some parents react very sharply and more than ordinarily punitively toward some behaviors. A never-married mother of three had had her first out-of-wedlock child when she was 19. As a consequence, she had to give up her school plans after considering, but failing to obtain, an abortion. The mother beat her 6-year-old daughter after the child was raped by a boy in the neighborhood. The mother saw the child as willful and headstrong.

She's a very bright child but she's got this idea of having her way that when she grows up, at the age of 14, she going to do what she wants to do and I don't want that. I want her to grow up to make something of her life. I don't want my daughter to be like me.

Positive identification with one child can intensify negative identification of another child who is then high risk for abuse.

A divorced mother with a girl of 8 and a boy of 9 saw the boy as the favorite of his father and of the grandparents. The girl, with whom the mother identifies, is given less consideration. "She's pushed aside and left out." In addition, the mother saw the boy as very much like his father, from whom she is divorced. As a consequence, the mother admitted she tends to blame the boy for anything that goes wrong between him and his sister. He tends to be made the scapegoat.

PERSONALITY DISTURBANCES

We also obtained some evidence on personality disturbances manifested by respondents, since this too is regarded as a factor which contributes to, and helps explain, abuse. This content was, however, less systematically explored with respondents as contrasted with explicit questions regarding stress, identification, relationships to their own parents, and experience as an abused child; pregnancy and delivery experiences; and physical and emotional problems of the abused child.

We were alert to, but did not ask direct questions about, arrest record, mental illness, suicide attempts, general, atypical, consistent, impulsive, and/or aggressive behavior.

A limited number of the respondents (about 20 percent) shared this kind of relevant information. The fact that some 80 percent of the respondents did not volunteer any comparable information is, of course, no guarantee that they were free of such problems. We can only say that, in an interview which was conducted so as to encourage open sharing with an interviewer who had no authority over them, most interviewees indicated, by omission, that they had not experienced arrests, mental illness, suicide attempts, etc.

Three respondents had a record of arrests, 4 had been mentally ill or felt sufficiently disturbed that they had seen a psychiatrist. One 22-year-old stepfather, perhaps the most severely disturbed of the respondents, had been in and out of psychiatric hospitals, alcoholic clinics, orphanages, foster homes, group homes since he was 8. "I've sat in reform schools twice, once for armed robbery or strong-armed robbery, and the first time was for two counts of burglary, one count of grand theft." He described himself as "uncontrollable" as a child, having a violent temper as an adult, and ruling his home with an "iron hand." At one point in his life, he attempted suicide.

None of the respondents was overtly psychotic at the time of the event. The closest approximation to this was a mother who was interviewed, but whose interview was not included in the final count because there was no incident of actual abuse. The mother had called Parents Anonymous and involved the agency when she made tentative and abortive attempts to smother her 2-year-old boy with a pillow. "It had been coming for a long time. I had been thinking about doing it. I was hallucinating, and I think that's what brought it on. I was hallucinating that he was here to punish me. It was in me to hurt him. I don't know why, I just kept telling myself to hurt him."

Less serious, but of relevance, is the fact that some parents describe themselves as having a "short fuse," a "strong temper," being "easily arousable."

Having resorted to violence as the problem-solving option of choice in other situations, these parents have engaged in a process of symbolic interaction which has resulted in their perception of themselves as "violent," "easily angered," "hot tempered." Their self-image and sense of identity includes a picture of themselves as predisposed to violence. Describing themselves to themselves as well as to others in this way reduces inhibitions against acting abusively. In doing so, they are being true to themselves.

Summary

1. The findings supported the broad general hypothesis that child abuse is almost invariably precipitated by some behavior on the part of the child which initiates a disciplinary interaction culminating in abuse. In no instance studied was the child a passive participant in an event initiated by the parent and sustained primarily, if not exclusively, by the parent. The child through his behavior is an active agent in the abuse interaction.

The specific behaviors related to abuse varied with the age of the child—the children involved in the study ranged from 9 months to 16 years, mean age being 8½. Behavior included truancy, stealing, fighting, lying, enuresis, prolonged crying, failure to do chores, persistent disobedience, unacceptable habits, exit-entrance behaviors.

While other factors were identified as being related to the abuse-event process, they were of less immediate significance in determining the behavior of participants in the incident and in giving direction to the interaction. These included situational stress factors such as marital conflict, financial need, illness, poor housing, unemployment, the parent's own experience with abuse in childhood, and previous developmental experiences with the abused child. Unlike the child-behavior and parent-reaction factors present in every case, each of these factors was present in a more limited number of cases.

2. Parents' first reaction to incidents which initiated the interaction was general, a low-level noncorporal response—an admonition, threats, scolding, discussion, repetition of the request or demand for a modification of the child's behavior, time out, etc.

3. The child's behavior in response to the parent's initial intervention stimulated escalation of the subsequent parental response in the direction of greater punitiveness. Children talked back, ignored initial parental intervention, challenged the parent, failed to respond in the expected direction. Feeling frustrated by the child's response, as well as by the behavior which instigated intervention in the first place, the interaction escalated toward abuse.

4. In most instances, parents had a deliberate, explicit disciplinary objective in mind in involving themselves in the interaction culminating in abuse. Their instrumental intent was to obtain a modification of the child's behavior which they perceived as needing changing. Less frequently, parents had an expressive objective in mind—relieving anger and frustration, satisfaction in punishing the child, pleasure in the cathartic release of feelings.

5. The largest percentage of parents reacted negatively to their own behavior in the abusive incident, feeling anxiety, guilt, a sense of shame at their loss of control. Despite this, in some instances, if given the opportunity to relive the incident, they indicated that they would have repeated their behavior with the proviso that they would not have gone so far, would have been more controlled and temperate. While they see corporal punishment as ineffective in achieving their objectives, they see alternative disciplinary procedures as having been tried with equal futility.

6. Even after the event and the intervention of, and contact with, the protective-service agency, parents tended to perceive their behavior as having an essentially disciplinary intent rather than being abusive. While the community, as represented by the agency, sees the behavior as expressive and unsanctioned, the parents see their behavior as instrumental and having sanction in accordance with parents' rights and responsibilities.

CHAPTER 7

CONCLUSIONS AND IMPLICATIONS FOR PRACTICE

THE STUDY IS CONCERNED WITH a descriptive analysis of the stimulus-response interaction of the parent-child participants in a clearly identified abuse event, from the point of initiation of the interaction culminating in abuse to termination of the interactional episode.

Some of the explicit intent in selecting our focus for study was the effort to redress what we regard as a serious imbalance in the child abuse literature.

To a very considerable extent, the child abuse literature focuses almost exclusively on the parent and the parent's behavior. The child is a shadowy ghostlike figure who figures primarily, when he does come into focus, as the passive recipient of the parent's aggressive action. The event is described and analyzed with the parent's abusive behavior as the starting point. The child's antecedent behavior to which the parent's behavior is a response is almost totally ignored, as though it were a matter of indifference. Yet it is impossible to understand the parent's behavior, from the parent's point of view, unless we have some understanding of the situation which evoked the parent's abusive response.

We indicated in chapter 2 that we took a bidirectional orientation to parent-child relationships generally, and that such an orientation was a potentially productive focus for studying child abuse. We thought that abuse might be seen as the product of bidirectional transactions between parents and children—neither party totally passive, but each actively contributing in some measure to the event as it started, developed, and terminated.

We visualized the abuse event not as the exclusive product of either abuser or abused, but as the result of a complex interactive process between them. Neither is totally responsible; neither is totally innocent. The behavior of each of the participants in the abuse event is both a response to, and a stimulus for, the behavior of the reciprocal.

Furthermore the literature on child abuse has paid far more attention to the more peripheral psychodynamic developmental, social, and cultural variables in attempting to explain child abuse, with an almost total indifference to the immediate, contextual, phenomenological variables.

Our supposition is that the more remote the locus of the variable from the abuse event itself, the more attenuated is the effect of the impact of that variable in determining the actual behavior in the event. This suggested not only a focus on bidirectional interactional aspects of abuse, but some choice in the point selected for study in the ongoing relationship between parent and child. We chose, as our focus, the details of the abuse incident itself. The immediate specifics related to the incident itself are seen as time-limited and episodic, set apart from the day-to-day routine, from the typical interaction which characterizes the parent-child relationship. For a moment in time, several different considerations come together which result in child abuse—one atypical interaction in the thousands of repetitive interaction episodes between parent and child. Abuse is a specifically delimited behavioral event with identifiable points of starting and ending.

As Frude notes:

Since abuse is an action, an event with typically rather specific and discrete time characteristics . . . it is necessary to focus on a more limited time base . . . seeing abuse as an aggressive reaction to the immediate situation rather than focusing on more "distant" salient variables. (1979:903)

Abuse episodes have some of the characteristics of short-lived crisis situations. There is, for a limited period of time, a pivotal break in the usual procedure in coping with a difficult situation, and a period of instability associated with a decisive change in behavior.

The abuse incident itself is in the nature of a crisis event—a sharp upsetting change from a steady state. An equilibrium, however tenuously established and maintained, comes apart over a limited period of time; a period of disequilibrium follows during which abuse is initiated, acted out and terminated, and a new equilibrium is established after the end of the abuse event.

As in any crisis situation, some problem, some stress is encountered (in this case, the behavior of the child which requires a response) which does not yield to the utilization of the customary, familiar methods of problem solving. The problem remains unresolved after the habitual responses have been unsuccessfully applied. The stressful situation, per se, is perceived as threatening—to ego, to status, to self-esteem—triggering aggressive feelings. Further, the inability to resolve it satisfactorily intensifies feelings of tension, frustration, inadequacy, helplessness, and hopelessness, which further intensify feelings of anger to a higher level, more accurately described as rage. Such feelings in crisis situations have been noted to result in "some regressions of ego function to a more primitive level and to more childlike types of behavior" (Golan 1978:66).

As in other crisis situations, stress is more likely to lead to loss of equilibrium and homeostatic balance if the subject encounters the precipitating incident when he is in a vulnerable state. The precipitating factor—in the case of abuse, the child's behavior—is generally a link in the "chain of stress-provoking events that convert a hazardous state into disequilibrium" (*Ibid*:66), a state of active crisis. The same behaviors encountered by the subject when he was not as vulnerable to being negatively affected by them might not have precipitated any sharp change, and a previous equilibrium might have been successfully maintained.

This, in general, was our orientation and focus: what was happening between parents and children that initiated a particular series of interactions which eventuated in clearly defined incidents of abuse.

The project was concerned with a review of 830 substantiated reports of physical child abuse perpetrated by parents in 1974 and 1975 in Wisconsin, and with detailed interviews with 66 parents identified as abusive. A comparison of information available on the parents, the children, and the abuse incident selected for study with information available in national reports on physical child abuse indicates that the study group is representative of abuse families nationwide.

In studying the state reports and in the extended interviews, which employed a structured pretested format, our focus was on the details of the abuse incident itself and the parent-child interaction in the incident.

The principal general conclusion which emerges from the study is that abuse incidents initiate with some behavior on the part of the child, which the parent, correctly or incorrectly, justifiably or unjustifiably, perceives as aversive, and as requiring some intervention to change. In many of the cases, there were other factors noted, some remote, some immediate, associated with the abuse incident—situational stress factors, psychodynamic factors, cultural factors. But no factor was so universal, so ubiquitous, as some identifiable behavior on the part of the child which precipitated the parent-child interactional sequence culminating in abuse. In 91 percent of the abuse incidents noted in the 830 reports, and in each one of the 66 interviews, such a behavioral antecedent of the abuse event was identified.

The principal finding that some particular behavior on the part of the child perceived as aversive by the parent is a necessary starting point for an interactional episode culminating in abuse is supported by a study by Libbey and Bybee (1979). The general configuration presented in the interviews of an interactional sequence, initiated by some aversive or noxious behavior on the part of the child, in which parental intervention, implementing instrumental intentions, become progressively more punitive, receives some support from other studies (Minton, Kagan, and Levine 1971).

Not only were children's behaviors, both as a stimulus and a response to parental behaviors, a factor in initiating the particular interaction that culminated in reported abuse, but, further, children's behaviors affected the course of the interaction during the process from initiation to termination of the incident.

There is little evidence in these interviews that unwarranted malice, deliberate sadism, or deep-rooted, persistent animosity toward the child prompted parental abuse. Invariably, there was some behavior on the part of the child which served to instigate an interactional, stimulus-response chain of interdependent actions culminating in abuse. Rarely does the parent's behavior appear to be primarily arbitrary or based on whim.

The picture of a parent with a generalized anger searching for a target and selecting the child as scapegoat because he is conveniently available, and because he has an inordinate degree of power over the child, needs some correction.

As this point, it might be necessary to make clear what we are *not* saying. First, we are not saying that children are "to blame" for being abused. Secondly, we are not saying that factors other than the behaviors of parents and children that do not immediately relate to the abuse event itself are inconsequential or unimportant in furthering our understanding of abuse.

Here, as elsewhere in dealing with social problems, the least productive approach is to be concerned with assigning blame. Our effort is to understand as fully as possible the nature of the situation we have some responsibility for changing. Further, the fact that the child might, in fact, be an active participant in the interactional process which results in abuse does not in any way excuse parental abuse. The fact that seven children in the interview study had to be hospitalized for treatment of their injuries is testimony to the danger such situations present for children. While the findings may enable the worker to empathize more adequately with, and understand more clearly, the parent's reaction, it does not absolve the parent from the responsibility of intervening in a less destructive manner.

The fact that both parents and children are active participants in the abuse event does not imply that they are co-acting equals or co-equal actors. It is clear that parents have more authority and power to direct the action, that they have more experience and ability in directing the action and that they have more responsibility for directing the action. The child is objectively dependent on the parent. Legal sanction, control of, and authority over, the child rests with the parent. Parents are in a stronger, more potent, position to influence the child, to enforce compliance, to require that the child adjust and adapt to them rather than the reverse. The available evidence confirms the fact of this difference in power potential in favor of the parents (Hoffman, 1975) and supports the hypothesis that while the parent-child relationship is interactional, the parents' characteristics and attitudes are generally more saliant than the child's characteristics, or objective behavior, in determining how the interaction will proceed (Minton, Kagen, Levine 1971; Vaughn, Dienard, Egeland 1980).

It might be said that the nature of the child's behavior can be regarded as inconsequential. A parent predisposed to abuse in response to his/her own needs will see *any* child behavior, however innocuous, as an appropriate stimulus for aggression, and retrospectively justify abuse by citing the child's behavior, whatever it is, as sufficient instigation. It does not take much of a precipitant to start an explosion in a gas-filled room.

To do further justice to the complexity of the problem, it should be recognized that the child's behavior is objectively neutral. It is the parents' perception of the behavior, and their attitude toward the behavior, which define it, for them, as aversive or not, and which then determine their feelings in response. But it also should be recognized that most parents have been socialized in the same cultural matrix which imposes some standards regarding the reciprocal functions and responsibilities of parent and child in the parent-child relationships. Consequently there are many kinds of child behaviors which, for a very large percentage of parents, are uniformly perceived as noxious and aversive. Persistent disobedience, prolonged crying and nagging, persistent negativism, destructiveness, lying, stealing, sassing, aggressive behavior toward parents, siblings, and peers, failure to perform chores, school failure and truancy, precocious or atypical sexual behavior, pot smoking, drinking, etc., can be expected to evoke angry, anxious, disapproving responses in most parents. In very few instances in the study was the abuse event interaction initiated by what might be consensually defined as "inconsequential" behavior.

Traditionally social workers have attempted an understanding of those groups in the population whose behavior has been regarded by the general community as atypical, non-normative, tending toward deviance. This is an element of the value system of the profession but, in addition, has a strong pragmatic component. Since social workers are charged with the responsibility of working with the delinquent, the alcoholic, the drug abuser, the unmarried mother, the homosexual, the mentally disabled, etc., our efforts to understand their behaviors is a practice requirement. Without such understanding, efforts to effect change are likely to fail.

Some of the public negative attitude toward social work results from the effort to communicate to the public our understanding of where such groups of people are coming from. The statement of understanding is received as a statement of exculpation, excusing the behavior to which the community reacts negatively. Social workers were members of the general community before they became social workers and as social workers retain some component of lay attitudes. Social workers find it easier to understand, and show a greater readiness to understand, some kinds of non-normative behavior than other kinds. We extend ourselves further in efforts to understand the unmarried mother, the alcoholic, the mentally disabled than we do in efforts to understand the rapist, the wife batterer, and the child abuser. There is, even for social workers, a hierarchy of understandable behaviors since, for us too, understanding suggests forgiveness, exoneration. Some of the previous reluctance in exploring the aspects of child abuse reviewed here might be related to these considerations.

The risk that a focus on the active participation of both parties in the child abuse event might be misinterpretated as "excusing" inexcusable behavior is a danger that needs to be recognized. Such a risk is exceeded only by the potential damage resulting from failure to achieve a more accurate understanding of the abuse event deriving from a reluctance to consider possibly significant factors because such consideration might violate our ideological preconceptions or preferences. This is an abrogation of professional responsibility and, ultimately, a disservice to the client group.

Second, in making explicit what we are *not* saying, noting that both the record review and interview data suggest that child-abuse interactions begin as a consequence of some noxious, aversive behavior on the part of the child is not to say that other considerations are unimportant. Developmental, situational, and ideological factors were operative in behaviors generated during the abusive incident, and were illustrated in interview data. Such factors give direction to the way anger is expressed, and they are incremental elements in the intensity of feeling expressed. But, in each case, these factors, when present, were activated in aggressive behavior directed toward the child only when there was some manifestation of aversive behavior on the part of the child, which aroused aversive feelings. Developmental, situational, and ideological factors serve as latent, inactive potentials for abuse. The child's behavior serves to energize these factors. The sine qua non for initiation of an abusive event was, in each instance studied, some behavior on the part of the child. This is the decisive, compelling, essential factor; other considerations are accessory, supplementary, subsidiary factors. In the absence of a precipitant in the form of some child behavior, predispositions may not be manifested in abuse.

While the child's behavior was not always the sole factor determining the pattern of interaction, and while there were often other contributing factors which shaped the outcome, the child's behavior was in the very largest percentage of instances the necessary, if not always the sufficient, factor in the abuse configuration.

Reading and analyzing the interview develops a greater respect for the potency of the most immediate contextual variables, as against developmental or situational stress variables, in determining the interaction in an episodic event such as child abuse. What is happening at the moment, the immediate interactional configuration—the immediate stimulus instigating and requiring an immediate response—seems to be much more significant for determining how the interaction unfolds than are the more remote psychodynamic, ideological, situational factors. This, once again, is not an either-or statement. It does not suggest that ideological developmental or situational stress factors are not incrementally significant in shaping the interaction which eventuates in abuse. It merely points to the *relatively* greater importance of immediate contextual variables in explaining why an abuse sequence should get started at some particular point in time. The most parsimonious explanation lies in interaction in the event itself.

This parallels Clifford's findings in a home controlled-observation study of child discipline which attempted to assess the relative potency of "extrinsic factors considered to be external to the disciplinary situation per se, but which might be expected to affect it," as compared with factors relating to the disciplinary situation itself. The data "pointed conclusively to the fact that extrinsic factors have very little bearing on the occurrence of discipline" (1959:78).

In understanding abuse, then, we would need to give greater consideration to the immediate contextual variables that shape the abuse event as it is instigated and as it develops. The explanation of the event more nearly lies in the event itself.

The fact that we made a deliberate effort to explore the presence of these additional factors in the incidents which were the subjects of our interview indicates that we do not mean to discount them. However, we think these factors need to be put in a different perspective and the immediate contextual variables given some greater visibility and priority.

The findings suggest, then, that to a greater extent than is generally given recognition, a component of child abuse behavior is immediate context-derived and context-contingent.

It suggests a modification of, or an amendment to, the approach to child abuse which now gives clear prominence, if not exclusivity, to the personality characteristics and attributes of participants and the long term social situation as the pre-potent explanatory variables by the need to give additional consideration to situational specifics related to the abuse event.

This is not to engage in the "state" versus "trait," "dispositional" versus "situational," controversy on the side of situationalism (Bowen, 1973). There is no question for us that the abuse event is affected both by the personality and character participants bring to the event and by their interaction with the immediate situation.

The most consensually accepted axiom in social work is that behavior is codetermined—a function of both the person and the environment. But environment can refer to the persistent enduring macro-environment of job, housing, income, or it can refer to the immediate episodic, micro-situation in which a person finds himself and to which he needs to respond. It is this later definition of environment, the immediate antecedent stimuli in the person-environment equation, that we are raising for greater visibility here.

Having been introduced to the event after the culmination expressed as abuse, the very natural tendency of the protective service worker is to perceive the event from that vantage point. Attempting to see the process sequentially, as we have attempted here, provides an additional, different perspective.

Lennard and Bernstein present an analogy which is instructive:

A man who is trying to get out of a crowded parking lot may initially be observed as careful in his moves, making way for other cars and in good humor. He remains unaggressive in the face of contradictory directions and commands coming to him from other impatient drivers. After a series of episodes, however, he becomes less careful, less willing to let others pass, and less willing to be told whether to move forward or back. Finally, he loses his temper (passes a stochastic threshold) and drives recklessly through the traffic, shouting at the other drivers to move here and there. An observer coming upon the scene at this time might infer that the driver was an unstable person, with little control over his impulses and reckless in his disregard for the rights and safety of himself and others. . . .

This model, involving a cumulative effect, appears to be relevant to the understanding of many interaction systems . . . Consider a parent's instruction to a child to clean his room, which is repeatedly disregarded. The longer the parent's command is ignored, the more likely the parent is to lose his temper and start to scold. An observer's judgment of a given parent's patience and stability would depend upon what phase of the interaction he witnessed—whether he was there from the start or happened on the scene at a late phase in the sequence of disregarded instructions. (1969:35)

We recognize that this approach to the child-abuse event, with the emphasis on the immediate process and on the joint contributions of parent and child, fails to do justice to the complexity of the abuse situation. But then, given the profound heterogeneity of abusive parents, abused children and abuse situations included under the rubric, we would seriously question whether any one approach, however comprehensive, can by itself provide an adequate explanation. We need a variety of complementary perspectives and offer this as one which has some explanatory potency. It may act as a corrective, sensitizing the observer to factors which previously had been given limited consideration.

On Validity of the Data

It might be expected that parents identified as abusive might attempt to excuse themselves by shifting responsibility for the event onto the child. The child's behavior might be cited in exculpation of disciplinary excesses. Or they might seek to redefine their behavior so that it is more likely to be sanctioned by appeal to higher principles. The "abuse" is perceived "as part of necessary and morally justified discipline, the intent of discipline being to establish appropriate social and moral conduct" (Parke and Collmer 1975:32).

There may very well be some element of this in the parents' descriptions of the abuse event. It is said that everyone has his excuses, and heart and mind are imaginatively employed so that we feel justified in what we have done and find it acceptable to ourselves. This process was, of course, operating here in the parents' recapitulation of their experiences. However, the fact that the interview material and agency record material, when checked against each other, showed a high level of congruency, the fact that the interviewers, social workers with considerable clinical experience, rated the information obtained in most of the interviews as reliable, would suggest that there is considerable validity in the interview data. The fact that the parents so often shared unflattering aspects of their lives suggested that they were not highly concerned with being self-protective and self-serving. The researchers were strangers who, representing a university research group, had no possibility of either harming or helping. This may have freed the parents to share the "truth" as they saw it.

The interview procedure was designed to facilitate retrospective introspection and to reduce distortion due to forgetting. The accepting, empathic approach of the experienced social work interviewers was designed to reduce deliberate falsification. Unconsciously motivated distortions are more difficult to correct.

To some extent, there is a double standard regarding child abuse inter-view information. The literature accepts without much reservation the abusive parents' accounts of their own childhood abuse experiences. The generally accepted axiom that abused children grow up to become abusive parents is based primarily, and without question, on interview data obtained from parents about events remote in time and concerned with poorly defined behaviors. None of the studies which cite such data provide any objective records or observational validating material. It is a tribute to our ideological biases that we readily accept these accounts in which abusive parents have a defensive interest, since it tends to "excuse" their behavior, while being critically predisposed to reject the validity of the parent's account of the abuse event shared in the interview, where this involves the child as an active participant in the event.

Implications for Practice: Toward Empathic Understanding

One of the cardinal principles of the helping professions is the necessity of starting where the client is. The problem lies in understanding where the client is to start with. Studies of client and social-worker perceptions of their joint endeavors often reveal a very wide gap between the client and worker's definition of the same situation (Mayer and Timms 1970; Maluccio 1979a).

This appears to be the case in the protective service encounter regard-ing physical abuse. One principal implication of this study for protective service practice is that of calling attention to the difference in definition of the situation as expressed by parents in the interviews as compared with the worker's definition of the situation.

Violence does not mean any use of force in a social situation; other-wise, the policeman's use of force would be regarded as violence. Vio-lence is the use of force in situations where the community defines the use of such force as illegitimate. Unless there is agreement that the use of force in a particular situation is illegitimate, it is not defined as violence (Rule et al. 1975; Rule and Nesdale 1976). We can expect the violent person to change his behavior only if he accepts the community's defini-tion of his behavior as violent and hence unsanctioned. Abuse is a partic-ular form of violence. Whether or not the use of force in parent-child relations is regarded as violence depends on whether the community defines the use of force in the parent-child relationship as without legitimate sanction. Throughout most of history, the use of force in the parent-child relationship context was not defined as violence, because the use of force by parents against children was regarded as legitimate. Presently, while the community defines such a use of force as violence, hence, abuse, the parent may not. The community and the agency definition of abuse may be very much at variance with the parent's definition of his behavior. Given his view of the situation as a legitimate employment of force for disciplinary reasons, he is not likely to feel any need to change his behavior.

What the agency defines as abuse—force without any legitimate sanction engaged in to satisfy the needs of the parents—may be defined by the parent as legitimate force engaged in to serve the ultimate needs of the child.

The largest percentage of the parents interviewed saw their intent as primarily instrumental and the largest component of their behavior as a manifestation of legitimate use of force. This is in contradiction to the agency and worker categorization of their behaviors as expressive and illegitimate, beyond community sanction.

However much we may disagree with the abusive parent's definition of the situation, unless we are aware of the way such parents may define the situation, we are very unlikely to be able to empathically discuss their behavior with them with any hope of effecting change. The fact is that unless we understand the event from the parents' point of view, we cannot understand their lack of motivation to change. From the point of view of the reporting agency, it is abuse. But from the point of view of the parent, it may be a justifiable and necessary exercise of parental responsibility and authority. Rather than acting as irresponsible parents, they may see themselves as responding to the child's behavior as responsible parents concerned with maintaining domestic tranquility, with public morality, and with the child's future. When such behavior is defined by others as abuse, in defense of the child, these parents may see themselves as abused and controlled by the child and abused and controlled by the agency. The fact that a large percentage of the parents interviewed said they would do the same thing again—albeit perhaps with greater moderation and control—even after they had already been in contact with the agency for some time, indicates the fact that they had not accepted the worker's definition of the situation.

The difference in definition and the resistance this difference evokes is vigorously expressed by one mother. Her child, a girl of 15, had reported the fact that her mother slapped her face to the school social worker and the agency had intervened. The woman asks:

> What right has a parent got? According to Annie's law, Annie's way of thinking, you have—all right, you're my mother. You're my dad. But you have no right to hit me, you have no right to discipline me, you have no right to tell me when to come home. You have no right to tell me how late to work. Well, then, what am I here for, as a parent? Then Annie might as well be living by herself. I says to the fellow from the Child Protective Agency, I says, you mean I have no right to discipline my child? He said, "That's what I'm telling you." I said, "Then tell me what I'm supposed to do." Because I felt I have a right as a parent. I have a right to tell my daughter what time she comes—how late she works, because she is only 15. And then I also felt that I have a right to tell her what time she has to come home at night if she does go out to a show or anything. 'Cause there is 11 o'clock curfew law, and Annie feels that she can come and go as she wants, do what she wants. So what am I supposed to do if she doesn't listen?

As Maluccio notes in an interview study of clients and workers in a family service agency,

clients and workers come to their encounter with different frames of reference which influence their involvement in the process and their views on its outcome, in persistent and impressive ways. There is need to consider the potential significance for practice these findings have. (1979b:400)

Viewing the encounter from widely different points of views makes communication between worker and client very difficult and makes some degree of misunderstanding inevitable.

Acceptance of corporal punishment as a disciplinary procedure is directly related to child abuse. Most instances of child abuse encountered in this study were, in effect, extensions of disciplinary actions, which, at some point and often inadvertently, crossed the ambiguous line between sanctioned corporal punishment and unsanctioned child abuse. While parental use of force is accepted, "excessive" use of force is not. There is no clear definition, however, which would indicate when the quality or quantity of force employed becomes excessive.

The point of transition from which socially sanctioned corporal punishment becomes a socially deviant activity—child abuse—has yet to be clearly defined.

At the extreme ends of the continuum of parental care-taking behavior there is some consensual agreement as to what is "clearly acceptable" and what is "clearly unacceptable." Unfortunately, only a small percentage of physical abuse instances fall in the clearly defined areas of the continuum. The largest percentage of reports fall in the gray zones where a decision has to be made, using controversial, ambiguous and shifting guidelines as to what is 'excessive discipline,' 'inappropriate discipline,' when parental prerogatives have been exceeded and the child's inherent rights have been denied. It is difficult to define deviation from the cultural norms of child care where such norms lack clear consistency and coherence. Court decisions and school practices support a general acceptance of corporal punishment as a disciplinary procedure. Legal decisions suggest that when corporal punishment is moderate and reasonable, when it is engaged in with the ultimate welfare of the child as its principal purpose, when discretion and good judgment are used, it is sanctioned as being a prerogative of parents and parental agents, such as teachers. It is evident, upon reading, that the statement is loaded with ambiguous terms open to a variety of interpretations.

Asked to rate a series of seven vignettes describing different incidents of physical abuse, over 300 professionals concerned with child abuse agreed on the level of seriousness of five incidents. There was "complete disagreement" on two incidents, which indicated controversy on the threshold of mistreatment—when sanctioned physical discipline became child abuse (Giovannoni and Becerra 1979:136). Few professionals defined commonplace spanking as child abuse ("The parents usually punish their child by spanking him with the hand, leaving red marks on the child's skin").

Since the authorities themselves differ on the boundary of transition between acceptable corporal punishment and unacceptable physical abuse, it is to be expected that parents may often be in doubt. They may, therefore, contest in their own mind the agency's definition of their action as child abuse. The lack of consensus makes for a heterogeneity of norms from which the parent can select the one toward which he is disposed.

There is considerable controversy as to whether corporal punishment as a disciplinary procedure is equally acceptable to nonwhite parents as contrasted with white parents, lower-class parents as compared with middle-class parents. For our purposes here, the important distinction of difference should be made between the attitudes toward corporal punishment of the protective service workers and the client group of parents. In a study in which both social workers and members of the lay community were asked for their reactions to a series of vignettes regarding child maltreatment, social workers ranked physical abuse as the most serious of the varieties of maltreatment presented. Community respondents ranked physical abuse as lowest in seriousness of the forms of maltreatment. Their level of rating was considerably below that of the social workers (Giovannoni and Beccera 1979:51, 194).

Parents do not share, to the same degree of intensity, some of the feelings about corporal punishment which might inhibit the use of such a disciplinary option if the same situation were to have been encountered by the worker.

The definition of "abuse" has been progressively broadened so that parental behavior previously tolerated or ignored is now the subject for community intervention. Disciplinary procedures which were previously regarded as normative for some groups in the population or defined merely as different, are now defined as deviant. But a large percentage of the target population of "abuse" interventions has not made the same shift in redefinition of their behavior. The discrepancy in perception of the event between worker and client make effecting change difficult, if not unlikely.

We need to give more recognition to the fact that the parent, in dealing with his child, knows the situation much more definitively than we can ever know it. The parent tests our definition of the situation against his own more intimate, detailed knowledge of the child, the child's behavior, the limits of what he sees as possible and feasible, the situational context in which the parent-child relationship is enacted, etc. Propositions which seem conclusive and defensible to us may seem inappropriate or erroneous to them. The parent's "ordinary" knowledge of the situation may conflict with our, perhaps more scientifically based, procedures. "Ordinary" knowledge in such a case has more validity for the parent and however polite and outwardly receptive he may appear to be to what we are saying, it may have limited credibility to him (Lindblom and Cohen 1979). Discrepancies between the agency's and the parent's perception may be perceived by the parent as a lack of understanding on the part of agency representatives. Viewing the agency as naïve and misguided, the parent has little confidence in the worker's communications and they have little power in influencing him.

This is particularly true if we fail to include in our definition of the situation some consideration of what is perhaps the most salient factor for the parent's definition, namely, the child's behavior as the instigating antecedent of the abuse event. When this factor is given active consideration, the definition of the situation for the professional tends to shift closer to that of the parents.

Where the child's behavior preceding and related to abuse is given greater explicitness and visibility in an account of abuse, professionals are likely to be much less inclined to label parental behavior as abuse, and their definition of the situation shifts closer to that of the client parent group. Thus, when descriptions of children's unacceptable behavior were included in vignettes offered 313 professionals (lawyers, social workers, police, pediatricians), this tended to decrease their ratings of seriousness of the parent's abusive response (Giovannoni and Becerra 1979:111).

Hopper similarly found, in presenting a series of incidents taken from protective-service files to 82 professionals, that the percentage of the group classifying a situation as child abuse was lowered when a description of aversive child behavior associated with abuse was included (1976:143).

Libbey and Bybee raise this question in discussing the physical abuse of adolescents. "Is a bruise from being hit by a belt 'discipline' rather than abuse *if* the incident was preceded by rule-breaking or law-breaking behavior?" (1979:104).

Questions of "provocation" and "justification" are generally not raised in discussions of child abuse primarily in response to the erroneous perception that the very largest majority of abused children are infants or very young children. For such children there is neither "provocation" nor "justification" for abuse. However, questions regarding "provocation" and "justification" may be considered more relevant variables with increasing age of the abused child. The presumption of complete child passivity becomes less tenable with increasing age of the abused child into adolescence.

There is substantial evidence that while corporal punishment and other power assertive disciplining procedures have some value in the socialization process under limited conditions and in specific contexts, they are, by and large, less effective and certainly less equitable than other procedures in achieving the objectives of parenting. However, abusive parents who were interviewed frequently perceived corporal punishment as instrumentally effective. Gelles also found that parents use violence instrumentally to "teach and control" and as a "form of discipline to punish misbehavior" (1972:63) and that corporal punishment is often "used when no other method works" (p. 65).

Steinmetz found a pattern of escalation in the disciplinary procedures of families she interviewed which replicate our findings. "Spanking frequently was seen as a method of last resort" (1977:67). While corporal punishment was considered to have failed to resolve the parent-child conflict in 14 percent of the cases, it was regarded by parents as a "successful" intervention in 64 percent of the cases and partially successful in 14 percent of the cases (1977:69).

Lytton and Zwirner charted the parent child disciplinary interaction on the basis of 6 hours of observation of 136, 2-3 year old white boys. The researchers attempted to discover the response of the child to different parental interventions in disciplinary situations. Analyzing a variety of verbal and behavioral interventions by the mother on the complaint or noncompliant behavior of the child, the authors found that physical control (slap or physically restraining or restricting) had a more powerful effect on the child than other kinds of interventions ("command," "prohibition," "suggestion," "reasoning") both for compliance and noncompliance (1975:773–777). Physical intervention made things happen. The researchers, interestingly enough, are somewhat apologetic about their "antihumanist conclusion" (p. 779). They further note that their study was "situation bound" so that long range effects which might be negative were not studied. However, the relevance of this study for our discussion is that physical interventions do have potency for immediate accomplishment of parental disciplinary objectives—something that parents frequently discover on their own in single-subject-design, disciplinary "experiments." This, once again, points to a difference in definition of the situation between worker and client which needs to be taken into consideration in our approach to them.

The high failure rate of protective service agency interventions noted in chapter 2 (pp. 29–37) may be, in part, attributable to these difference in the definition of the situation. Interventions have been most successful with a limited selective group of abusive parents—the Parents Anonymous membership—who have accepted the agency's definition of the situation. Membership requires accepting the label of abusive parent as this is generally defined by the literature.

Such acceptance is not true of the very largest percentage of abuse-reported parents. For the bulk of abusive parents, expectations of internally motivated change would initially require, it seems to us, meeting the client first on his own ground, seeing the situation more clearly as he sees it. This does not imply accepting the abusive parent's views of the situation. But an effective dialogue leading toward change cannot even begin until the worker understands the abuse event as the parent experienced it. What we have offered here is an explication of the abuse event as described by the parent so as to contribute toward such a more emphatically effective understanding of the client's situation on the part of the worker.

Protective service workers often note that it is difficult to be empathically understanding and accepting of abusive parents. Services suffer as a consequence of the inevitable limits of even the best worker's level of tolerance. Understanding and acceptance might be enhanced if workers were more sensitive to the stressful provocation encountered by some abusive parents as a consequence of the child's behavior. A better understanding of the totality of the abuse configuration might then result in more effective service to abusive parents as workers develop greater empathy and acceptance. Such information might be included in in-service training programs of protective service workers, and as content in educational supervision, to heighten sensitivity to the interactional nature of child abuse and correct an overdetermined unidirectional focus.

If empathic understanding is one of the crucial facilitating prerequisites for guiding protective service workers' interventions so that there is some probability of having a therapeutic impact, if a variety of procedures frequently employed by protective service workers in interactions with abusive parents (i.e., verbal following, reflecting, summarizing, interpreting, supporting) depend on a clear undersatnding of clients in interaction with their social situation, if we are admonished, correctly, that it is necessary to start where the client is, then, despite behaviors which are difficult to accept, the obligation is to understand as objectively as possible.

In trying to understand more fully "where the parents are coming from," we may not have fully appreciated the extent to which the family context is inherently high risk for violence. Gelles and Straus (1979) have pointed to some of the relevant considerations to which parents often alluded in the interviews. These characteristic aspects of family organization and interaction make for decidedly different interpretations of the same behavior, depending on whether one is inside the family system, as is the client, or outside the family system, as is the worker.

We recognize the family setting as the legitimate context for the display and expression of the strongest, most intimate feelings and behaviors. Emotional interchange is more intense here than in any other setting. This is true for both positive and negative emotions. The people with whom we have the most highly charged emotional relationship have the greatest power to delight us, to move us, to hurt us. We can tolerate with more comfortable indifference behaviors of other children which provoke emphatic responses in us when displayed by our own children. Because of affectional ties, children have greater power than others to hurt, to shame, to excite guilt and anxiety.

The vehemence of response to the child's behavior is further intensified by the generally expressed idea that the parent's capacity in parenting is reflected in the child's behavior. Aversive, unacceptable child behavior is not only a matter of concern in its own right, but is further a source of shame and derogation of the parent.

It is difficult for someone not affectively tied to the child—like the worker—to appreciate the intensity of feelings of pain and/or shame aroused by what appears to the observer to be rather inconsequential behavior. To say that the behavior elicits an "inappropriate" or "excessive" response is the assessment made by a neutral observer not affectively connected with the child and not being subjected to the actual pressures of the child's behavior. It is a normative statement made at some distance removed in time, place, and emotionality from the behavior as it impacts on the parent. To the parent, the same behavior may be perceived as considerably more aversive and provocative.

The parental role requires continuing exposure to aversive stimuli without the possibility of removing oneself from impact. One can leave a job that is aversive; terminate contact with an acquaintance who annoys us; divorce a spouse who provokes anger. Parents cannot divorce a child, terminate the relationship.

Parents cannot ignore the child's behavior; they cannot opt out of dealing with it, or walk away from the situation. They cannot easily negotiate compromise or conciliation with the child, particularly the younger child. They are locked into the necessity of dealing with recurring aversive situations requiring their continuing response.

The parent is forced to remain rather consistently in contact with the child; there is limited possibility of reducing the level of instigation to aggression by decay or dissipation of aroused feelings. Undissipated residuals of previous frustrating experiences summate with newly experienced frustration to keep the overall level of instigation to aggression high. A series of noxious experiences between parent and child may not result in abuse until the fifth or eighth incident, when a sufficiently high additive level of instigation to aggression is reached to overcome the summation of all factors inhibiting the expression of violence. The aversive behavior most immediately related to the reported abuse in and of itself may not appear to be of any consequence, and the response may appear "excessive" and "inappropriate" to any reasonable objective observer. But this perception of the situation ignores the less immediate, but actively operative, instigations to aggression previously experienced.

Most social roles are concerned with a limited sector of activities. Being an employee, a student, a member of a political, religious, or social organization, involves contact with others around a particular group of activities. The parent-child relationship covers a much wider variety of activities—eating, sleeping, playing, working, toileting, teaching, and learning. The possibilities for conflict are consequently increased. Possibilities for conflict are further intensified by the fact that most other social roles involve participants of the same age and often of the same sex. The family involves interaction between participants of various ages and both sexes, increasing the possibilities for misunderstanding. Differences in needs, in perceptions of the same situation, in preferences, are apt to be wider here than in other social situations. The "Generation Gap" is an exemplification of this additional inherent aspect of family life, making it high risk for violence.

Parents and children may differ in their perception of the child's ability to engage in certain activities and the level of probability of danger for the child. The child may be overconfident; the parent may be excessively cautious. Parents, as a consequence of life experience and often their own personal history, are often more aware of both the immediate and long-range consequences for the child of certain behaviors. The child cannot have the long-range perspective the parent brings to the situation. But beyond all this, while children do suffer the consequences of a misjudgment of their abilities and their readiness for certain experiences, the parents are more directly blamed for this; and the parents have to pick up the pieces, deal with the situation, incur the expenses, inconvenience, and emotional hurt that may result from such misjudgments.

Reciprocal role responsibilities in the parent-child relationship system are inherently tilted in the direction of high risk of parental aggression against children. The exchange ratio is such that the parents give more than they get for a long period of time during the child's dependency. Parents generally accept this without feeling unduly exploited. But when the child, through his behavior, increases the costs of being a parent and decreases the rewards, this activates latent feelings of being treated unfairly, of being abused, and arouses strong feelings of anger. Exchange theory would suggest that such a configuration predisposes to aggression.

Parents bring ideas of distributive justice and reciprocity to the parent-child relationship. Within some general limitations set by age and level of development, they expect a child to do his part in contributing to satisfactions in the relationship, in the maintenance of the relationship. If the child makes demands that are greater than normatively anticipated, or when a child fails to cooperate and reciprocate when cooperation and reciprocation might legitimately be expected, punitive responses may seem justified to redress the balance.

While having some choice as to whether to have a child or not, the parent has no choice with reference to the actual child he does get. Parents are obligated to accept what nature offers and to regard all their children as equally acceptable. The reality of differential preferences creates a conflict for the parent between what he wants to do and what he has to do, generating anger against the less preferred child.

The family provides outlets for safer displacement of aggressive feelings originating outside of the family. This is true for both children and parents. Parents' hostility against a supervisor on the job, a fellow worker, acquaintance in the community, can be more safely discharged against children and spouse. The hostility children might feel toward a teacher or a peer may once again be expressed at lower risk against parents and siblings. The obligation to, and expectation of, acceptance and understanding of normatively unacceptable behavior by family members of each other allows them to let their hair down and be, less guardedly, their uninhibited selves.

As compared with other kinds of social settings in which people are repetitively involved—the work situation, social friendship groups, community or religious organizations—family interaction is less formally structured. The rules which dictate what one should or should not do are not as clearly delineated in the case of family interaction. Consequently, the limits of permissable behavior are broad and ambiguous. This gives sanction to, or at least does not interdict, more uninhibited behavior in the family situation.

Nuclear family housing arrangements generally guarantee a high measure of privacy, protecting the parents from any outside observation of their behavior, and thus freeing them from any inhibitions to aggression that might derive from the negative opinion of others.

In the privacy of the family, external restraints have very limited impact; inhibition of overt expression of aggression depends primarily on internally imposed restraints. An aggressive response to a particular child behavior manifested in the home would be inhibited in response to the same behavior in the supermarket or park, in the sight of community witnesses. Inhibitions to questionably acceptable responses to the child are thus weaker in the home as a consequence of privacy. Living with each other in unremitting intimacy and minimal privacy makes retreat and concealment of true feelings and behavioral impulses more difficult. Nuclear family arrangements not only ensure a greater measure of privacy but also diminish the number of potential alternative caretakers immediately available to offer relief to overburdened, overstressed parents.

The family, thus, requires forced, continuous contact in a wide variety of situations between individuals who feel very strongly about each other, and who, because of generational differences and different role responsibilities, may misunderstand each other. Instigation to aggression is higher in the family; inhibition against expression of aggression is lower in the family; nonviolent alternatives to overt expression of aggressive feelings in acts of violence are more limited in the family. The family setting couples maximum instigation to aggression with maximum opportunity for its expression. There should be little surprise, then, that the family is the scene of much violence.

There are, of course, strong forces inhibiting the expression of aggression within the family. Love and concern and empathy for the child, the caring evoked by helplessness and dependency, are countervailing forces. These are strengthened and supplemented by external constraints in the general social disapproval of parents who injure the child and neglect his needs—a disapproval expressed in the ultimate sanction involved in the legal possibility of termination of parental rights. Respect for a worker with whom a positive relationship has been established, and a desire to retain the worker's acceptance, act to inhibit violence against a child.

The deliberate emphasis here, for more empathic understanding, is on the instigations to parental aggression rather than the inhibiting variables. There is another reason related to the responsibilities given protective service agencies for the problem of child abuse for this selective emphasis. It suggests that agencies need to be more sanguine and conservative in what they can lead the public to expect in terms of problem resolution.

The problem is difficult not only because of elements intrinsic to the family context which predispose toward violence but also in terms of the statistical odds. The material we have presented suggests that the abuse event is a residual event. Parents have frequently tried to deal with the problems in a less punitive manner; and where such interventions succeed, abuse does not take place. Abuse is a testimonial to the failure of other procedures.

The number of disciplinary situations in which parents are involved over the course of the year is astronomical. There were some 64 million children under 18 in the United States in 1979. It is hard to know exactly how many disciplinary incidents are encountered by parents during the course of any one week. Clifford (1959), for instance, noted that parents, recording such incidents using standardized instructions, reported 3-year-old children involved in disciplinary incidents on the average of approximately once a day; 6 year olds every other day; 9 year olds every fourth day. If we, very conservatively, estimate ten incidents a year per child, there are 640 million incidents requiring resolution—incidents in which the child does something, or fails to do something, which impacts adversely on the parent, arousing anger, causing concern.

Employing the most varied disciplinary intervention, starting with the least punitive, the very largest number of these incidents are resolved by some procedure short of abuse. At the very least, the parent may suppress any feelings of anger or concern and ignore the situation, or the parents may intervene, employing the most benign procedures—praising alternative behavior, discussing, reflecting, feeling, empathically understanding. And a sizable percentage of the incidents requiring intervention may yield to these procedures, ending any need for further discipline. In the case of some incidents, with some children, these procedures prove to be ineffective and parents then move on to appealing, admonishing, coaxing; further, to nagging and shouting; and further still, to threatening. Another sizable percentage of the total number of incidents requiring discipline yield to these interventions. In the residual group of incidents, where previously cited procedures prove ineffective, the parent might employ progressively more punitive procedures—shaming, ridiculing, withholding love, withdrawing privileges, time-out. And an additional group of incidents are resolved, leaving a still smaller number of incidents requiring, or perceived as requiring, some action on the part of the parent. Having failed with the less intrusive, less punitive interventions, parents may employ mild, nonabusive corporal punishment, such as slapping and spanking. All of these less-than-abusive disciplinary procedures, from discussion, reflection, empathic understanding, through mild corporal punishment may be, in aggregate, successful in resolving the situation perceived as requiring discipline in 99 percent of the cases. This still, then, leaves some 6,400,000 situations—1 percent of the conservatively estimated 640,000,000 incidents requiring disciplinary intervention in the United States each year—that need to be dealt with by parents when all disciplinary interventions from the most benign to mild corporal punishment have been ineffectively attempted.

If parents had a success rate of 99 percent with all of the suggested procedures other than procedures which risk abuse—a phenomenal success rate for programs of intervention—it would still leave more than six million residual disciplinary events unresolved. In these instances, having employed without success those interventions which are progressively more punitive, parents in puzzlement and desperation are at high risk for abuse.

The numbers involved suggest the magnitude of the problem. To promise that the problem of child abuse can be resolved in any large measure is likely ultimately to result in loss of agency credibility.

Additional Implications, for Practice

Suggestions for practice at a less global level might be made, following from the findings:

1. We have noted the kinds of behaviors that are most frequently associated with abuse. Children who emit such behaviors with atypical frequency might then be regarded as high risk for abuse. Knowing that parents are particularly sensitive to, and more than ordinarily likely to be

aroused by such behaviors, might enable one to prepare parents in advance as to the anger they are likely to feel when they encounter such behaviors. Professionals in contact with such children might be alerted to the potentialities for abuse in such situations. We might, as a precautionary measure, familiarize the parents of such children with the availability of such services as relief surrogate parents if things get tense, or with the services of the local unit of Parents Anonymous. Identification of high-risk child behaviors is a necessary precursor of anticipation and preparation.

The practitioner oriented to behavior modification would, in working with parents, be in a better position to develop a hierarchy of desensitization to projected abusive events, with a clearer imagery of the nature of reciprocal interaction which leads to such incidents. Knowledge of the parent-child interaction in abuse incidents provides this.

2. We noted in chapter 1 that there are currently two general approaches toward effecting desired change in the abuse situation. One approach is directed toward effecting change in the parents, strengthening their ability to cope with stress, modifying their patterns of coping with stress through counseling, psychotherapy, casework. A second general approach is directed toward reducing stress impinging on the abuser family unit through provision of social utilities, social supports, facilitative services and broader opportunities. The research suggests a third approach in supplementation of those currently utilized. Aware of the kinds of behaviors which "provoke," "incite," and "instigate" abuse, efforts might then be made to help the child change his activities so that the child, as possible victim, imposes less stress on the parent as potential abuser. Behavior modification might be employed by the therapist, and by the parents as "cotherapists," to reduce the incidence of the child's parent-frustrating behaviors. More traditional psychotherapies might be employed to help the child toward clarification of, and insight into, those responses which create a danger for him in his interaction with his parents. Greater emphasis might be given to the child as the target of change. The simplest, quickest, and most effective way of reducing the possibility of child abuse is to eliminate those stimuli which elicit the instigations initiating the interaction which risks culminating in abuse— namely, the aversive behavior of the child.

Given the older age of the largest percentage of the children involved in abusive incidents, it is feasible to consider a program of instruction to

children as to how to respond to an aroused parent. Many nonabused children are nonabused because they have learned to deal with potentially abusive situations so as to ensure their safety. They have learned how to "psych out" their parent, knowing how far they can go before things begin to get dangerous, when to cool it, when to shut up. The abused child has often failed to learn what he needs to know in order to adapt to his parents. Perhaps the agency can teach this.

This puts part of the responsibility for preventing abuse on the child. But with increasing rights accorded the child, it is reasonable to expect greater responsibility of the child for the interaction in disciplinary events.

3. Further, the program of instruction developed on productive fair-fighting between marriage partners might be duplicated on the parent-child relationship level. Recognizing that we are not likely to be able to eliminate conflict between parents and children, such intervention would be directed toward reducing the probability of escalation toward abuse, once a conflict interaction has been initiated. The suggestion derives from the finding that many of the incidents escalated toward abuse not so much as a consequence of the behavior which initiated the interactional event but rather as a result of the defiant, retaliatory, aggressive responses manifested during the interaction.

4. We noted that very often the child's response to the parent is negative following the abuse event. Since abuse results in intensification of conflict and bad feeling between the parent and child, the parents are hurting as well as the children.

As Goode (1971) notes, the costs of the use of force in parent-child relationships—even if effective in achieving parental objectives—are high, because such force may destroy the possibility of achieving goals other than mere conformity, e.g., spontaneous affection and respect.

The parent's own perception of the frequent negative consequence of abuse might be employed as a lever to motivate him or her toward change. If procedures with less disadvantageous consequences can be employed by the parents to achieve their objectives, this may be of interest to the parents. The point of entree for the worker lies in the fact that for the most part, parents are not happy with what they have done to themselves, to the children, and to their relationship with their children. Bruises, welts, broken bones, and fractures represent not only regrettable damage to the child but are an advertisement visible to others, and to

themselves, of parents' inadequacies and loss of control. If possible, parents would prefer other, less damaging procedures.

5. The finding that abuse is not synonymous with total rejection provides the worker with another point of entree for effecting change. There is, for most of these parents, a positive component in their ambivalent attitude toward the child. There is affection and pleasure in the relationship. The worker can make these aspects of the relationship explicit and build on them in motivating the parent toward change.

6. Changing the child's behavior was, for many parents, the motive prompting abuse. For many, too, the intervention failed to achieve the objective. Parents felt frustrated as a consequence. Recognizing the disjoint between parents' objectives and achievement, the worker can, once again, utilize this as an entree for engaging parents in treatment. Accepting the parent's motives, the worker would help the parent develop skills in procedures that might be more effective.

7. We noted that parents have unsuccessfully tried a variety of interventions before resorting to abuse.

Rather than assuming that parents lack knowledge and skills in alternative interventions, it might be well for the worker to inquire about the use of other procedures. To suggest a disciplinary approach that the parent has already attempted without success, without having first checked with the parent, results in a loss of confidence in the worker.

8. Despite our tendency to reject the idea, it should be recognized, if we are to understand the parent, that in some percentage of cases punitive corporal discipline does achieve its objectives. It gets the behavior changed. Parents have experienced this in their own lives as they describe changes they made in response to parental corporal discipline. They experience it in their own life with their children as such punishments get some behavior stopped, other behavior started. To deny this is to reduce our credibility, once again, in the eyes of the client. It might be well for the worker to be aware of this possibility.

9. Part of the current effort of social workers is designed to induce acceptance by the abusive parents of a redefinition of the situation. We redefine the child's behavior so that it will not be perceived as a willful, consciously motivated attack on the parent—as the parent may define it. We redefine the child's behavior so that it can be seen as appropriate for a child of that age, correcting parents who have excessive expectations of a child. It may be necessary to more actively consider such an approach of

redefining the situation directed toward the parent's behavior. Parents who define their behavior as "discipline" and, as such, acceptable and sanctioned, may have much stronger inhibitions against engaging in "abuse." If the same behavior now defined as "discipline" can be redefined in the mind of the parent as "abuse," he might mobilize stronger constraints against doing the same things. While it was clear that the agency throughout was talking the language of "abuse," many of the parents interviewed were talking the language of "discipline." A belt, an extension cord, a coat hanger, a wooden spoon can be benignly defined as a weapon of "discipline" or more unacceptably as a weapon of "abuse."

Actions taken to "correct the child," "teach the child a lesson," defined as "instrumental aggression," have fewer inhibitions associated with them than "expressive aggression"—aggression engaged in to satisfy the emotional needs of the parents. Many of these parents saw their behavior as justified because they defined their actions as having an instrumental intent, being designed to achieve some good for the child. If reported behavior can legitimately and appropriately be redefined by the worker so that parents accept the expressive aggressive component in their actions, they may feel a greater sense of shame and guilt, a stronger inhibitions, in engaging in the behavior.

These then are some additional protective services practice implications deriving from the study.

REFERENCES

Bowen, Kenneth. 1973. "Situationalism in Psychology: An Analysis and a Critique." *Psychological Review* (September), 80(5):307–36.

Clifford, Edward. 1959. "Discipline in a Home-Controlled Observational Study." *Journal of Genetic Psychology,* 95:45–82.

Frude, Neil. 1979 "The Aggression Incident: A Perspective for Understanding Abuse." *Child Abuse and Neglect: The International Journal,* vol. 3.

Gelles, R. 1972. *The Violent Home.* Beverly Hills, Calif.: Sage Publications, 3:903–6.

Gelles, Richard and Murray A. Straus. 1979. "Determinants of Violence in the Family: Toward a Theoretic Integration." In Wesley R. Burr, Reuben Hill, F. Ivan Nye, and Ira L. Reiss, eds., *Contemporary Theories About the Family,* pp. 549–81. New York: Free Press.

Giovannoni, Jeanne M. and Rosina M. Becerra. 1979. *Defining Child Abuse.* New York: Free Press.

Golan, Naomi. 1978. *Treatment in Crisis Situations.* New York: Free Press.

Goode, William S. 1971. "Force and Violence in the Family." *Journal of Marriage and the Family,* 33:624–36.

Hoffman, Martin. 1975. "Moral Internalization, Parental Power and the Nature of Parent Child Interaction." *Developmental Psychology,* 11:228–39.

Hopper, Mark A. 1976. *A Concept Analysis of the Abused Child.* Ed.D. dissertation. Utah State University.

Lennard, Henry L. and Arnold Bernstein. 1969. *Patterns in Human Interaction.* San Francisco: Jossey-Bass.

Libbey, Patricia and Roger Bybee. 1979. "The Physical Abuse of Adolescents." *Journal of Social Issues,* 35(2):101–25.

Lindblom, Charles E. and David K. Cohen. 1979. *Useable Knowledge, Social Science, and Social Problem Solving.* New Haven: Yale University Press.

Lytton, Hugh and Walter Zwiner. 1975. "Compliance and its Controlling Stimuli Observed in a Natural Setting," *Developmental Psychology* 11(6):769–79.

Maluccio, Anthony N. 1979a. *Learning from Clients.* New York: Free Press.

—— . 1979b. "Perspectives of Social Workers and Clients on Treatment Objectives." *Social Casework* (July), 60(7):394–401.

Mayer, John E. and Noel Timms. 1970. *The Client Speaks: Working Class Impressions of Casework.* London: Routledge and Kegan Paul.

Minton, C., S. Kagen, and S. A. Levine. 1971. "Maternal Control and Obedience in the Two Year Old." *Child Development,* 42:1873–94.

Rule, B. J., R. Dyck, M. McCard and A. R. Nesdale. 1975. "Judgments of Aggression Service Personal and Pro-Social Purposes." *Social Behavior and Personality—An International Journal,* 3:55–63.

Rule, Bredon G. and Andres R. Nesdale. 1976. "Moral Judgements of Aggressive Behavior." In R. G. Green and E. O'Neal, eds., *Perspectives on Aggression,* pp. 37–60. New York: Academic Press.

Steinmetz, S. K. 1977. *The Cycle of Violence,* New York, Praeger.

Vaughn B., A. Deinard, and B. Egeland. 1980. "Measuring Temperament in Pediatric Practice." *Journal of Pediatrics* (March), 96(3):510–14.

APPENDIX A

SCHOOL OF SOCIAL WORK

THE UNIVERSITY OF WISCONSIN—MADISON

425 HENRY MALL
MADISON, WISCONSIN 53706

Dear Parent:

We are a research group from the University of Wisconsin-Madison studying what happens when parents discipline their children. We are very interested in talking with you about this. The interview will take about an hour. We will pay you $25.00 for your time. We will be glad to come to your home for this at any time that is convenient for you.

Whatever you might say in the interview will be only between us and will be strictly confidential. Our only contact with the Department of Public Welfare is our asking them to send you this letter.

In sharing your experience with us, you will be helping other parents and children to live together more comfortably. We hope that you will be willing to participate with us in this important research.

If you are willing to have us visit with you, please fill out the attached postcard with your name and telephone number and mail it to us. When we receive the card, we will call you to arrange a time for the interview.

If you have any questions about the project and would like to talk with one of us, please do not hesitate to call collect at any one of the numbers given below.

We look forward to receiving a postcard from you letting us know that you are interested.

Sincerely,

COUNTY OF ROCK

DEPARTMENT OF SOCIAL SERVICES

P. O. BOX 1649
306 W. MILWAUKEE ST.
JANESVILLE, WISCONSIN 53545

Dear

A research group at the University of Wisconsin-Madison is studying parent-child conflicts and has asked our agency to send you the attached letter. The research group wishes to interview natural parents, adoptive parents, step-parents and foster parents who have come to our attention because of a disciplinary problem with their child. Only the parent who administered the discipline will be interviewed, and you will be paid Twenty-Five Dollars ($25.00) for the interview.

In order to protect your privacy and freedom to refuse the interview, you have NOT been identified to the researchers. Your name will become known to them ONLY if you return the post card to them and give them permission to see you for an interview. Your relationship with the Department of Social Services will not be affected in any way by whether or not you decide to participate in the study.

Our agency does regard this as a worthwhile project, and we encourage you to give the request your favorable consideration. If you choose to participate in the research, we believe that your involvement will be a meaningful experience for you and a help to all parents and their children.

Very truly yours,

(Mrs.) Judy A. Bablitch, Director

JAB:es

Attachments:
1) Letter of Invitation, University of Wisconsin
2) Post card

APPENDIX B

REPORT OF ALLEGED CHILD ABUSE
FS-SS-40(CA) (Rev. 9-76)

Original of half sheet: Send to DFS immediately
Copy of half sheet: For county Use.
1st Copy of full sheet: Send to DFS within 90 days
2nd Copy of full sheet: For County Use.

PART I. CASE IDENTIFICATION See instructions on back of form

1. Child's Name (Last, First, Middle)		10. Legal Mother's Name (Last, First, Middle)	14. Alleged Abuser(s) Name(s) If Multiple Alleged Abusers, See Instructions on Back of Form	
2. Date Received	4. Received from: 1 Reporter directly	Street Address Circle if Child Lives Here	Street Address	
3. County	2 Law Enforcement	Birth Date / City or Town	Age(s) and Sex (as many as apply) / City or Town	
5. First Reporter (to Law Enforcement or Agency)		Maiden Name (Last) / Prev. Married Name (Last)	1st 2nd 3rd 4th age (sex) age (sex) age (sex) age (sex)	
Street Address		11. Legal Father's Name (Last, First, Middle)	15. Alleged Abuser(s) Relationship to Child	
Organization / City or Town		Street Address Circle if Child Lives Here	1st 2nd 3rd 4th 1 1 Natural parent 1 1 2 2 Adopt. parent 2 2	
6. Reporter's Occupation or Relation. to Child	7. Child's Birth Date	Birth Date / City or Town	3 3 Step parent 3 3 4 4 Foster parent 4 4	

01 Physician
02 Nurse
03 Social Worker
04 School Administrator
  Counselor, Teacher,
  Soc. Wkr, Nurse
05 Hosp. Administrator
06 Dentist
07 Law Enf. Officer
08 Parent
09 Relative
10 Friend/Neighbor
11 Other specify
	8. Child's Sex
	1 Male
	2 Female
	
	9. Child's Race
	1 White
	2 Black
	3 Amer-Indian
	4 Latin-American
	5 Asian-American
	6 Other specify
	9 Unknown
		12. Caretaker(s) (other than legal parents) Mother or Father Substitute in Household Where Child Lives
		Street Address Circle if Child Lives Here
		Age(s) / City or Town
		—— (Male) —— (Fem.)
		13. Caretaker(s) Relationship to Child
		Male Female
		1 1 Step parent
		2 2 Foster parent
		3 3 Relative
		4 4 Other: specify
		8 8 Not Applicable
			5 5 Sibling 5 5
			6 6 Other relative 6 6
			7 7 Other specify 7 7
			
			8 Not applicable 8 8
			9 9 Unknown 9 9
			
			16. Worker's Immediate Plan
			1 Emergency (Investigate within __ Hrs.)
			2 Urgent (Follow-up within 24 Hrs.)
			3 Action needed (Follow within __ days)
			4 No plan
			give reason	

17. CASE STATUS after follow-up 1 No injury or abuse 2 Injury but no abuse 3 Abuse still uncertain 4 Abuse appears certain 5 Abuse legally established If Case Status 1 or 2, Stop Here If Case Status 3, 4 or 5, Complete Entire Form 18. Case Type circle all that apply 01 One child reported 02 More than one reported 04 More than one alleged abuser 08 Fatality	**PART II. CHILD'S FAMILY BACKGROUND** 19. Father or Substitute's Occupation / Education _____ Use Codes From Item 29 Below. 20. Mother or Substitute's Occupation / Education _____ Use Codes From Item 29 Below.

PART III. CHILD'S HOUSEHOLD At Time of Alleged Abuse

PART IV. ALLEGED ABUSER'S BACKGROUND * For Additional Alleged Abusers, Use Space at Bottom of Page

21. No. of Persons	24. Other Children Residing in Household No. Other Children/No. Previous Abused		25. Abuse History	26. Birth Date	29. Education (circle one code)
22. No. of Rooms	Natural Siblings _____		a. Previous alleged abuse to child		0 None
	Siblings by Adoption _____		1 Same child 2 Other child(ren) 3 Same and other child(ren) 9 Unknown	27. Race 1 White 2 Black 3 Amer.-Indian	1 8 years or less 2 9-11 years 3 H.S. grad 4 Some College 5 College grad
23. No. of Adults ___ Legal Parents ___ Grandparents ___ Aunts, Uncles ___ Other related ___ Unknown if related ___ Not related	Half-Siblings _____ Other related _____ Foster Children _____ Other non-related _____ No. Older than child. ___ / Age of Oldest Child (if any older) ___ No. Younger than child. ___ / Age of Youngest Child (if any younger) ___		b. Abuse to adults 1 Yes or alleged 2 No 9 Unknown c. Abused as a child 1 Yes or alleged 2 No 9 Unknown	4 Latin-American 5 Asian-American 6 Other specify 9 Unknown 28. Occupation	6 Vocational School in lieu of H. S. 7 Other specify 9 Unknown

* Additional Alleged Abusers use codes shown in Part IV

2nd	25.	26.	27.	28.	29.
3rd Hist-		Birth	Race	Occu-	Edu-
4th ory a.___ b.___ c.___		Date _____		pation _____	cation _____

REPORT OF ALLEGED CHILD ABUSE
DCS-SS-40(CA) (Reissued 10-77)

Original: Send to DCS within 90 days **PAGE 2**
Copy: For County Use

PART V. ALLEGED ABUSE

CHILD'S NAME _____

30. Judgment of Injuries	32. Judgment of Incident	33. Judgment of Stress Just Before Incident Affecting Alleged Abuser	34. Judgment of On-Going Stress of or affecting Alleged Abuser
01 Bruises, welts	01 Beating with hands, slapping	Reacting to	Adjustment problems
02 Sprains, dislocations	02 Beating with instruments	01 Family break-up	01 Personal-Emotional
04 Bone fracture (not skull)	04 Kicking	02 Job loss or demotion	02 Marital
08 Internal injuries	08 Throwing, pushing, dropping	Involved in recent	04 Work related
16 Skull fracture	16 Biting, hairpulling	04 Argument	08 Community related
32 Brain damage	32 Tying up, locking in	08 Physical fight	16 New baby in home
01 Psychological, emotional	01 Strangling, suffocating	Under influence of	32 Absence of essential family member
02 Suffocation	02 Drowning	16 Alcohol	64 Other
04 Burns, scalding	04 Burning, scalding	32 Other drug	Health problems
08 Abrasions, lacerations	08 Poisoning	Over reacting to child's:	01 Physical illness or injury
16 Cuts, punctures	16 Shooting	01 Incessant crying	02 Incapacitating mental deficiency
32 Dismemberment	32 Stabbing, slashing	02 Disobedience	04 Recent discharge from mental hospital
01 Freezing, exposure	01 Deliberate neglect, exposure to danger	04 Hostility or provocation	08 Currently receiving treatment of Mental Health Clinic
02 Malnutrition	02 Freezing, exposure to weather	08 Other child behavior	16 Alcohol addiction
04 Sexual abuse	04 Malnutrition		32 Other drug addiction
	08 Sexual abuse	Other Immediate stress	64 Other
08 Other		16 _____	Financial Conditions
	16 Other	00 None apparent	01 Inability to live on income
00 None apparent		99 Unknown	02 Heavy indebtedness
	99 Unknown		04 Unemployment

31. Evidence of previous abuse	30. ☐☐ ☐☐ ☐☐		08 Receiving income maintenance
1 Yes	**FOR STATE OFFICE USE**		16 Other
2 Not apparent	32. ☐☐ ☐☐ 33. ☐☐ ☐☐ 34. ☐☐ ☐☐		99 Unknown
9 Unknown			

PART VI. ACTIONS TAKEN WITHIN 90 DAYS (circle code or codes)

35. Medical Attention to Child	37. Placement of Child	39. Juvenile Court Action	40. Criminal Court Action
1 None given	1 Removed from home but later returned	1 No court referral	1 No referral to D.A.
2 Attention given, care not required	2 Moved to relative's home	2 Petition dismissed	2 Referral to D.A., no court referral
3 Medical care given as outpatient: Number of days ___	3 Moved to foster home	3 Child at home under supervision	3 Complaint dismissed
4 Child hospitalized: Number of days ___	4 Institutionalized	4 Custody transferred	4 Legal sentence
		5 Guardianship transferred	
36. Welfare Services to family	5 Indeterminate, child still hospitalized	6 Petition: no action taken	5 Referral to court: no action taken
001 Casework Services	6 Child died	7 Other	6 Other
002 Guidance Clinic or Counseling Clinic	7 Child not placed, remained at home.		
004 Financial Assistance and planning	8 Other	**41. Please add a paragraph on:**	
008 Public Medical Care	9 Unknown	1) What precipitated the alleged abuse	
016 Maternity Care	**38. Placement of other Children**	2) The alleged abuse incident	
032 Day Care Services	1 All removed from home		
064 Homemaker Services	2 Some removed from home		
128 Other	3 No (other) children removed		
	8 Not applicable, no other children.		
000 Services never given	9 Unknown		
999 Unreported			

STATE OFFICE USE
36.

REPORT OF ALLEGED CHILD ABUSE
DCS-SS-40(CA) (Reissued 12-77)

Original of half sheet: Send to DCS immediately Page 1
Copy of half sheet: For county Use.
1st Copy of full sheet: Send to DCS within 90 days
2nd Copy of full sheet: For County Use.

PART I. CASE IDENTIFICATION

1. Child's Name (Last, First, Middle)		10. Legal Mother's Name (Last, First, Middle)		14. Alleged Abuser(s) Name(s)			
2. Date Received	4. Received from: 1 Reporter directly	Street Address		Street Address			
3. County	2 Law Enforcement	Birth Date	City or Town	Age(s) and Sex (as many as apply)	City or Town		
5. First Reporter (to Law Enforcement or Agency)		Maiden Name (Last)	Prev. Married Name (Last)	1st 2nd 3rd 4th ( ) ( ) ( ) ( )			
Street Address		11. Legal Father's Name (Last, First, Middle)		15. Alleged Abuser(s) Relationship to Child			
Organization	City or Town	Street Address		1st 2nd		3rd 4th	
6. Reporter's Occupa- tion or Relation. to Child	7. Child's Birth Date	Birth Date	City or Town	1 1 Natural parent 2 2 Adopt. parent 3 3 Step parent 4 4 Foster parent		1 1 2 2 3 3 4 4	
01 Physician	8. Child's Sex	12. Caretaker(s) (other than legal parents)		5 5 Sibling		5 5	
02 Nurse	1 Male			6 6 Other relative		6 6	
03 Social Worker	2 Female	Street Address		7 7 Other		7 7	
04 School Administrator							
Counselor, Teacher, Soc. Wkr, Nurse	9. Child's Race	Age(s)	City or Town	8 Not applicable		8 8	
05 Hosp. Administrator	1 White 2 Black	(Male) (Fem.)		9 9 Unknown		9 9	
06 Dentist	3 Amer-Indian	13. Caretaker(s) Relationship to Child		16. Worker's Immediate Plan			
07 Law Enf. Officer	4 Latin-American	Male Female		1 Emergency (Investigate within ___ Hrs.)			
08 Parent	5 Asian-American	1 1 Step parent		2 Urgent (Follow up within 24 Hrs.)			
09 Relative	6 Other	2 2 Foster parent		3 Action needed (Follow within ___ days)			
10 Friend/Neighbor		3 3 Relative		4 No plan			
11 Other	9 Unknown	4 4 Other: ____ 8 8 Not Applicable					

17. CASE STATUS		**PART II. CHILD'S FAMILY BACKGROUND**
1 No injury or abuse		19. Father or Substitute's Occupation / Education
2 Injury but no abuse	18. Case Type	
3 Abuse still uncertain	01 One child reported	20. Mother or Substitute's Occupation / Education
4 Abuse appears certain	02 More than one reported	
5 Abuse legally established	04 More than one alleged 08 Fatality abuser	

PART III. CHILD'S HOUSEHOLD At Time of Alleged Abuse

PART IV. ALLEGED ABUSER'S BACKGROUND *

21. No. of Persons	24. Other Children Residing in Household No. Other Children/No. Previous Abused	25. Abuse History a. Previous alleged abuse to child	26. Birth Date	29. Education (circle one code)
	____ Natural Siblings ____	1 Same child		0 None
22. No. of Rooms		2 Other child(ren)	27. Race	1 8 years or less
	____ Siblings by Adoption ____	3 Same and other child(ren)	1 White	2 9-11 years
23. No. of Adults		9 Unknown	2 Black	3 H.S. grad
____ Legal Parents	____ Half-Siblings ____	b. Abuse to adults	3 Amer.-Indian 4 Latin-American	4 Some College
____ Grand- parents	____ Other related ____	1 Yes or alleged	5 Asian-American	5 College grad 6 Vocational School in lieu of H. S.
____ Aunts, Uncles	____ Foster Children ____	2 No	6 Other	7 Other
____ Other related	____ Other non-related ____	9 Unknown		
____ Unknown if related	No. Older than Age of Oldest Child child. ___ (if any older) ___	c. Abused as a child	9 Unknown	9 Unknown
____ Not related	No. Younger than Age of Youngest Child child. ___ (if any younger) ___	1 Yes or alleged 2 No 9 Unknown	28. Occupation	

* Additional Alleged Abusers

2nd	25.	26.	27.	28.	29.
3rd	Hist-	Birth	Race	Occu-	Edu-
4th	ory a. ___ b. ___ c. ___	Date ___	___	pation ___	cation ___

REPORT OF ALLEGED CHILD ABUSE
DCS-SS-40(CA) (Reissued 10-77)

Original: Send to DCS within 90 days **PAGE 2**
Copy: For County Use

CHILD'S NAME _____

PART V. ALLEGED ABUSE   Circle <u>all</u> codes that apply |ITEMS 30 -34 ARE BASED ON SOCIAL SERVICE WORKER'S JUDGMENT

30. Judgment of Injuries
Use Medical Reports if Available
- 01 Bruises, welts
- 02 Sprains, dislocations
- 04 Bone fracture (not skull)
- 08 Internal injuries
- 16 Skull fracture
- 32 Brain damage

- 01 Psychological, emotional
- 02 Suffocation
- 04 Burns, scalding
- 08 Abrasions, lacerations
- 16 Cuts, punctures
- 32 Dismemberment

- 01 Freezing, exposure
- 02 Malnutrition
- 04 Sexual abuse   specify
  _____
- 08 Other
     specify _____
- 00 None apparent

31. Evidence of previous abuse
circle <u>one</u> code only
- 1 Yes
- 2 Not apparent
- 9 Unknown

32. Judgment of Incident
- 01 Beating with hands, slapping
- 02 Beating with instruments
- 04 Kicking
- 08 Throwing, pushing, dropping
- 16 Biting, hairpulling
- 32 Tying up, locking in

- 01 Strangling, suffocating
- 02 Drowning
- 04 Burning, scalding
- 08 Poisoning
- 16 Shooting
- 32 Stabbing, slashing

- 01 Deliberate neglect, exposure to danger
- 02 Freezing, exposure to weather
- 04 Malnutrition
- 08 Sexual abuse   specify
  _____
- 16 Other
     specify _____
- 99 Unknown

33. Judgment of Stress Just Before Incident Affecting Alleged Abuser

Reacting to
- 01 Family break-up
- 02 Job loss or demotion

Involved in recent
- 04 Argument
- 08 Physical fight

Under influence of
- 16 Alcohol
- 32 Other drug

Over reacting to child's:
- 01 Incessant crying
- 02 Disobedience
- 04 Hostility or provocation
- 08 Other child behavior specify
  _____

Other Immediate stress specify
- 16 _____
- 00 None apparent
- 99 Unknown

34. Judgment of On-Going Stress of or affecting Alleged Abuser

Adjustment problems
- 01 Personal-Emotional
- 02 Marital
- 04 Work related
- 08 Community related
- 16 New baby in home
- 32 Absence of essential family member
- 64 Other specify
  _____

Health problems
- 01 Physical illness or injury
- 02 Incapacitating mental deficiency
- 04 Recent discharge from mental hospital
- 08 Currently receiving treatment of Mental Health Clinic
- 16 Alcohol addiction
- 32 Other drug addiction
- 64 Other specify
  _____

Financial Conditions
- 01 Inability to live on income
- 02 Heavy indebtedness
- 04 Unemployment
- 08 Receiving income maintenance
- 16 Other specify
  _____
- 99 Unknown

30. [| | | | |]
32. [| | | |]   33. [| | | |]   34. [| | | |]   **FOR STATE OFFICE USE**

PART VI. ACTIONS TAKEN WITHIN 90 DAYS (circle code or codes)

35. Medical Attention to Child
circle <u>one</u> code only
- 1 None given
- 2 Attention given, care not required
- 3 Medical care given as outpatient: Number of days _____
- 4 Child hospitalized: Number of days _____

36. Welfare Services to family
circle <u>all</u> codes that apply
- 001 Casework Services
- 002 Guidance Clinic or Counseling Clinic
- 004 Financial Assistance and planning
- 008 Public Medical Care
- 016 Maternity Care
- 032 Day Care Services
- 064 Homemaker Services
- 128 Other specify _____
- 000 Services never given
- 999 Unreported

STATE OFFICE USE
36.

37. Placement of Child
circle <u>one</u> code only
- 1 Removed from home but later returned
- 2 Moved to relative's home
- 3 Moved to foster home
- 4 Institutionalized   specify
- 5 Indeterminate, child still hospitalized
- 6 Child died
- 7 Child not placed, remained at home.
- 8 Other specify _____
- 9 Unknown

38. Placement of other Children
circle <u>one</u> code only
- 1 All removed from home
- 2 Some removed from home
- 3 No (other) children removed
- 8 Not applicable, no other children.
- 9 Unknown

39. Juvenile Court Action
circle <u>one</u> code only
- 1 No court referral
- 2 Petition dismissed
- 3 Child at home under supervision
- 4 Custody transferred
- 5 Guardianship transferred
- 6 Petition: no action taken
- 7 Other specify

40. Criminal Court Action
circle <u>one</u> code only
- 1 No referral to D.A.
- 2 Referral to D.A., no court referral
- 3 Complaint dismissed
- 4 Legal sentence
  specify date
- 5 Referral to court: no action taken
- 6 Other specify

41. Please add a paragraph on:
1) What precipitated the alleged abuse
2) The alleged abuse incident

APPENDIX C

TABLE C.1
Family Characteristics

Abusive Parents:			
Relationship to child (N = 830)	83% parents (691)	15% step-parents (122)	2% adoptive parents (17)
Gender (N = 830)	59% fathers (492)	41% mothers (338)	
Age (N = 784)	15% 19–24 (121)	63% 26–39 (490)	22% 40+ (173)
Parent status by gender (N = 774)	25% of fathers single parents (115)	61% of mothers single parents (195)	
Abused Children:			
Gender (N = 828)	45% boys (373)	55% girls (455)	
Age (N = 800)	29% 0–5 (233)	36% 6–12 (284)	35% 13–17 (283)
Age by gender[a] (N = 799)	58% age 0–5 boys (135)	54% age 6–12 boys (153)	25% age 13–17 boys (71)
Age by gender of parent[b] (N = 800)	51% age 0–5 abused, by fathers (118)	53% age 6–12 abused, by fathers (151)	71% age 13–17 abused by fathers (201)
Race (N = 819)	81% white (659)	14% black (115)	5% other (45)
Sibling position (N = 605)	50% oldest (302)	39% middle (235)	11% youngest (68)

TABLE C.1 (continued)

Abusive Family:

Number of parents (N = 773)	40% single parent (310)	60% two parents (463)	
Family size (N = 699)	13% 1 child (94)	44% 2–3 (307)	43% 4+ (298)
Social class index (N = 633)	10% class I–III (61)	29% class IV (184)	61% class V (388)
Receiving financial assistance (N = 694)	23% yes (156)	78% no (538)	
Financial problems affecting abuse (N = 694)	53% yes (371)	47% no (323)	

[a]$X^2 = 70.51$ [b]$X^2 = 27.56$
d.f. = 2   d.f. = 2
p = .0000   p = .0000

Note: Totals less than 830 indicate missing data.

TABLE C.2
The Abuse Incident

Abuse Method Used (N = 802)	81% beaten with hand, instrument (650)	13% kicked, thrown, punched (100)	7% tied up, burned, stabbed (52)
Psychological Abuse (N = 829)	18% yes (148)	82% no (681)	
Type of Injury (N = 754)	79% minor; bruises, welts (596)	16% moderate: abrasions, cuts, sprains (122)	5% severe: fractures, burns, suffocation (36)
Medical Care (N = 827)	86% none (710)	9% outpatient (70)	6% hospitalized (47)
Abuse Method by Age of Child			
Beat with hand (N = 276)	43% age 0–5 (95)	27% age 6–12 (73)	39% age 13–17 (108)
Beat with instrument (N = 351)	36% age 0–5 (80)	57% age 6–12 (155)	42% age 13–17 (116)
Tied up, pushed, thrown (N = 74)	14% age 0–5 (30)	7% age 6–12 (20)	9% age 13–17 (24)
Kicked (N = 29)	1% age 0–5 (2)	4% age 6–12 (11)	6% age 13–17 (16)
Medical Care by Age of Child			
Hospitalized (N = 47)	16% age 0–5 (36)	3% age 6–12 (8)	1% age 13–17 (3)

Note: Totals less than 830 indicate missing data.

TABLE C.3
Family Violence

Abuse History (N = 830)	21% to this same child (174)	6% to sibs (50)	14% to child & sibs (118)	59% none or don't know (488)
Abuse to Adults (N = 393)	37% Yes (146)	63% No (247)		
Abuse to Adults by Abuse History[a] (N = 393)				
Adult abuse found (146)	21% history: abuse to 1 child (30)	6% history: abuse to sibs (9)	36% history: abuse to child and sibs (52)	38% no abuse history (55)
No adult abuse (247)	22% history: abuse to 1 child (55)	6% history: abuse to sib (15)	7% history: abuse to child and sibs (17)	65% no abuse history (160)
Abuser Abused as Child (N = 302)	68% yes (206)	32% no (96)		

[a] $X^2 = 55.60$
d.f. = 3
p = .0000

Note: Totals less than 830 indicate missing data.

TABLE C.4
Ongoing Stresses Affecting the Alleged Abuser

Personal Emotional Problems (N = 761)	70% yes (531)	30% no (230)
Other Health/Mental Health Problems (N = 751)		
Recent discharge from mental hospital	2% yes (13)	98% no (738)
Mental health clinic treatment	5% yes (34)	96% no (717)
Incapacitating mental deficiency	3% yes (25)	97% no (726)

Mental deficiency by gender of abuser[a]	5% of women, yes (17)	2% of men, yes (8)
Physical illness or injury	10% yes (75)	90% no (676)
Alcohol addiction	12% yes (87)	88% no (664)
Alcohol addiction by gender of abuser[b]	7% of women, yes (23)	15% of men, yes (64)
Other drug addiction	1% yes (8)	99% no (743)

Family Problems
(N = 761)

Marital adjustment problems	43% yes (326)	57% no (435)
Marital problems by gender of abuser[c]	37% of women, yes (116)	47% of men, yes (210)
Absence of essential family member	9% yes (66)	91% no (695)
Absence of essential family member by gender of abuser[d]	17% of women, yes (53)	3% of men, yes (13)
New baby in home	5% yes (38)	95% no (723)

Community Related
Adjustment Problems
(N = 761)   8% yes (60)   92% no (701)

[a] $X^2 = 6.29$ [c] $X^2 = 7.87$
d.f. = 1   d.f. = 1
p = .0121   p = .0050

[b] $X^2 = 8.71$ [d] $X^2 = 43.02$
d.f. = 1   d.f. = 1
p = .0032   p = .0000

Note: Totals less than 830 indicate missing data.

TABLE C.5
Agency Involvement with the Family

Social Services Provided (N = 815)	96% yes (781)	4% no (34)	
Type of Services Provided			
Casework services	89% yes (728)	11% no (87)	
Guidance clinic, counseling clinic	25% yes (204)	75% no (611)	
Financial assistance and planning	19% yes (156)	81% no (659)	
Financial assistance by gender of abuser[a]	23% of women given assist. (77)	16% of men given assist. (79)	
Public medical care	12% yes (99)	88% no (716)	
Public medical care by gender of abuser[b]	15% of women given care (50)	10% of men given care (49)	
Maternity care	1% yes (6)	99% no (809)	
Maternity care by gender of abuser[c]	2% of women given care (6)	0% of men given care (0)	
Day care	3% yes (27)	97% no (788)	
Homemaker services	4% yes (36)	96% no (779)	
Homemaker services by gender of abuser[d]	6% of women given assist. (21)	3% of men given assist. (15)	
Juvenile Court Action (N = 828)	77% no court referral (635)	1% petition dismissed (11)	5% supervision of child in home (37)
	11% custody transfer (90)	0% guardianship transfer (2)	2% petition— no action yet (14)
	5% other (39)		

Juvenile Court Action by
Age of Child[e]
(N = 747)

| (Action taken: custody, supervision, guardianship transfer) | 24% age 0–5, action taken (52) | 14% age 6–12, action taken (39) | 13% age 13–17, action taken (33) |

Juvenile Court Action by
Gender of Abuser[f]
(N = 775)

| | 17% of women, action taken (53) | 16% of men, action taken (76) | |

Criminal Court Action
(N = 825)

| | 82% no referral to D.A. (673) | 11% no court action (87) | 1% complaint dismissed (7) |
| | 2% legal sentence (14) | 2% no court action yet (20) | 3% other (24) |

Criminal Court Action by
Age of Child[g]
(N = 754)

| (Action taken: legal sentence) | 3% age 0–5 action taken (7) | 2% age 6–12, action taken (6) | 0% age 13–17, action taken (1) |

Criminal Court Action by
Gender of Abuser[h]
(N = 781)

| | 0% of women, action taken (1) | 3% of men, action taken (13) | |

Placement of Child
(N = 826)

| | 10% placed and returned (85) | 8% with relatives (68) | 11% in foster home (90) |
| | 2% institutionalized (17) | 4% other (32) | 65% not placed (534) |

Placement of Child by
Age of Child[i]
(N = 765)

| | 33% age 0–5, placed (72) | 25% age 6–12, placed (68) | 40% age 13–17, placed (108) |

Placement of Siblings
(N = 670)

| | 5% all removed (36) | 7% some removed (49) | 87% none removed (585) |

Placement of Siblings by
Age of Abused Child[j]
(N = 648)

| | 13% age 0–5, all removed (20) | 5% age 6–12, all removed (12) | 1% age 13–17, all removed (3) |

[a]$X^2 = 5.51$	[c]$X^2 = 6.49$	[e]$X^2 = 12.27$	[g]$X^2 = 5.87$	[i]$X^2 = 15.41$
d.f. = 1	d.f. = 1	d.f. = 2	d.f. = 2	d.f. = 2
p = .0189	p = .0108	p = .0022	p = .0530	p = .0005
[b]$X^2 = 4.01$	[d]$X^2 = 4.10$	[f]$X^2 = .01$	[h]$X^2 = 5.44$	[j]$X^2 = 28.34$
d.f. = 1	d.f. = 1	d.f. = 1	d.f. = 1	d.f. = 4
p = .0453	p = .0429	p = .9112	p = .0197	p = .0000

Note: Totals less than 830 indicate missing data.

TABLE C.6

Child Behaviors: Second and Third Precursors

Behavior Category	Second Precursor		Third Precursor	
	Percent	*Number*	*Percent*	*Number*
Aggressive behavior	3.9	32	.2	2
Lying, stealing	2.0	17	.5	4
Entrance/exit behavior	2.7	22	.2	2
Behavior involving food, elimination, sleeping	.7	6	0	0
Performance of household chores	1.2	10	.2	2
Defiance of parental orders	1.9	16	.2	2
Crying, whining	.4	3	0	0
Disapproved habits	1.4	12	.2	2
Dating, sexual behaviors, disapproved friends	1.1	9	.2	2
School-related problems	1.3	11	.1	1
Overactivity	.7	6	0	0
Other and unspecified misbehavior	3.5	29	.4	3
No misbehavior mentioned	79.2	657	97.6	810
Total	100%	830	100%	830

TABLE C.7
Age and Behavior of Abused Children
(*proportion of cases behavior is present*)

Behavior Category	Early Childhood	Latency	Adolescence	
Aggressive behavior	11.2% (26)	16.9% (48)	32.9% (93)	$X^2 = 40.65$ d.f. = 2 p. = .0000*
Lying, stealing	2.1% (5)	16.9% (48)	6.7% (19)	$X^2 = 36.82$ d.f. = 2 p = .0000*
Entrance/exit behavior	1.7% (4)	4.6% (13)	12.4% (35)	$X^2 = 26.53$ d.f. = 2 p = .0000*
Behavior involving food, elimination, sleeping	15.0% (35)	6.3% (18)	1.1% (3)	$X^2 = 38.56$ d.f. = 2 p = .0000*
Performance of household chores	1.7% (4)	4.2% (12)	7.4% (21)	$X^2 = 9.58$ d.f. = 2 p = .0083*
Defiance of parental orders	4.3% (10)	5.3% (15)	2.8% (8)	$X^2 = 2.18$ d.f. = 2 p = .3357
Crying, whining	11.6% (27)	1.1% (3)	0% (0)	$X^2 = 56.39$ d.f. = 2 p = .0000*
Disapproved habits	.9% (2)	3.5% (10)	5.3% (15)	$X^2 = 7.76$ d.f. = 2 p = .0206†
Dating, sexual behaviors, disapproved friends	1.3% (3)	1.4% (4)	7.1% (20)	$X^2 = 18.31$ d.f. = 2 p = .0001*
School-related problems	.4% (1)	3.9% (11)	4.9% (14)	$X^2 = 8.84$ d.f. = 2 p = .0120†
Overactivity	6.0% (14)	2.8% (8)	.7% (2)	$X^2 = 12.39$ d.f. = 2 p = .0020*
Other misbehavior	7.3% (17)	7.4% (21)	3.5% (10)	

TABLE C.7 (continued)

Behavior Category	Early Childhood	Latency	Adolescence
Unspecified misbehavior	12.4% (29)	13.0% (37)	6.0% (17)
No misbehavior mentioned	24.0% (56)	12.7% (36)	9.2% (26)

Note: N = 800 for each behavior category; there are 30 missing data cases.
* Results significant. P ≤ .01.
† Results suggestive .01 < P ≤ .05.

TABLE C.8
Gender and Behavior of Abused Children
(proportion of cases behavior is present)

Behavior Category	Male	Female	
Aggressive behavior	16.9% (63)	24.0% (109)	$X^2 = 5.80$ d.f. = 1 p = .0161†
Lying, stealing	10.2% (38)	7.7% (35)	$X^2 = $ N.S.
Entrance/exit behavior	4.0% (15)	9.0% (41)	$X^2 = 7.32$ d.f. = 1 p = .0068*
Behavior involving food, elimination, sleeping	8.8% (33)	5.1% (23)	$X^2 = 4.09$ d.f. = 1 p = .0431†
Performance of household chores	2.9% (11)	6.2% (28)	$X^2 = 4.00$ d.f. = 1 p = .0454†
Defiance of parental orders	5.6% (21)	3.1% (14)	$X^2 = $ N.S.
Crying, whining	3.2% (12)	4.2% (19)	$X^2 = $ N.S.
Disapproved habits	2.9% (11)	3.7% (17)	$X^2 = $ N.S.
Dating, sexual behaviors, disapproved friends	.5% (2)	5.5% (25)	$X^2 = 14.44$ d.f. = 1 p = .0001*
School-related problems	4.6% (17)	2.2% (10)	$X^2 = $ N.S.
Overactivity	3.5% (13)	2.6% (12)	$X^2 = $ N.S.

Note: N = 828 for each behavior category.
* Results significant. P ≤ .01.
† Results suggestive .01 < P ≤ .05.

INDEX

Abortion: in preventing child abuse, 27; abusive parent's consideration of, 236, 238

Abused children: in history, 1–2; national concern for, 2; growing interest in, 3; hospitalization of, 4, 147; severity of injuries to, 6, 9–10, 108, 147; in America, prevalence of, 7–9; substantiated cases of, 9; families of, 10; and parental role reversal, 15; and parental expectations of, 15; as parents, 19–20; and use of nurseries, 23–24; previous abuse of, 30; effects of preschool programs on, 34; development of, through treatment, 34–36; effects of foster care on, 35; unidirectional view of, 47; bidirectional view of, 48, 49, 74–75, 78–80; parental scapegoating of, 70, 72, 109–10, 239–41; parent's perception of, 70, 72–73, 184–88, 240–43, 244–47; as initiating abuse, 74–75, 78–80, 114–15, 116–29 *passim*, 130–31, 142–43, 148–62; transferred custody among, 113; placement of, 113–14, 134; and prevalent behaviors by age, 129–31; and behaviors by sex, 130–31; and severity of abuse determined by behaviors of, 132–35; in response to parent's nonpunitive interventions, 164–65, 166–68, 170–72; as ignoring parental interventions, 172–74, 181–82; accidental abuse of, 182–83; as terminating abuse, 200; and reactions to abuse, 201, 205–6, 211–13; injuries of, as eliciting parental guilt, 202; parent's reconciliation with, 205–6; and reactions to abusive parent, 211–13; as learning from abuse event, 214–15; and nonabused

sibling, 239, 240–42; as less preferred, 240–43; negative identifications with, 246–47; counselling of, 275–76

———— *profiled*: average age of, 9, 78, 107, 146–47, 240, 266; sex of, 9, 107, 146; common characteristics of, 11, 62–63, 64, 68–70, 146–47; congenital defects among, 63; infant characteristics of, 63–66, 67; as physically handicapped, 63–64, 69, 72, 239; as mentally handicapped, 63–64, 72, 187, 239; as premature, 63–64, 73, 239; retardation among, 64, 66, 69; atypical social status of, 66; as illegitimate, 66–67, 135–36; as unplanned, 66–67, 235, 237–38; as depressive, 67–69; temperamental characteristics of, 67–69, 70–73, 240–45; as hyperactive, 67–68, 70, 72, 239; aggression in, 67–68, 68–71, 116–20, 128–29, 130–31, 149, 154, 157, 174–77, 181; as negativistic, 67–68, 69; problem behaviors among, 68–69, 70–73, 74, 119–31 *passim*, 148–62 *passim*, 239, 253, 256–57; truancy among, 69; as runaways, 69; stealing among, 69, 120–22, 130–31, 149, 158–59; physical attractiveness of, 70; intelligence of, 70; racial breakdown of, 107, 146; destructive activity among, 119–20, 149, 154, 157; lying among, 120–21, 130–31, 149, 151, 155, 178–79; entrance-exit behavior among, 122–23, 130–31, 149, 151; biological functioning of, 123–24, 128, 130–31, 156; crying among, 124, 131, 135, 149, 158; parental defiance of, 124–25, 128, 130–31, 149,

Abused children (Continued)
150, 152–53, 155, 159; and school-related behaviors, 125, 149, 150, 153–54, 157, 159, 187–88; sexual behavior among, 125–26, 151–52, 160, 187; drinking among, 125–27, 128, 149, 150, 159; disapproved habits of, 125–27, 128, 130–31, 149; drug use among, 126, 128, 149, 150, 159; as uncommunicative, 172–73, 185; negative birth situation of, 235–37; as first-born, 238, 240

Abuse event: identification of, 142; as idiosyncratic, 142; as an interactional process, 142–43, 218–24; and methods of abuse, 147; and typical place of occurrence, 147; and time of occurrence, 147; severity of, 147; interactions preceding, 148–49, 150–62; as initiated by child, 148–49, 150–62, 254, 256, 257; etiology of, 165–68, 170–82, 218–23; as accidental, 182–83; parent's intentions during, 188–99; and intervention of witnesses, 199–200; termination of, 199–207; parental feelings toward, 201–7; reconciliation following, 205–6; outcomes of, 207–18; positive parental perception of, 208–9, 213; negative parental perception of, 208–13; consequences of, for parent-child relationship, 210–12; as learning situation, 214–16; and complexity of factors involved, 218–23; as result of situational stress, 226–30, 253, 257–58; as crisis situation, 252–53; as linked to extrinsic factors, 257–58; as immediate context-contingent, 257–58

Abusive families: profile of, 10, 106–7, 141, 146; psychodynamic model of, 15; sociological stresses on, 15–16; marital discord in, 16, 112; effects of Bowen project on, 34; aversive behavior in, 71; extent of abuse in, 73–74; research of, techniques involved, 92, 94–95; violence patterns in, 109–111; and loss of members, 112; and social services provided, 112–13

Abusive parents: and initiation of protective services, 11–12; role reversal among, 15; as perceiving the abused child, 15, 28, 70, 72–73, 240–43, 244–47; sociological

stresses on, 15–16, 109, 230; recidivism among, 26, 30, 32–33; attempted identification of, 27–28, 35–36, 66–67, 275; early rejection of child by, 28; unidirectional view of, 47; bidirectional view of, 48, 49; unplanned pregnancy among, 66–67; insensitivity of, to abused child, 70; and scapegoating of abused child, 70, 72–73; interviews with, 93–94, 99–103; as misrepresenting abuse, 102–4; and methods of abuse, 107–8, 132–34, 147; previous abuse by, 109; and distribution of abuse, 109–110; and violence patterns of, 109–111; stresses on, 111–12, 114–15, 226–30, 239, 253; criminal prosecution of, 113, 134–36; as responding to child's behaviors, 114–29, 148–49, 150–62, 162–64, 166–68, 254, 256, 257; as responding to child's aggression, 116–20, 128–29, 174–77, 181; as reacting to child's lying, 120–21; as reacting to child's stealing, 120–22; as reacting to child's entrance-exit behavior, 122–23; as responding to child's crying, 124, 131, 135; as responding to child's defiance, 124–25; responses determined by sex of, 131; and initial responses to child's misbehavior, 162–64, 166–68; disciplinary repertoire of, 163–64; nonpunitive interventions of, 163–65, 166–68; and failure of initial interventions, 165–67, 170–72, 179–80; as reacting to uncommunicative child, 172–73, 185; child's indifference to, 172–74, 181–82; accidental abuse by, 182–83; as interpreting child's misbehavior, 184–88; as empathic, 184–88; expressive intentions of, 189, 196–97; instrumental intentions of, 189–99 passim; as desiring authority, 197–98; as dissociated from abusive behavior, 199; and termination of abuse, 200–1; inhibitory effects on, 200–1; as feeling justified, 201, 207; as negatively perceiving abuse, 201–6, 208–213; guilt of, 202–3; self-image of, 204–5; attempted reconciliation by, 205–6; as positively perceiving abuse, 208–9, 213, 262–63; as perceived by child, 211–13; as learning from abuse, 214–16; job-related stresses on, 219, 221,

226, 227; financial stresses on, 226; emotional stresses on, 226–27; situational stresses on, 226–30, 239, 253; perception of corporal punishment by, 232–34, 265, 266–67; negative birth situation among, 235–37; as resisting abortion, 236, 238; as identifying with abused child, 246–47; as perceiving social workers, 265
—— profiled: age of, 10, 106; class affiliation of, 10–11; common traits of, 14–17, 107, 145–46; mental-health problems of, 15, 17, 111–12, 248–49; social isolation of, 16; immaturity of, 16; marital discord among, 16, 112, 226, 228; childhood abuse of, 19–20, 111, 231–34, 261; marital status of, 106, 112, 145–46, 230, 235–36; sex of, 106, 145–46; economic status of, 106–7, 145–46; criminal activity among, 112, 248; education of, 145–46; alcoholism among, 226; as violence-prone, 249
—— treatment of: approaches involved in, 21; resistance to, 22; and internalizing new attitudes, 22–23; and Parent Effectiveness Training, 23; behavior modification in, 23; shared parenting as, 23; nurseries used in, 23–24; and temporary shelters, 24; behavioral changes following, 31–33; and Bowen Project, 34; and preschool programs, 34; and Parents Anonymous, 34–35; extensive programs in, 36; client's responses to, 37; social services provided in, 112–13; protective service agency's role in, 213–14; social worker's role in, 256–57, 261–68; see also Child abuse, treatment of
Adolescents, as prone to abuse, 146–47
Adoption, abusive parent's consideration of, 236
Adoptive parents, as abusive, 106
Aggressive children: as abused, 68–70, 70–71; as initiating abuse, 116–20, 128–29, 130–31, 149, 154, 157; average age of, 130–31; as intensifying parent's anger, 174–77, 181
Alcoholism, 256; among abusive parents, 112, 114, 226; among abused children, 125–27, 128
American Academy of Pediatricians, 3

American Bar Association, child abuse defined by, 6
American Humane Association, 3
American Medical Association, 3
Assertiveness Training, in treating abuse, 36

Battered Child Syndrome, 4; identification of, 3; as distinguished from child abuse, 6
Behavior Modification: in treating abuse, 21, 23, 275; success of, in abuse situations, 32
Bible, on disciplining children, 1
Bidirectionality: in explaining child abuse, 48–49, 74–76, 78–80, 251–52, 254–55; abuse researcher's ambivalence toward, 76–79; as ideologically unattractive, 77–79
Blind children, parental response to, 54
Bowen Project: and treatment of abusive families, 34; success of, 34

Casework counselling, in treating abuse, 10, 113
Child abuse: as American concern, 2–3; legislation directed at, 3; public interest in, 4; medically oriented interest in, 4; varieties of, 4–5; definitions of, 6, 8, 74–75; prevalence of, 7–9, 274; substantiated cases of, 9; reporting of, 10, 95–97; perpetrators of, 10; and abusive family distinguished, 10; the diagnostic configuration of, 13–14; recurrence of, 26; abortion as preventing, 27; prevention of, 27–28; and high risk cases, 62–64; research of, techniques involved, 92, 94–96; parent's misrepresentation of, 102–4; in Wisconsin, extent of, 105; and methods of, 107–8, 132–34, 147; distribution of, 109–111; and juvenile court proceedings, 113; and criminal proceedings, 113, 134–36; dangers of generalizing about, 142; and age of abused, 146–47; as accidental, 182–83; parent's intentions in, 188–99; parent's perceptions of, 189–99 passim, 201–7, 209–213; witness's interventions in, 199–200; consequences of, for parent-child relationship, 210–12; complexity of factors involved in, 218–24;

Child abuse (*Continued*)
as limited to one child, 239–43; as crisis situation, 252–53

———— *etiology of*: as class affiliated, 10–11; factors associated with, 14–18, 20–21; and the psychodynamic explanation, 15, 17; sociological explanations regarding, 15–16, 109; psychosocial theories regarding, 18; intergenerational theory regarding, 19–20, 231–34; unidirectional theory regarding, 47, 76–77; bidirectional explanation of, 48, 49, 74–76, 251–52, 254–55; child as factor in, 74–75, 114–15, 116–29, 142–43, 148–49, 150–62, 254, 256–57; and the microsystem, 91; and the macrosystem, 91; ecosystem as variable in, 91; stresses associated with, 111–12, 114–15; child's aggression linked to, 116–20, 128–29; child's lying associated with, 120–21; and child's entrance-exit behaviors, 122–23; and child's biological functioning, 123–24; child's defiance as factor in, 124–25; and disapproved behaviors of child, 125–26; and the interactional sequence, 142–43, 148, 218–24, 251–52, 254–55; situational pressures linked to, 226–30, 253, 257–58; negative birth experiences associated with, 235–39; extrinsic factors associated with, 257–58; as immediate context-contingent, 257–58

———— *history of*: prior to the eighteenth century, 1; an overview, 1–2; in nineteenth-century America, 2; and the formation of protective service agencies, 2; and current concern, 3–4

———— *physical*: various contexts of, 5; differing cultural definitions of, 5; accepted definition of, 5–6; intentionality in, 6; national prevalence of, 8–9; substantiated cases of, 9; and severity of reported injuries, 9, 10; in Britain, 10; diagnostic studies of, 14

———— *treatment of*: social services offered in, 10, 112–14; approaches in, 21–26; parental resistance to, 22; effects of, 22; social worker's role in, 22–23, 261–68; and emergency relief funds, 24; and agency resources, 25–26; and family planning, 27; and parent education, 27; and outcome-evaluation research, 29–33; and recidivism rates, 30, 32–33; length of, as determining success, 33; and impact on child, 34–36; role of foster care in, 35; and attempted identification of abuser, 35; success of, 36–37; and placement of child, 113–14; *see also* Abusive parents, treatment of

Child abuse legislation: and the growth of protective services, 3; rapid adoption of, 3; recent provisions of, 3; and mandatory reporting of abuse, 3, 12; as politically attractive, 4; *see also* Federal Child Abuse Prevention and Treatment Act

Child abuse reports: sources of, 10, 11; by socioeconomic groups, 10–11; as initiating protective services, 12; as legally required, 12; unsubstantiated, 13; as research tool, 96–97

Child counselling, in treating abuse, 36

Child neglect: causes of, 17–18; as distinguished from abuse, 17–18

Children: historical status of, 1–2; contemporary rights of, 4; socialization process of, 48–50; active role of, in parent-child relationships, 48–53, 58–59; hyperactive, 52, 55, 67–68, 70, 72, 239; aggressive behavior of, 52–53, 62; early social behavior of, 54; temperamental groups among, 54–55, 59–60; and separation anxiety, 55–56; handicapped, 56; mentally disturbed, 56, 60–61; as self-regulated, 56; consciously rejected, 57; sleeping difficulties among, 57–58; emotionally disturbed, 58–59; activity levels of, in determining discipline, 59; as responding to discipline, 62; premature, 63–64

Children's Bureau: and child protection, 3; resources of, 4

Corporal punishment: historical status of, 1, 262; as socially sanctioned, 6–7, 261–62, 264; parental attitudes toward, 7; prevalence of, 7; in public schools, 7; abusive parent's attitude toward, 15, 265, 266–67; proposed elimination of, 27; in Sweden, 27; parental alternatives to, 163–65, 166–68; as climax of earlier interventions, 165–68, 170–71; and parental intentions, 193–95, 197–98; as form of communication, 194; and parental control, 197–98; arguments against, 208; as positively perceived, 208–9, 213, 215–17, 232–34; as negatively perceived, 209–213, 233; social worker's perception of, 64–65

Counselling clinics, in treating abuse, 113

Criminal activity: among abused children, 120–22, 149; of abused child, as initiating court action, 135; among abusive parents, 248

Criminal court proceedings: in abuse cases, 113; as linked to child's behaviors, 134–36

Crisis Nurseries, in treating abuse, 23–24

Day care services, in treating abuse, 10, 21, 113

Disciplinary interventions, variety of, among parents, 163–65, 166–68

Drug abuse, 256; among abusive parents, 114; among abused children, 125–26, 128, 149, 150

Ecosystem, as influencing child abuse, 91

Emergency Relief Funds, in alleviating abuse, 24

Emotional problems: among children, 58–59, 61; among abused children, 63; among abusive parents, 220, 226–27, 228

Entrance-exit behaviors, of abused children, 122–23, 130–31

Expressive intentions, of abusive parents, 189, 196–97

Extended family center, function of, 24

Family-planning services, in treating abuse, 27, 36

Federal Child Abuse Prevention and Treatment Act, provisions of, 3

First-born children, as abused, 238, 240

Foster care: prevalence of, in abuse cases, 10; in preventing abuse, 21; in treating abused children, 26, 56, 113, 230; as abuse treatment, success of, 35; parent-child relationships in, 56–57; view of child in, 79

Foster parents, as responding to foster child, 56–57

Goal Attainment Scaling, in treating abuse, 33

Homemaker services, 25; in treating abuse, 10, 21, 113

Hospitalization, of abused children, 133–35, 147

Household chores, as factor in abuse, 124–25, 130–31, 136

Hyperactive children: bidirectional explanation of, 52; parental response to, 55; as abused, 67, 68, 70, 72, 239

Illegitimate children, as abused, 235–36

Instrumental intentions, of abusive parents, 189–99 passim

Intergenerational abuse, 231, 234, 261; theory of, 19; empirical studies of, 19–20; evidence for, 20; as unconfirmed, 111

Interview Procedure: in social science research, 92, 94; in treating abusive parents, 93–94, 99–103; respondent reliability in, 93–94, 102–4; as reliable, characteristics of, 94–95; validity of, 260

Live-in treatment, as aid to abusive parents, 24

Macrosystem, as influencing child abuse, 91, 259

Marital stresses, among abusive parents, 226, 228

Mental illness, 256; in children, parental response to, 56–57; among abusive parents, 248–49

Mental retardation: among abused children, 63–64, 66, 69, 187, 239; among abusive parents, 111–12

Microsystem, as variable in abuse, 91, 259

National Center for Child Abuse and Neglect, 9; formation of, 3

National Education Association, 7

National Society for the Prevention of Cruelty to Animals, 2

National Society for the Prevention of Cruelty to Children, 10; birth of, 2; growth of, 2

National Study on Child Abuse and Neglect: on the prevalence of abuse, 8–9; abuse explained by, 17–18

Parent-child relationships: unidirectional view of, 47; bidirectional view of, 48–52;

Parent-child relationships (*Continued*)
child's influence on, 48–51, 62; complementary dispositions in, 51–52; dissonance in, 51–52; and child abuse, 53; affect of child's social behaviors on, 54; observational studies of, 54–60; as affected by child's temperament, 54–55, 59–60, 67–68; reciprocity in, 55, 56–57; as affected by physical handicaps, 56; as affected by mental illness, 56–57; in foster care, 56–57; as affected by sleep disturbances, 57–58; as influenced by child's activity level, 59; as influenced by child's psychosis, 60–61; aggressive behavior in, 62; effect of prematurity on, 63–64; as emotionally charged, 269–70; prevalence of conflicts in, 270–72

Parent Education, in preventing abuse, 27; success of, 32

Parent Effectiveness Training, in treating abusive parents, 23

Parents: historical status of, 1; as influenced by child's behaviors, 48–51, 58–59; disciplinary techniques of, 53, 163–64; as responsive to child's social behavior, 54; as responsive to child's temperament, 55, 59–60; as reacting to handicapped children, 56; as reacting to mentally disturbed children, 56–57, 58–59, 60–61; of consciously rejected children, 57; of sleepless children, 57–58; of premature children, 63–64

Parents Anonymous, 267; as preventing abuse, 21; function of, 24–25; formation of, 24–25; membership of, 25; success of, 32, 34–35

Pediatricians: reports of, in child abuse, 3; and abused child as client, 4; as rediscovering child abuse, 4

Physically handicapped children: parental response to, 56; as abused, 63–64

Premature children: as abused, 63–64, 73, 239; parental response to, 63–64; requirements of, 64; causes of, 64; characteristics of, 64–65

Protective service agencies: decline of, 2; shifting orientation of, 2; recent growth of, 3; legislation's effects on, 3; publicizing of services by, 11–12; as initiating aid, 11–12; availability of, 11–12; abusive

situation assessed by, 13; as influencing abusive parents, 21–22; as treating abuse situation, 21–26; and emergency relief funds, 24; necessary resources of, 25–26, 37; court action by, 26–27; success of, in treating abuse, 29–33, 36–37, 213–14; services provided by, 113–14; failed interventions of, 267

Psychotherapy: of abusive parents, 21; in treating abuse, 36

Questionnaires: identifying abusive parents through, 28, 35; and research on families, 92

Sexual behaviors, of abused children, 125–26, 128, 130–31, 151–52, 160, 187

Shared parenting, abusive parents relieved by, 23

Social workers: child protective functions of, 2; as assessing abusive situation, 13; abusive situations treated by, 21–22; in relation to abusive parents, 22–23; as role model, 22–23; responsibilities of, 256; as understanding of atypical behaviors, 256–57; and client, as differently perceiving abuse situation, 261–63, 264–65, 266, 267; necessary empathy of, for abusive parent, 262, 268; as perceiving corporal punishment, 264–65; as perceived by abusive parent, 265

Surrogate mothers, as supervising abusive parents, 24

Sweden, corporal punishment in, 27

Truancy, among abused children, 149, 159

Unidirectionality, in explaining abuse, 47, 76–77

Unplanned children, as abused, 235–36, 237–38

Violence: as factor in abuse, 109–111; abusive parents as prone to, 249

Wisconsin: cases of child abuse in, 105; profile of abusive parent in, 106, 111–12; profile of abused child in, 107; hospitalization of abused children in, 107; violence among abusive families in, 110–11

Child abuse studies traditionally focus on the parent and his behavior. "The child," Alfred Kadushin and Judith A. Martin write in their conclusion to *Child Abuse—An Interactional Event*, "is a shadowy, ghostlike being who figures primarily, when he does come into focus, as the passive recipient of the parent's aggressive action.... The child's antecedent behavior to which the parent's behavior is a response is almost totally ignored.... Yet it is impossible to understand the parent's behavior, from the parent's point of view, unless we have some understanding of the situation which evoked the parent's abusive response."

Incorporating earlier approaches to the subject into their study, Kadushin and Martin offer a comprehensive critical review of research on psychological factors and types of social deprivation affecting abusive parents. Using this exhaustive critique as a point of departure, the authors develop a systematic study of parent-child behavior leading to physical abuse.

In order to categorize the types of child behavior which trigger parental violence, the authors investigated over 800 child abuse cases. They also conducted in-depth interviews with 66